DATE DUE

Unless Recalled Earlier

DEMCO 38-297

Laboratory experiments have become an important source of data in economics. Hundreds of journal articles, dozens of surveys, and several books report what laboratory experiments have helped economists discover about commodity and asset markets, industrial organization, committees and voting, laws and rules, inflation, individual choice, games, and many other fields. Until now, existing literature has provided little guidance to the researcher about the actual design and conduct of economic experiments.

This primer is the first readily accessible, self-contained summary of experimental method and technique for students and researchers in economics. The authors touch on broad conceptual issues and discuss the basic principles but emphasize concrete procedures for successful experimentation: picking an interesting and important problem, creating a laboratory environment, choosing and motivating subjects, designing and conducting experiments, collecting and analyzing the data, and reporting the results. It will help beginners to avoid making mistakes in organizing an experiment and to increase the experiments' scientific returns.

EXPERIMENTAL METHODS

Experimental methods
A primer for economists

DANIEL FRIEDMAN
University of California, Santa Cruz

and

SHYAM SUNDER
Carnegie Mellon University

CAMBRIDGE
UNIVERSITY PRESS

Published by the Press Syndicate of the University of Cambridge
The Pitt Building, Trumpington Street, Cambridge CB2 1RP
40 West 20th Street, New York, NY 10011–4211, USA
10 Stamford Road, Oakleigh, Melbourne 3166, Australia

First published 1994

Printed in the United States of America

Library of Congress Cataloging-in-Publication Data

Friedman, Daniel, 1947–
    Experimental methods : a primer for economists / Daniel Friedman,
Shyam Sunder.
        p.   cm.
    Includes bibliographical references and index.
    ISBN 0-521-45068-3. – ISBN 0-521-45682-7 (pbk.)
    1. Economics – Methodology.   2. Economics – Simulation methods.
3. Economics – Research.   I. Sunder, Shyam.   II. Title.
HB131.F75   1994
330'.01'1 – dc20   93–8005
                                                                                        CIP

A catalog record for this book is available from the British Library.

ISBN 0-521-45068-3 hardback
ISBN 0-521-45682-7 paperback

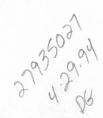

CONTENTS

v

FIGURES AND TABLES

PREFACE

Laboratory experiments have become an important source of data for economists. Hundreds of journal articles, dozens of surveys, and several books report what laboratory experiments have helped us discover about commodity and asset markets, industrial organization, committees and voting, laws and rules, inflation, individual choice, games, and many other institutions and phenomena.

Information on how to conduct experiments has not kept pace with economists' interest in this new method of gathering empirical evidence. The published literature focuses on substantive results and provides little guidance about how to do your own experiments, especially if you are trying something new. Most experimental economists have learned their craft through apprenticeship. There has been no readily accessible, self-contained summary of experimental method and technique for students and researchers in economics. This primer is intended to bridge that gap.

In this primer, we take you through the entire process of conducting economic experiments. We touch on broad conceptual issues and discuss the basic principles, but we emphasize concrete procedures for successful experimentation. Picking an interesting and important problem, creating a laboratory environment, choosing and motivating subjects, designing and conducting experiments, collecting and analyzing the data, reporting the results – these are the key tasks. It is easy for beginners to make mistakes, at considerable cost in money, time, and effort. The purpose of this book is to help you lower these costs and increase your scientific returns.

This primer grew out of our class notes, and more recently from our methodological papers, Friedman (1988) and Sunder (1991). It collects and distills information from numerous published sources. It also draws on the oral traditions of experimental economists and on our own personal experience. On controversial points we offer our opinions, but not to the exclusion of other views. We have tried to make the material self-contained and reasonably thorough.

In order to help make the material accessible to economists at the advanced undergraduate level and beyond, we adopted an informal second-person style; we hope you won't mind.

We aimed this primer at teaching, practicing, and apprentice economists. It should be especially helpful to undergraduate or graduate economics students who are (or wish they were) enrolled in an experimental economics course. This primer should be combined with readings of surveys and primary articles, demonstration experiments, and with projects that require students to design and conduct experiments. To that end, we discuss applications only as illustrative examples in the body of this book. Several appendixes contain reading lists from recent experimental economics courses at the undergraduate and graduate level, a glossary of experimental jargon, and procedures and instructions for classroom demonstrations as well as research experiments. This format provides ample material for an instructor to design a learn-by-doing course in a flexible format.

Please send your comments and suggestions for improving the primer to either author, or by electronic mail to primer@cash.ucsc.edu.

ACKNOWLEDGMENTS

In preparing this manuscript we benefited from the financial support of the National Science Foundation (Grants IRI88–12798 and SES90–23945 to Friedman and SES89–12552 to Sunder) and the support of Richard M. and Margaret Cyert Family Funds to Sunder. We owe a great debt to coauthors and colleagues who helped us learn and improve our experimental technique over the years, especially Charles Plott, Glenn Harrison, Tom Copeland, Edward Prescott, and Ramon Marimon.

More directly, we are indebted to Vernon Smith, Charles Plott, Arlington Williams, Colin Camerer, Glenn Harrison, Ron King, and Andrew Schotter for reading an earlier version of the text and suggesting many improvements. They and others (Tom Reitz, Jim Andreoni, Jim Cox, Mark Isaac, Antoni Bosch, John Kagel, Tom Palfrey, Rob Porter) helped us immensely by sharing with us their reading lists, instructions, laboratory plans, or other materials included in the appendixes of this volume. Martin Weber, Graham Loomes, and Shawn LaMaster helped us compile the list of universities where experimental economics research is being conducted. The task of tracking down the references and quotations was done superbly by Yeong-Ho Suh. Betty Cosnek, Traci Yanovich, and Bonnie Schultz worked indefatigably to complete the endless revisions of the manuscript. Scott Parris, Louise Calabro Gruendel, and Alan Gold of Cambridge University Press worked closely with us to get the manuscript to print. Our wives and children (Penny and Sara and Ben Friedman, and Manjula and Richa and Neal Shyam) gave us the precious time and support that allowed us to complete the book.

The publishers of the articles listed on the next page gave us permission to reproduce their copyrighted material. But most of all, we are grateful to hundreds of experimental subjects, mostly university students, for their patience and fortitude in putting up with our errors, and giving us a chance to learn.

We dedicate this book to our parents, Martin and Marion Friedman and Murari Lal and Yashoda Devi, who encouraged us to experiment and to learn from our mistakes.

The authors are grateful for permission to use the following material:

> Cox, James, "Syllabus for Economics #506 for Fall of 1992," pp. 1–2, and "Economics 506: Core Reading List," pp. 1–6.
>
> Fiorina, Morris, and Plott, Charles, "Committee Decisions under Majority Rule: An Experimental Study," *American Political Science Review* 72 (June), pp. 594–6.
>
> Issaac, Mark, "Syllabus for Economics 406, Introduction to Experimental Economics, Spring 1994," pp. 1–2.
>
> Palfrey, Thomas, and Porter, Robert, "Guidelines on Submission of Manuscripts on Experimental Economics," *Econometrica* 59:4 (July), pp. 1197–8.
>
> Plott, Charles, "Experimental Political Economy Reading List by Category," February 1990.
>
> Plott, Charles and Smith, Vernon, "An Experimental Examination of Two Exchange Institutions," *Review of Economic Studies* 45:1 (February), pp. 147–53.
>
> Sunder, Shyam, "Market for Information: Experimental Evidence," *Econometrica* 60:3 (May), pp. 692–4.

EXPERIMENTAL METHODS

1

Introduction

1.1 Economics as an experimental discipline

One possible way of figuring out economic laws . . . is by *controlled experiments*. . . . Economists [unfortunately] . . . cannot perform the controlled experiments of chemists or biologists because they cannot easily control other important factors. Like astronomers or meteorologists, they generally must be content largely to observe. (Samuelson and Nordhaus, 1985, p. 8)

Samuelson and Nordhaus echo a widely shared view that some disciplines are inherently experimental, but others (including economics) are not. History has not been kind to this view. In Aristotle's day some 2,000 years ago, even physics was considered nonexperimental. About 400 years ago, innovators such as Bacon and Galileo established a tradition of controlled experiments, mostly in physics. Experiments in related disciplines such as chemistry followed. For a long time biology was considered inherently nonexperimental because its subject was living organisms, but Mendel, Pasteur, and others introduced new experimental techniques in the nineteenth century. Modern biology certainly is an experimental science. Even psychology, whose mental subject matter might seem least accessible to laboratory study, has evolved a distinctive experimental tradition over the last century.

History suggests that a discipline becomes experimental *when innovators develop techniques for conducting relevant experiments*. The process can be contagious, with advances in experimental technique in one discipline inspiring advances elsewhere. Still, each discipline must innovate for itself. Even closely related disciplines differ in their intellectual focus, so wholesale transfer of experimental technique across disciplinary boundaries is seldom possible.

1

It took a long time but economics has finally become an experimental science. Most economists have heard about the experimental work of Vernon Smith, Charles Plott, Reinhard Selten, and others in the last three decades. (Indeed, in later editions of their text Nordhaus and Samuelson edited out the remarks we quoted.) Experiments are now commonplace in industrial organization, game theory, finance, public choice, and most other microeconomic fields. Some aspects of macroeconomic theory recently have been examined experimentally, although full-scale macroeconomic experiments do not seem feasible for budgetary and political reasons. (We refer to true, controlled experiments; uncontrolled macroeconomic "experiments" are all too common in recent years!) Perhaps macroeconomics too, like meteorology and astronomy, will become an indirectly experimental discipline, one that relies on experimentally verified results in constructing its central theories, although the central theories themselves are not amenable to direct experimental examination.

The methods as well as the substance of experimental economics are new in some respects. In the last few years the substantial findings of experimental economics have been expertly surveyed; see the annotated bibliography in Appendix I, pp. 143–74. However, no readily accessible, self-contained summary of experimental method and technique has yet been written for students and researchers in economics. The purpose of this primer is to bridge that gap.

Chapters 2 through 8 examine specific methods and techniques for economic experiments. The final chapter takes a look at the emergence of experimental economics in the last thirty years. The present chapter touches on some preliminary but fundamental issues: the interaction between theory and empirics, the differences between experimental and nonexperimental data for empirical work, and the diverse purposes of experiments. Since this book is a primer and not a theoretical treatise, we barely skim the surface of the deeper philosophical issues.

1.2 The engine of scientific progress

Theory organizes our knowledge and helps us predict behavior in new situations. In particular, theory tells us what data are worth gathering and suggests ways to analyze new data. As theory progresses, it guides us in refining our use of data and in selecting questions we should ask.

Conversely, data collection and analysis often turn up regularities that are not explained by existing theory. Such empirical regularities spur refinement of theory, usually as minor adjustments and sometimes as revolutionary changes. Kuhn (1970) and Lakatos (1978) discuss how

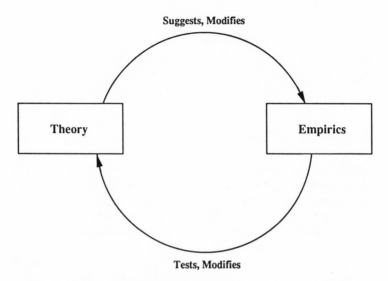

Fig. 1.1   Theory and empirics.

data and theory interact over time. The alternation of theory and empirical work, each refining the other, is the engine of progress in every scientific discipline. (See Figure 1.1.) Economics is no exception. Traditionally, observations from naturally occurring economic phenomena were the only source of data to stimulate revision of theory. If data relevant to an economic proposition could not be captured from naturally occurring conditions, then the proposition went without benefit of empirical refinement. In recent years, experimental methods have given economists access to new sources of data and have enlarged the set of economic propositions on which data can be brought to bear.

1.3 **Data sources**
Data for empirical work can be drawn from several types of sources, each with distinctive characteristics, advantages, and disadvantages. A key distinction is between *experimental data,* which are deliberately created for scientific (or other) purposes under *controlled* conditions, and *happenstance data,* which are a by-product of ongoing *uncontrolled* processes. A less important but still useful distinction can be drawn between *laboratory data,* which are gathered in an artificial environment designed for scientific (or other) purposes, and *field data,* which are gathered in a naturally occurring environment.

All combinations are possible. For example, an experimenter may

	Happenstance	Experimental
Field	Rate of Inflation in U.S.	Income Maintenance Experiments
Laboratory	Discovery of Penicillin	Laboratory Asset Markets

Fig. 1.2   Examples of data sources.

intervene in a naturally occurring process and record the outcomes; such data are field-experimental (FE). An economic example is the income-maintenance experiments in Denver, Seattle, and elsewhere (see Killingsworth, 1983; Pencavel, 1986). Traditionally, almost all empirical work in economics has used field-happenstance (FH) data such as national income accounts, commodity prices, or corporate financial statements. The story goes that penicillin was discovered in a laboratory when controls failed in a nutrient experiment, so this is an example of rare laboratory-happenstance (LH) data. Of course, this primer focuses on the last type of data, laboratory-experimental (LE). In this and later chapters, we often loosely refer to LE data as laboratory data or as experimental data and often ignore LH and FE data, but we make the finer distinctions when necessary.

Experimental data (LE or FE) are especially valuable for scientific purposes because they are relatively easy to interpret. If outcome Y (say, highly efficient allocations) is always associated with institution X (say, a certain kind of auction market) as institutional and other environmental variables are manipulated in a well-designed experiment, then we can confidently conclude that X causes Y. Happenstance data can't support such confident causal conclusions. Given the absence of control, an observed correlation between X and Y may be due to Y indirectly causing X, or may be due to some unobserved variable Z causing both X and Y. Leamer (1983, p. 31) makes the point while satirizing Monetarists and Keynesians in his delightful "Luminist versus Aviophile" parable. Aviophiles explain the higher crop yields found under trees in terms of bird droppings, while Luminists explain the same finding in terms of light intensity. Their quarrel is unresolvable with the "field" data because the two explanatory variables are completely confounded – that is, shade and bird droppings go together. The process-control example in Box, Hunter, and Hunter (1978, p. 487ff) provides a more elaborate discussion of the same point. We defer discussion of the underlying statistical issues until Chapter 7.

The other main issues in comparing experimental and happenstance data are cost and validity. Flexible, controllable laboratory environments usually are expensive to build, maintain, and operate, and each experiment requires further costs such as payments to human subjects. Thus both fixed (or sunk) costs and marginal costs may be significant for laboratory experiments, and typically are even higher for field experiments. Of course, it is also costly to obtain new field-happenstance data. The costs of gathering FH data on individual choice behavior, for example, are about the same as for LE data. Obviously it is least expensive to use data previously collected by someone else, such as a government agency.

Validity (or relevance) is a crucial issue for all data sources. When the field environment is of direct interest, FH and FE data are automatically relevant. On the other hand, FH data are normally,

> collected by government or private agencies for non-scientific purposes.... [By contrast,] astronomers are directly responsible for the scientific credibility of their data in a way that economists have not been. In economics, when things appear not to turn out as expected the quality of the [FH] data is more likely to be questioned.... (Smith, 1987, p. 242)

Specifically, the validity of FH data often is impaired by the omission of the really interesting variables (necessitating use of crude proxies), by measurement error of unknown magnitude, or by skewed coverage.

Laboratory data pose different validity questions. First, there is the question of internal validity: Do the data permit correct causal inferences? As we will see in later chapters, internal validity is a matter of proper experimental controls, experimental design, and data analysis. Second, there is the question of external validity: Can we generalize our inferences from laboratory to field? The issue of external validity or relevance often troubles economists who are unfamiliar with experimental work, and it remains a concern for experimentalists. Chapter 2 begins with a discussion of the gentle art of designing relevant experiments. Parallelism, the last substantive topic in Chapter 2, deals directly with the general question of external validity. For now, suffice it to say that, in economics as in other experimental disciplines, external validity has been firmly established in a diverse set of laboratory studies.

Sometimes data from computer simulations or surveys are improperly labeled as experimental economic data. Computer simulations of a theoretical model (no human decision makers involved except in writing the computer code) are best regarded as a type of theoretical results rather than as empirical data. Traditionally the investigator uses deductive logic and mathematical derivations to discover the implications of a theoretical model. You may resort to simulation because you have an intractable theoretical model so you can't derive the relevant theorems. As computing power becomes cheaper and more convenient, computer simulations become increasingly attractive relative to formal derivations as a discovery method. Survey data (human responses to hypothetical questions) are empirical but, unless responses are economically motivated, their reliability as economic data is questionable. This last point is developed in Section 2.3.

1.3.1 Some evidence

Econometricians have devised many ingenious techniques to deal with the weaknesses of happenstance data. Direct opportunities to test the effectiveness of these techniques are rare, LaLonde (1986) being the prime example. (See Cox and Oaxaca, 1991, for a different kind of effectiveness test.) LaLonde obtained field-experimental earnings data on former participants and nonparticipants in a job-training program. Experimental control had been achieved by random assignment of individuals as participants or nonparticipants; this important technique is discussed in Section 3.2. Straightforward statistical procedures showed that participants' mean annual earnings were about $900 higher, a statistically significant difference.

LaLonde then treated the data as if it were happenstance and the "control group" of nonparticipants did not exist. He used standard data sources and several multiequation specifications (some involving self-selection) and several econometric procedures to estimate the earnings effect. Estimates of the job-training effect on earnings varied considerably and some even had the wrong sign. He concludes

> This study shows that many of the econometric procedures and comparison groups used to evaluate employment and training programs would not have yielded accurate or precise estimates of the impact of the National Supported Work Program. The econometric estimates often differ significantly from the experimental results. Moreover, even when the econometric estimates pass conventional specification tests, they still fail to replicate the experimentally determined results. (LaLonde, 1986, p. 617)

The point is that, when obtainable at comparable cost, experimental data allow more reliable inferences than happenstance data. There are many cases where happenstance data are adequate and cheap; then experiments are not worthwhile. In many other cases happenstance data are inadequate and experimental data can be obtained at reasonable cost. Such cases present the best opportunities for experimental work.

Different types of data can be complementary. You can combine evidence from computer simulations, field, and laboratory to get sharper conclusions than those obtainable from a single data source.

1.4 Purposes of experiments

Experiments have many possible purposes. The proper way to design and to conduct your experiment depends on your purpose. Before proceeding further, a review of the purposes of experiments is in order (see Plott, 1982, 1987).

Some experiments have been conducted to generate data that might influence a specific decision. For example, Grether and Plott (1984) report an experiment designed to provide evidence in an antitrust case. Hong and Plott's (1982) research arose from a case considered by Interstate Commerce Commission. Alger (1988), Alger, O'Neill, and Toman (1987a,b), Plott (1988), and Rassenti, Reynolds, and Smith (1988) discuss the experiments conducted to assist Federal Energy Regulatory Commission. Roth (1987a) refers to experimentation designed to influence policymakers as "whispering in the ears of princes."

Influencing authorities is not the only persuasive purpose for experiments. Innumerable laboratory and field experiments have been conducted in order to provide data on how best to influence the decisions of consumers, voters, and managers. Cohen (1992) reports that white American consumers are more responsive to advertisements for stereo equipment featuring Asian models. This responsiveness of demand for stereos, where Asian manufacturers have dominated the U.S. market, is not discernible in advertisements for pickup trucks. Recently several popular business magazines have discussed new field technology that allows accurate measurement of market response to product innovations or advertising campaigns. In U.S. presidential campaigns at least since 1988, laboratory studies of voter response to proposed television messages and campaign slogans have played an important part in the strategies of most major candidates. For example, Torry and Stencel (1992) report in the *Washington Post* that the Bush–Quayle campaign confirmed through focus groups that bashing trial lawyers was an effective vote-getting theme; see Payne (1992) for another typical example. The large (and apparently increasing) sums of money devoted to such marketing applications suggests that they do provide commercially valuable data.

This primer emphasizes the scientific purposes of experiments. Persuasion certainly is still in the picture (McCloskey, 1985), but specific immediate decisions are of less concern than the longer run views of the scientific community. One scientific purpose is to discover empirical regularities in areas for which existing theory has little to say. McCabe, Rassenti, and Smith (1993) and Friedman (1993), for example, compare the properties of several market institutions whose theoretical properties are as yet poorly understood. Smith (1982b) calls such experiments *heuristic*. In other areas, by contrast, several competing theories offer differing predictions and experiments can help map the range of applicability for each theory. For example, Fiorina and Plott (1978) study committee decisions in the laboratory and find that only a few of the sixteen models and variants considered are at all consistent with the data. Finally, there are areas for which only one model is applicable. Laboratory work can demonstrate whether there are any conditions under which the theory can account for the data, and if so, can test theory for robustness. "In Search of Predatory Pricing," by Isaac and Smith (1985) is a negative example. Smith (1982b) refers to the last two types of experiments as *boundary* experiments and refers to sets of experiments intended to establish definitive broad laws of behavior as *nomothetic*.

Some experimental economists have hesitated in recent years to describe the purpose of an experiment as a *test of theory*. From a formal point of view, a theory consists of a set of axioms or assumptions and definitions, together with the conclusions that logically follow from them. A theory is formally valid if it is internally consistent – that is, it does not lead to statements that contradict each other – and if the conclusions are indeed provable from the assumptions. What can be learned about theories by conducting experiments? Some experimentalists (including most psychologists) think of experimental data as a means of testing the descriptive validity of the assumptions about human behavior on which the theory is based. Others (including most economists) would readily grant that the behavioral assumptions of most economic theories do not and need not meet the descriptive validity criterion used in psychology. Instead they believe that a theory is of direct practical interest only to the extent that its conclusions provide good approximations (relative to alternative theories) of actual behavior even when its assumptions are not precisely satisfied. See Friedman (1953) and Koopmans (1957) for further discussion.

The proper job of the empirical scientist is to find regularities in observed behavior in a broad range of interesting environments and to see which theories can best account for these regularities. Whether this job is called "testing theories," or more circumspectly referred to as "seeing which theories best organize the data," it is a primary purpose of scientific experiments.

Experimental economists have become increasingly interested in recent years in using laboratory methods (including economic incentives) to measure individual (innate or "home-grown") characteristics in the population, such as willingness to pay for environmental amenities or risk aversion (see Cummings, Harrison, and Rutström, 1992). In a novel application of experimental technique, Forsythe et al. (1992) have introduced a computerized field market for candidate-contingent claims to predict the percentage of total vote received by each candidate in an election. Some experimentalists in previous decades tried to measure behavioral parameters or to simulate natural economic processes in the laboratory. For example, Hoggatt (1959) set out to measure oligopolistic "reaction functions," and Garman (1976) tried to simulate the New York Stock Exchange. Experimental economists now recognize that behavioral parameters usually vary with the institution and the environment, so the external validity of such measurements is questionable. As explained in Section 2.1, experimentalists no longer see simulation (in the sense of replicating a field environment as closely as possible) as a useful goal.

A related but more modest purpose for experiments has recently emerged. Aircraft engineers find it useful to study a small-scale model in a "test bed" before trying to build and fly a new plane. Likewise, economists and policymakers recently have found it useful to study new institutions in the laboratory before introducing them in the field. McCabe et al. (1991) describe "test-bed" experiments of computer-aided markets for composite commodities such as computer resources, and gas and electrical power grids. Given the accelerating pace of transformation in the formerly centrally planned economies and given continuing deregulation in Western economies, the scope for institutional engineering of this sort is large and increasing.

Finally, experiments have an important pedagogical purpose. The first recorded use of economics experiments, by Chamberlin (1948), was primarily pedagogical. Since the 1980s this use of economics experiments has grown steadily. Incorporating experimental demonstration of economic propositions into the high school and college curriculum is a natural accompaniment of the evolution of economics as an experimental science. Walker, Williams, and their colleagues at Indiana University, and Wells and his colleagues at the University of Arizona have developed many pedagogical economics experiments (see Wells, 1991; Williams and Walker, 1993).

2

Principles of economics experiments

How do you choose and present the rules governing an experimental economy? How do you choose and motivate subjects? The principles presented in this chapter will provide some guidance. We begin with by discussing the relations between laboratory experiments, formal models, and reality, then informally present the key concepts of economic agents and economic institutions. (See Smith, 1976, 1982b for a more formal presentation using the framework of Hurwicz, 1972.) The next few sections present induced-value theory (again based on Smith, 1976). After a general discussion of external validity or *parallelism,* we highlight some practical implications and apply the ideas to an important strand of literature on market experiments.

2.1 Realism and models

Unless you already are an experienced experimentalist, your first instinct in designing an experiment probably will be to pursue *realism* – design the laboratory environment to resemble as closely as possible a real-world environment of substantive economic interest. If you are interested in securities markets, for example, you might have some subjects serve as investors, some as floor brokers, and some as specialists, all following the rules of the New York Stock Exchange.

On the other hand, if you are a theorist, your first instinct might be to design an experiment that replicates as closely as possible the assumptions of a formal model of interest. For the securities market example, you would throw out the brokers and specialists and the New York Stock Exchange rules, and perhaps ask your subjects to reveal their optimal demand/supply schedules to a (Walrasian) auctioneer.

Which approach is right: to mimic reality or to mimic a formal model? The correct answer is *neither.* Your goal should be to find a design that

10

offers the best opportunity to learn something useful and to answer the questions that motivate your research. Usually an effective design is quite simple compared to reality, and in some respects simpler than relevant formal models.

It is futile to try to replicate in the laboratory the complexities of a field environment. Like fractals, reality has infinite detail; it is its own best model. No matter where you stop in building the details of reality into your laboratory environment, an infinite amount of detail will always remain uncaptured. A practical difficulty is that your budget probably won't let you get far in this direction. Before you get close, the laboratory environment will have become so complex that you will find it difficult or impossible to disentangle causes and effects. As in any other experimental discipline, simplicity enhances control. Try to find the simplest laboratory environment that incorporates some interesting aspects of the field environment. In the asset market example, to discover whether the market disseminates insider information, you will learn more if you begin with a single, simple, tradeable security and find an appropriate way to feed some traders inside information on its fundamental value.

It is equally futile to try to replicate in the laboratory the precise assumptions of a formal model. A practical difficulty is that most formal models leave out details, and you typically must make choices that are arbitrary in terms of the theory but important in terms of behavior. For example, in a rational expectations model, traders' orders theoretically are based on observed market-clearing prices. In the laboratory, do you announce market-clearing prices before traders place orders or after? Either way you fail to replicate the formal model.

Even if you succeed in creating a laboratory economy that closely replicates the assumptions of a formal model, you usually will not learn much from it. If the observed behavior in your economy is consistent with the implications of the formal model, you have only weak evidence of the model's explanatory power. The evidence would be stronger if you had observed the same behavior in a laboratory economy that relaxed the more stringent assumptions of the model. Suppose you somehow were able to recreate precisely the formal model in the laboratory. Data consistent with the model only tells you that there is no obvious logical flaw in the model – a hollow victory at best, since laboratory experiments are less efficient in detecting logical errors than mathematical analysis or computer simulation. On the other hand, if the observed behavior you report is inconsistent with a logically valid formal model, you face criticism that your design was inadequate or that your subjects failed to understand the environment or both. Unless your purpose is to demonstrate the model's narrow or empty range of applicability (as in Isaac and Smith, 1985), you can learn rather little from such an exercise.

An analogy may clarify the relationships between reality, formal models, and laboratory experiments. An artist wishes to express a human event, say the death of his brother. He is unable to reenact the real event (that brother is gone) and finds it undesirable for practical and aesthetic reasons (not to mention moral reasons) to replicate it closely. He chooses a medium of expression, perhaps canvas or stone. The quality of his painting will be judged by how well it simplifies reality to capture and communicate the essence of his loss. The stone sculpture also will be judged by its impact on the viewer, not by its fidelity either to reality or to the painting. Likewise, a laboratory experiment should be judged by its impact on our understanding, not by its fidelity either to reality or to a formal model.

2.2 Controlled economic environments

An experiment takes place in a controlled economic environment. Controlled or otherwise, an economic environment consists of individual economic *agents* together with an *institution* through which the agents interact. For example, the agents may be buyers and sellers and the institution may be a particular type of market. Another example, drawn from politics, has voters as agents and majority rule as an institution.

Agents are defined by their economically relevant characteristics: preferences, technology, resource endowments, and information. Your subjects have their own home-grown characteristics, but often you want to examine theories that assume specific characteristics that may or may not correspond to those of available subjects. You might think at first that agents' characteristics are difficult to observe, much less control. The next subsection explains how induced-value theory (Smith, 1976) identifies sufficient conditions for experimental control, conditions that are often easy to satisfy in practice.

An economic institution specifies the actions available to agents and the outcomes that result from each possible combination of agents' actions. Achieving experimental control over the institution is conceptually straightforward: The experimenter explains and enforces the rules. Specific techniques are discussed later.

2.3 Induced-value theory

The key idea in induced-value theory is that proper use of a reward medium allows an experimenter to *induce* prespecified characteristics in experimental subjects, and the subjects' innate characteristics become largely irrelevant.

Three conditions suffice to induce agents' characteristics:

1. *Monotonicity.* Subjects must prefer more reward medium to less, and not become satiated. Formally, if $V(m,z)$ represents the subject's unobservable preferences over the reward medium (m) and everything else (z), then the monotonicity condition is that the partial derivative V_m exists and is positive for every feasible combination (m,z). This condition seems easy to satisfy by using domestic currency as the reward medium.

2. *Salience.* The reward Δm received by the subject depends on her actions (and those of other agents) as defined by institutional rules that she understands. That is, the relation between actions and the reward implements the desired institution, and subjects understand the relation. For example, a \$5.00 fixed payment to subjects for participating is not salient because the payment does not depend on the subjects' choice of actions in the laboratory after she shows up. On the other hand, a payment of one cent for every point of profit earned in a market experiment is salient because the payment depends on subjects' actions.

3. *Dominance.* Changes in subjects' utility from the experiment come predominantly from the reward medium and other influences are negligible. This condition is the most problematic of the three since preferences V and "everything else" z may not be observable by the experimenter. Dominance becomes more plausible if the salient rewards Δm are increased and if the more obvious components of z are held constant. For example, subjects often care about the rewards earned by other subjects. If the experimental procedures make it impossible to know or estimate others' rewards (Smith calls this *privacy*) then a component of z is neutralized. Demand effects, arising from subjects' efforts to help (or hinder) the experimenter, are a second example. As the experimenter, avoid revealing your own goals and you neutralize another component of z.

When the three conditions are satisfied, the experimenter achieves control over agents' characteristics. To illustrate, suppose you want to induce some specific smooth preferences (e.g., Cobb-Douglas) represented by the utility function $U(x,y)$. You pick convenient objects such as colored slips of paper, say x = number of slips of red paper and y = same for blue, and clearly explain to the subject (e.g, using a table of rewards with columns indexed by x and rows by y) that her payment will be $\Delta m = U(x,y)$. Then the induced preferences are $W(x,y) = V(m_0 + U(x,y), z_0 + \Delta z)$, where (m_0, z_0) is the subject's unobservable initial endowment of money and everything else, and Δz summarizes the subject's nonpecuniary proceeds from the experiment. By Hicks's Lemma (1939, appendix) we may conclude that two utility functions represent the same preferences if their marginal rates of substitution always coincide. We have

$$MRS^W = \frac{W_x}{W_y} = \frac{V_m U_x + V_z \Delta z_x}{V_m U_y + V_z \Delta z_y} = \frac{V_m U_x}{V_m U_y} = \frac{U_x}{U_y} = MRS^U$$

with the first and last equalities following from a standard property of marginal rates of substitution, the second equality from salience and the chain rule of calculus, the third equality from (complete) dominance, and the fourth equality from monotonicity. Thus the prespecified preferences represented by U and the induced preferences represented by W are indeed the same.

The intuition is that the experimenter can freely choose any relationship between intrinsically worthless objects and the reward medium. As long as he can explain the relationship clearly to the subjects (salience) and subjects are motivated by the reward medium (monotonicity) and not other influences (dominance), then the experimenter can control subjects' characteristics to implement the chosen relationship in laboratory. A standard example is sellers' cost in a market experiment. If you want to implement increasing marginal costs, say $c_1 < c_2 < c_3$ for three indivisible units, you simply tell the subject that she will receive m units of the reward medium, where $m = (p_1 - c_1) + (p_2 - c_2) + (p_3 - c_3)$, if she sells the units at successive transaction prices p_1, p_2, and p_3.

The concept of salience differentiates surveys from controlled economics experiments. A typical survey asks respondents to report some aspects of their personal characteristics, historical actions, or events. U.S. Bureau of Labor Statistics gathers, classifies, and reports a great deal of such happenstance data. In addition, survey technique is sometimes used to ask respondents to make choices in hypothetical situations. Controlled economics experimentation must not be confused with this latter class of surveys; since no salient rewards are offered in such surveys, respondents are not making economic choices under conditions within the control of the researcher. A laboratory procedure that pays subjects a flat participation fee to respond to hypothetical choices, properly speaking, is a survey and not a controlled economic experiment, because rewards are not salient. (See Kotlikoff, Samuelson, and Johnson

1988, for an example.) What people say they would do in hypothetical situations does not necessarily correspond to what they actually do (see Bishop, 1986). On the other hand, a field "market survey" that offers a choice between brand X and brand Y is a controlled economic experiment if respondents know they get to keep the brand they choose.

We should note that some economics experiments, especially early pilot studies, continue to be conducted and reported without salient rewards. Sometimes salient rewards substantially alter the experimental outcomes and sometimes they don't; Jamal and Sunder (1991) find that the use of salient rewards tends to increase the reliability of results; see Smith and Walker (1992) for a recent summary of the evidence. In any case, an experimentalist who uses unmotivated subjects can anticipate that many economists will challenge the results.

2.4 Parallelism

Some economists question the external validity of laboratory data and feel that such data somehow is not representative of the real world. For example, in 1987 an anonymous referee of a paper on laboratory asset markets discounted the relevance of the work on the grounds that "experienced traders used to dealing with large sums of money [may not] use the same heuristics, etc., exhibited by rather naive students who may or may not take this seriously." Bohm raises the issue in motivating his field experiment: "If a given mechanism can be shown to work ... in one, two or three laboratory tests, how can we be sure it will work in the fourth instance when we want an important decision to be determined by it?" (1984, p. 137).

Experimentalists in other disciplines have encountered similar skepticism. Galileo's critics did not believe that the motion of pendulums or balls on inclined planes had any relation to planetary motion in the celestial sphere. More recently, some people question whether substances found to be toxic in large doses for laboratory rats will harm human beings exposed to small doses over longer periods of time.

Deductive logic does not provide the basis to reject such skepticism. From the mere fact that you have observed the sun rise every morning for twenty years you can't really deduce the proposition that it will rise again tomorrow morning. Yet people do make the leap of faith that the sun will rise. This is *induction*.

The general principle of induction is that behavioral regularities will persist in new situations as long as the relevant underlying conditions remain substantially unchanged. Theory suggests what is "relevant" and what is a "substantial" change, but the principle itself is an assumption (an "axiom" or "maintained hypothesis," if you prefer), not a deducible proposition.

Vernon Smith refers to the induction principle in the present context as the "parallelism precept":

> Propositions about the behavior of individuals and the performance of institutions that have been tested in laboratory microeconomies apply also to nonlaboratory microeconomies where similar *ceteris paribus* conditions hold. (1982b, p. 936)

According to parallelism, it should be *presumed* that results carry over to the world outside the laboratory. An honest skeptic then has the burden of stating what is different about the outside world that might change results observed in the laboratory. Usually new experiments can be designed and conducted to test the skeptic's statement. For example, in the past both authors have heard colleagues argue that laboratory asset market data are "artificial." When pressed, the colleague usually cites the large number of traders or the high stakes and the professionalism of traders in the real world as the important differences. The appropriate response is to conduct experiments with more traders or more experienced (or professional) traders or to increase the salient rewards. The idea is to use the skepticism to promote constructive research, and not to engage in sterile arguments.

For scientific purposes, the simplicity and small scale of laboratory environments relative to field environments are virtues. Charles Plott makes the case as follows.

> The art of posing questions rests on an ability to make the study of simple special cases relevant to an understanding of the complex. General theories and models by definition apply to all special cases. Therefore, general theories and models should be expected to work in the special cases of laboratory markets. As models fail to capture what is observed in the special cases, they can be modified or rejected in light of experience. The relevance of experimental methods is thereby established. (1982, p. 1520)

In the same article, Plott deals with general concerns regarding external validity as follows:

> While laboratory processes are simple in comparison to naturally occurring processes, they are real processes in the sense that real people participate for real and substantial profits and follow real rules in doing so. It is precisely because they are real that they are interesting. (p. 1486)

2.5 Practical implications

A few minutes' reflection on induced-value theory yields some basic practical advice for beginners on the conduct of economic experiments. Among the more important do's and don't's:

1. To create controlled economic environments in laboratory, motivate subjects by paying them in cash. (Grades may also work for student subjects; see Chapter 4). Most of the payment should be sensitively linked to subjects' actions in the experiment. The average payment should exceed subjects' average opportunity cost. Such payments promote monotonicity and salience.
2. Find subjects whose opportunity costs are low and whose learning curves are steep, in order to achieve dominance and salience at moderate cost. Undergraduate students are usually a good bet.
3. Create the simplest possible economic environment in which you can address your issues. Simplicity promotes salience and reduces ambiguities in interpreting your results. Check instructions carefully for accuracy and clarity. Verify subjects' understanding in "dry runs" or quizzes.
4. To promote dominance, avoid loaded words in instructions. In a prisoner's dilemma experiment, for example, label the choices A and B rather than Loyal and Betray. Use neutral terms for subjects' roles – for example, buyer and seller or player A and player B rather than czar and serf or opponent.
5. If dominance becomes questionable and your budget permits, try a proportional increase in rewards. A systematic change in observed outcomes suggests that dominance had not been achieved at the lower level of rewards.
6. When feasible and appropriate for your research, maintain the privacy of subjects' actions and payoffs, and of your own experimental goals. Subjects' homegrown (i.e., innate) preferences may have rank-sensitive malevolent or benevolent components that will compromise dominance when privacy is not maintained.
7. Do not deceive subjects or lie to them. It is true that social psychologists have sometimes run interesting experiments based on deception (e.g., Stanley Milgram, 1974). However, experimental economists require complete credibility because salience and dominance are lost if subjects doubt the announced relation between actions and rewards, or if subjects hedge against possible tricks. Deception harms your own credibility and that of

other experimentalists, thereby undermining the ability to achieve experimental control.

These rules are not ironclad. For example, there are advantages to using unpaid subjects in early pilot experiments. Later chapters will delve more deeply into the art of writing instructions, the circumstances in which privacy is appropriate, and so on. We suggest that you feel free to break these rules, but only when you are confident that you understand the underlying issues and that you can convince most skeptics that your reasons are sufficient.

2.6 Application: The Hayek hypothesis

The efficiency of competitive equilibrium (CE), popularly known as Adam Smith's Invisible Hand Theorem, is universally acknowledged as a central proposition in economics. However, economists differ sharply on the conditions necessary for the attainment of CE and therefore on the practical significance of the proposition. The usual textbook explanation, and perhaps the majority view among economists, is that the conditions are quite stringent, including (a) large numbers of buyers and sellers, each small relative to the market, who possess (b) perfect or at least very good information about demand and supply conditions. Other economists, an influential minority, believe the proposition holds given only a moderate number of buyers and sellers with little or no public information other than current prices. Friedrich Hayek, for example, states:

> The most significant fact about this [price] system is the economy of knowledge with which it operates, or how little the individual participants need to know in order to be able to take the right action. (1945, pp. 526–7)

Edward Chamberlin, an influential proponent of the majority view, addressed this range-of-applicability controversy in one of the earliest laboratory studies in economics. He created a simple classroom environment that incorporated what he viewed as key aspects of ongoing field markets: fairly large numbers of transactors (dozens) with imperfect information and no central auctioneer to coordinate trade. Chamberlin assigned (as private information) single unit values and costs to students who acted as buyers and sellers. The sellers and buyers searched for counterparties and set transaction prices in bilateral negotiations. Chamberlin reported considerable dispersion and some bias in transaction prices and significant inefficiency, due mostly to transactions involving either an extramarginal buyer or an extramarginal seller. He concluded:

My own skepticism as to why actual prices should in any literal sense tend toward equilibrium during the course of a market has been increased not so much by the actual data of the experiment before us – which are certainly open to limitations – as by failure, upon reflection stimulated by the problem, to find any reason why it should be so. It would appear that, in asserting such a tendency, economists may have been led unconsciously to share their unique knowledge of the equilibrium point with their theoretical creatures, the buyers and sellers, who, of course, in real life have no knowledge of it whatever. (1948, p 102)

Vernon Smith (1962) reported another set of simple laboratory markets based on a different view of the important aspects of ongoing field markets. Like Chamberlin, he used dozens of undergraduate buyers and sellers with privately assigned values and costs, but changed the laboratory environment in two important respects. Smith employed the double-auction (DA) institution in which buyers and sellers transact by making and accepting public bids and asks, rather than Chamberlin's bilateral search institution. Smith also used stationary repetition, in which value and cost assignments are held constant across several trading periods. He found that transaction prices converged reliably and fairly quickly to CE values. Plott and Smith (1978) discovered that the efficiency of such markets was always quite high, often 100 percent.

Thousands of experiments since then have corroborated Smith's results. Indeed, only a few buyers and sellers (two to four each) are required to achieve rapid convergence to efficient CE outcomes when subjects are paid according to the precepts of induced-value theory. Smith summarizes the findings in terms of what he calls the "Hayek Hypothesis: Strict privacy [regarding agents' value and cost characteristics] together with the trading rules of a market institution are sufficient to produce competitive market outcomes at or near 100% efficiency" (1982a, p. 167). The evidence strongly supports the hypothesis in simple stationary-repetitive environments using the DA institution. More complex laboratory environments using several alternative market institutions also generally support the hypothesis (but see Holt, Langan, and Villamil, 1986, and Davis and Williams, 1991, for some qualifications). Smith exercises caution in interpreting the findings:

> What has been established is, that in the simple environments studied to date, the attainment of C. E. outcomes is possible under much less stringent conditions than has been thought necessary by the overwhelming majority of professional econ-

omists. . . . But even if our Hayek hypothesis continues to out-perform its competitors in laboratory experiments, does this mean it will do comparably well in the "field" environment of the economy? On the assumption of parallelism, namely that the same physical (and behavioral) laws hold everywhere, it is a reasonable working hypothesis, provisionally, to make this extension, but independent field observations, or experiments, are the appropriate vehicle for testing the extended hypothesis. (1982a, p. 177).

Gode and Sunder (1992, 1993a,b) illustrate the fruitful interplay between experiment and computer simulation, and add a new twist on the Hayek hypothesis. The authors create zero-intelligence (ZI) computerized traders that bid or ask randomly subject to a no-loss constraint. They find that the double-auction institution produces highly efficient outcomes even with ZI traders! Perhaps the rationality assumption plays a smaller role in some market institutions than most economists have presumed.

3

Experimental design

How does the number of buyers and sellers affect market efficiency? Do consumers prefer the "new improved" product or the "classic" version? Whether your purposes are scientific or commercial, you probably are interested in the effects of only a few variables, the *focus* variables. Usually you must also keep track of several other variables of little or no direct interest, the *nuisance* variables, because they may affect your results.

Which variables are focus and which are nuisance in your experiment depends on your purpose. The number of buyers is a focus variable in some oligopoly experiments, but the same variable is a nuisance in experiments testing consumer response to new products.

This chapter will explain how to design experiments that sharpen the effects of focus variables and minimize blurring due to nuisance variables. It will also explain how to design experiments that allow you to disentangle the effects of different variables, that is, how to avoid *confounding* the effects of two or more variables.

The first two sections introduce control and randomization, the basic ingredients of proper experimental design. Sections 3.3 and 3.4 elaborate on these ingredients and discuss specific designs. Distilled practical advice appears in the next section, and the last section illustrates the main ideas while reviewing some "test-bed" market experiments.

A word of warning before we begin. This chapter contains technical jargon. We have tried to follow the most common practices, but the literature is not entirely consistent in how words are used. You can consult the glossary at the end of the book to see how we use these words, but be careful in reading the literature to check what the author really means.

3.1 **Direct experimental control: Constants and treatments**

In the laboratory you can directly control many variables. You can freely select cost and value parameters and trading rules in market experiments, or the choice set and the subject pool in individual choice experiments. By controlling important variables you produce experimental data rather than happenstance data.

The simplest way to control a variable is to hold it *constant* at some convenient level. For example, enforce the same double-auction trading rules throughout a market experiment. The main alternative is to chose two or more different levels that may produce sharply different outcomes, and to control the variable at each chosen level for part of the experiment (or subset of experiments). For example, use two different sets of cost parameters, one inducing highly elastic supply and the other inelastic supply. Perhaps because of their prevalence in medical experiments, variables controlled at two or more levels are called *treatment* variables.

There is a tradeoff between controlling variables as constants and as treatments. As you hold more variables constant your experiment becomes simpler and cheaper, but you learn less about the direct effects and the interactions among the variables. Section 3.5 offers some suggestions on managing this tradeoff.

Suppose you choose two treatment variables, say the market institution with levels PO (posted offer) and DA (double auction), and the demand elasticity with levels E (elastic) and I (inelastic). Despite your control, you will completely confound their effects if you always change the variables together, say PO-E combination half the time and DA-I combination the other half. Instead, if you run each treatment combination (PO-E, PO-I, DA-E, and DA-I) one quarter of the time, you can gauge the separate effects of the two treatments. The logic is quite general: *Vary all treatment variables independently* to obtain the clearest possible evidence on their effects (see Figure 3.1).

3.2 **Indirect control: Randomization**

Some variables are difficult or impossible to control. For example, weather is an important and uncontrollable nuisance in agricultural experiments. (And occasionally in economic experiments: One of the authors recalls snowstorms preventing subjects from showing up and the other author remembers watching helplessly as airconditioning failed and the room temperature rose above 100°F in an early computerized experiment.) For economists, subjects' expectations usually are more important than the weather and just as uncontrollable. Some potentially

A. Confounded Treatment Variables:

	Elastic Demand	Inelastic Demand
Posted Offer Auction	Observations (PO-E)	No Observations
Double Auction	No Observations	Observations (DA-I)

B. Independent Treatment Variables:

	Elastic Demand	Inelastic Demand
Posted Offer Auction	Observations (PO-E)	Observations (PO-I)
Double Auction	Observations (DA-E)	Observations (DA-I)

Fig. 3.1   Independent variation of treatment variables.

important nuisances, such as a subject's alertness and interest, are not even *observable* by the experimenter, much less controllable.

Uncontrolled nuisances can cause inferential errors if they are confounded with focus variables. The real cause of improvement in harvests in the year a new seed variety is introduced may be good weather. Efficiency may decline when elastic supply parameters are introduced late in a long experiment, but the reason may be subjects' fatigue. The problem is that you may attribute an observed effect to a focus variable when the effect actually arises from an uncontrolled nuisance.

How can you avoid confounding problems when you can't directly control some important nuisances? The advice offered at the end of the previous section provides a hint. Independence among controlled variables prevents confounding problems. We would solve the present problem if we could somehow make the uncontrolled nuisances independent of the treatment variables.

Randomization provides indirect control of uncontrolled (even unobservable) variables by ensuring their *eventual* independence of treatment variables. The basic idea is to assign chosen levels of the treatment variables in random order. For example, in a market experiment subjects' personal idiosyncrasies and habits are an uncontrollable and largely unobservable nuisance variable. When subjects arrive, don't assign all the early birds to the role of sellers and the late arrivals to the role of buyers. Randomize the assignment and you can be confident that observed profit differences between buyers and sellers arise from differences in the roles and not from differences in subjects' personal characteristics.

The simplest valid experimental design is called *completely randomized.* In this design, each treatment (or each conjunction of treatment variables) is equally likely to be assigned in each trial. (A *trial* is an indivisible unit of an experiment, such as a trading period in a market experiment.) Suppose you choose a completely randomized design for the two-treatment experiment illustrated in Figure 3.1. Then in each trial you might flip two fair coins to select each of the four treatments PO-E, PO-I, DA-E, and DA-I with probability 0.25 in each trial, independently of selections in previous trials.

Complete randomization is quite effective when you can afford to run many trials. Independence among your treatment variables and uncontrolled nuisance variables is "eventual" in the sense that only as the number of trials gets arbitrarily large does the probability of a given positive or negative correlation go to zero. You can occasionally get a large correlation between treatments and uncontrolled nuisances in a small set of randomized trials. Classical statistical techniques, discussed in Chapter 7, take this problem into account.

When uncontrolled nuisances produce little variation across trials, the completely randomized design is hard to improve upon. When controllable nuisances do significantly affect outcomes, however, designs that appropriately combine control with randomization are more efficient in the sense that they can produce equally decisive results from fewer trials. These designs ensure zero correlation among controlled variables even in small sets of trials.

Random block is the general name given to this improved design. The difference from the completely randomized design is that one or more nuisance variables are controlled as treatments rather than randomized.

Nuisance treatment variables are often called blocking variables, held constant within a block [subset of trials] but varied across blocks. The next two subsections provide examples.

3.3 The within-subjects design as an example of blocking and randomization

The purpose of the classic boys' shoe experiment (Box, Hunter, and Hunter, 1978, p. 97ff) is to see whether a new sole material lasts longer than the old. The focus is sole material, a treatment variable with two levels: old and new. Measured wear varies considerably, mostly from subjects' different activities and habits: Some boys are couch potatoes, others ride scooters using a shoe for a brake. Clever experimental design prevents these nuisances from obscuring the focus variable's effects: Each boy gets a pair of shoes with one sole of new material and the other sole of old. Thus subject identity in this design is a blocking (i.e., nuisance treatment) variable that captures the habits and activities nuisances, and *differences* in measured wear between left and right soles becomes the relevant performance measure. Random assignment of the focus variable (new material on left or right shoe) reduces confounding due to other nuisances, such as whether scooter brakers tend to be left or right footed.

Experimental designs that vary levels of the focus variable only across subjects are generically called *between subjects* designs and those that use several different levels for each subject are called *within-subjects* designs. The shoe experiment uses a special within-subjects design that allows all data to be expressed as differences across matched pairs. The matched-pair differences allow sharper inferences to the extent that individual subject variation is an important nuisance.

The same trick can be useful in economics experiments. For example, suppose you conduct individual choice experiments comparing the willingness to pay (WTP) for a gamble to the willingness to accept (WTA) a certain payment in lieu of the gamble. If you want to see whether your new "transparent" instructions will bring WTP and WTA closer together, then individual variability is an important nuisance you should take into account – for instance, some subjects may be more risk averse than others and report low WTP and low WTA. It would be appropriate to employ a within-subjects design as in the shoe experiment. Specifically, you could ask each subject for WTPs and WTAs in random order, and analyze the *differences* WTA − WTP across subjects for each gamble. That way you eliminate a potentially important source of noise, and the effects of your focus (instructions) then become more visible.

3.4 **Other efficient designs**

The within-subjects idea has two useful variants. A *crossover* design takes a subject or group of subjects and varies the levels, say A and B, of a treatment variable across trials. When you suspect your treatment variable has effects lasting several trials, you should consider the ABA crossover design. (The simpler AB design confounds time and learning with the treatment variable.) For example, suppose your focus variable is the market institution with A = the double auction and B = buyers' auction (sellers passive). The convergence behavior of a group of traders may carry over from one trading period to the next, so in one session you might conduct four A trading periods followed by eight B trading periods and finish with four more A periods (ABA), and use the complementary BAB design in a companion session. Then the difference in mean observed performance between the A and B periods would conservatively indicate the effect of your focus variable.

A second variant, the *dual trial,* is especially useful when individual or group idiosyncrasies may be an important nuisance. Kagel and Levin (1986), for example, suspected that individual random signals and the behavior of other bidders in a group could affect bidder behavior in first-price common-values auctions. To test cleanly the effects of the focus variable, group size with levels S(mall) and L(arge), they employed dual auctions: upon receiving her signal, each subject submitted two bids, one for a small-group auction and a second for the large-group auction. Their dual auction design allowed the authors to isolate the effect of group size by looking at differences ($b_L - b_S$) in the two bids across subjects and time periods.

The *factorial design* is perhaps the most important general method for combining randomization and direct control when you have two or more treatment variables. To illustrate, consider two treatment variables ("factors") labeled R and S, with three levels H(igh), M(edium) and L(ow) for R and two levels H(igh) and L(ow) for S. In the resulting 3×2 factorial design, each of the six treatments LL, LH, ML, MH, HL, and HH is employed in the same number k of trials. Thus $3 \times 2 \times 4$ = 24 trials are required to replicate the design $k = 4$ times. Randomization plays an essential role in that you must assign the six treatments in random order to the six trials in each replication.

When it is feasible, the factorial design is more efficient than the completely randomized design because it ensures that each treatment (combination) occurs an equal number k of times, and that the treatment variables all have zero correlations even for small replication numbers k. Among other things, this helps you to distinguish the direct effects of the treatment variables from interactions.

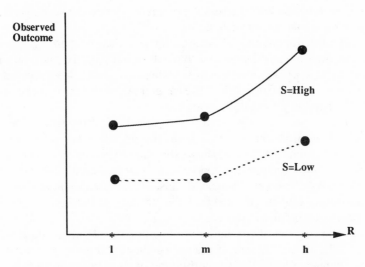

Fig. 3.2   Mean outcomes in a hypothetical factorial experiment.

Figure 3.2 uses the 3×2 example to illustrate direct and interactive effects. The vertical axis is the observed outcome, say market efficiency. The first treatment variable R, say elasticity of demand and supply, appears on the horizontal axis and the second variable S, say payoff intensity, shows up in the two curves labeled S = High and S = Low. The curves themselves connect the hypothetical mean outcomes in each treatment. The distance between the curves measures the direct effect of variable S. When the curves are parallel, there is no interaction between R and S, but when the gap between the curves widens as in Figure 3.1, there is a positive RS interaction. Chapter 7 will discuss the issue more extensively.

The factorial design is a bit less robust than the fully randomized design because experimenter errors in assigning treatments and missing trials (from computer glitches or no-show subjects, for instance) more seriously impair the data analysis. Indeed, if these problems are frequent, the factorial design becomes indistinguishable from the completely randomized.

Another problem with the basic factorial design is that the number of required trials increases quickly as the number of factors increases. Suppose, for example, you chose only two levels for each treatment variable. Even then, you need $2^4 = 16$ trials for 4 factors and $2^8 = 256$ trials for eight factors to run just a single replication! The problem is serious because there are many potentially important nuisance variables in some economic environments.

The fractional factorial design alleviates the problem. The basic idea is to run a balanced subset of the factorial design. To take the simplest example, suppose you have three variables, each with two levels denoted + and −, and can conduct only four trials. That is, you can run only half of the eight possible treatments (+ + +, + + −, + − +, + − −, − + +, − + −, − − +, and − − −). Your first thought might be just to run the first four treatments on the list, or every other treatment, but a moment's reflection shows that these choices are unbalanced because some variables are held constant or some pairs of variables are correlated. You get a balanced subset of treatments if you impose the restriction that the third sign is the product of the first two. Then the subset of treatments you run is + + +, + − −, − + −, and − − +. If you run this subset (in random order, of course!), then you have a half factorial $2 \times 2 \times 2$ design. If you are a geometric thinker, you can visualize the balance of this design by thinking of each possible treatment combination as a corner of the unit cube in the space of the three treatment variables. For example, + + − could label the upper left back corner and − − + label the lower right front corner. The chosen treatments' center of mass is the center of the cube, and the center of mass on each face is the center of the face. Each level of each treatment variable appears in the same number of trials (2) and each pair of treatment variables is orthogonal.

Conceptually (although not visually) it is straightforward to generalize to more treatment variables and to smaller replication fractions. For example, Copeland and Friedman (1987) use a half-factorial $2 \times 2 \times 2 \times 2$ design in an asset-market experiment, where the fourth treatment variable (infocontent, a focus variable that defines the informational complexity of the environment) is constrained to be the product of the first three treatment variables (two nuisance variables called learnops and paymethod and another focus variable called infoarrival). A more dramatic example is given by Box et al. (1978, p. 394). They present a 2^7 sixteenth-factorial design for determining which of seven variables (seat position, handlebar position, tire pressure, etc.) affect a bicyclist's performance. Only 8 trials are required, compared to 128 in the full once-replicated factorial.

The elegance and economy of the fractional factorial design come at a price. The design obviously is less robust than a randomized design; it loses appeal if you are not confident of your ability to conduct all trials flawlessly. (If you are confident, the design has a subtle advantage: You can complete the factorial design if it turns out you can run additional trials.) The other disadvantage is inherent in the design. The fractional factorial achieves balance in a subset of the possible treatments by systematically confounding some direct effects with some interactions. The simple half-factorial $2 \times 2 \times 2$ example confounds the third variable with the pairwise interaction of the first two variables, for instance. This disadvantage is not always serious. If you know that some pairwise or higher-order interactions are negligible, then you can harmlessly confound them.

We close this section with some background information for readers who wish to learn more about classical experimental design. R. A. Fisher and his colleagues developed most of the concepts presented in this chapter between 1910 and 1940. Much of the terminology comes from agricultural experiments; blocks, for example, originally referred to adjacent rectangular pieces of land, and a split-plot design (a type of randomized block) originally involved subdividing such a block for one treatment variable.

Statisticians with a combinatorial bent noticed that further efficiency gains theoretically arise from imposing additional symmetries on block and factorial designs. For instance, in testing four tire brands (*a, b, c,* and *d*) using four test cars, you could require not only the ordinary blocking condition that each car uses each brand, but also balance the assignment of tires to the four wheels of the test cars – say, use the order *abcd* for the four wheels in the first car, *dabc* in the second, *cdab* in the third, and *bcda* in the fourth car. This design is called Latin square after its diagrammatic representation, and it has higher-dimensional analogues called Graeco-Latin and hyper-Graeco-Latin designs. Such constructions quickly become quite Baroque and are not at all robust to missing trials and so forth.

The interested reader can find dozens of advanced books on experimental design, mostly of the 1950–70 vintage, in the QA279 section (under the Library of Congress system) and other sections of a good library. In writing this chapter we relied most heavily on Box et al., (1978) as well as Campbell and Stanley (1966), and Kirk (1982).

3.5 **Practical advice**

Theoretical considerations regarding experimental design do have practical consequences. Drawing on the theory, we offer some general advice regarding typical nuisance variables, the choice of constant and treatment variables, and the general conduct of experiments.

3.5.1 Chronic nuisances

Remember that the distinction between nuisance and focus variables depends on your purpose. Experience and learning, for example, are nuisances if you want to test a static theory but are focus variables if you want to characterize behavioral change over time. This chapter has already mentioned most of the important nuisance variables you typically face in conducting an economics experiment, and suggested ways for dealing with them. Chapters 4 and 7 provide a more systematic discussion, but a quick summary may be useful at this point.

1. Experience and learning: Subjects' behavior changes over time as they come to better understand the laboratory environment. When this is a nuisance, control it as a constant by using only experienced subjects, or control it as a treatment (blocking variable) by using a balanced switchover design.
2. Noninstitutional interactions: Subjects' behavior may be affected by interactions outside the laboratory institution. For example, sellers may get together during a break and agree to maintain high prices. Careful monitoring during the break, or a change in parameters after the break, therefore may be advisable.
3. Fatigue and boredom: Subjects' behavior may change over time simply as a result of boredom or fatigue. For example, after playing strategy A for 58 periods in a repeated prisoner's dilemma, a subject may choose strategy B (defect) just to relieve the tedium. We recommend occasional payoff switchovers and planned sessions of at most two hours for most experiments.
4. Selection biases: The subjects or their behavior may be unrepresentative because their selection was biased. For example, self-selection may upwardly bias self-reported sexual activity when only the most talkative choose to respond to your questionnaire. Experimenter selection may be biased when students in an advanced finance class are recruited for an asset-market experiment. Recognizing the problem is the key step in finding ways to deal with selection biases.
5. Subject or group idiosyncrasies: A subject's background or temperament may lead to unrepresentative behavior. A group of subjects somehow may reinforce each other in unusual behavior patterns. Replication with different subjects therefore is essential.

3.5.2 Disposition of variables
We offer the following suggestions on choosing treatment and constant variables.

1. Control all controllable variables. Otherwise your data will be less informative than they could be.
2. Control focus variables as treatments. Use widely separated levels to sharpen the contrasts. Use two levels and skip intermediate levels unless you are interested in possibly nonlinear effects.
3. When you suspect that a nuisance variable interacts with a focus variable, consider controlling the nuisance as a treatment. Two levels often suffice.
4. Control most nuisances as constants to keep down complexity and cost. Even a nuisance with large effects can harmlessly be held constant as long as its effects are independent of the focus variables' effects.
5. Vary your treatments independently to maximize the resolution power of your data and to avoid confounding.

3.5.3 Phases of experimentation

A laboratory investigation typically proceeds in phases. The preliminary phase identifies the specific issues to be investigated and the essential aspects of the laboratory environment. The next phase consists of one or more pilot experiments. Here you complete the specification of the laboratory environment, prepare instructions for subjects, and conduct the pilot experiments, perhaps with unpaid subjects at first. The results usually lead to improving (simplifying) the instructions and the environment. At this point you should choose the focus and important nuisance variables you will use as treatments; the suggestions in the previous subsection may help.

Now you are ready to begin the formal part of your research by conducting a set of exploratory experiments. You should pick a simple design capable of detecting gross effects of the treatment variables, perhaps a fractional factorial or a $k = 1$ factorial. When you analyze the data you may decide to hold constant some variables that seem to have no interesting effects or interactions. Possibly you will want to adjust the environment or introduce a new treatment variable on the basis of the exploratory data. If you are exploring a new area, you may well discover at this point that major changes in instructions or treatments are necessary. If so, you will probably relabel your work so far as preliminary, and try the second phase again.

The final phase consists of follow-up experiments intended to provide definitive evidence on your chosen issues. Try to reserve 50 to 75 percent of your budget for this phase. If the results of the exploratory experiments seem clear-cut, you may choose simply to replicate them in the follow-up phase. If the exploratory experiments suggest subtle but relevant direct effects or interactions among your variables, you may choose a more elaborate design.

A final piece of advice. Don't get too fancy in designing your experiments, especially in your first project. Begin with a proven design from related previous research by other authors, or use a simple version of one of the designs we have presented.

3.6 Application: New market institutions

We live in an era of rapid change in economic institutions. Existing markets have expanded and changed, and new markets have opened, in response to advances in computer and telecommunications technology and in response to political developments in Asia, and in Eastern as well as Western Europe. Even in the relatively stable markets of the United States, scandals and technological developments have spurred efforts to reform the primary market for U.S. government securities and the commodity exchanges.

How do we evaluate alternative market institutions? What kinds of market institutions will best promote efficient exchange in the new environments around the world? Existing economic theory and historical experience provide precious little guidance. Field experiments can be costly, as well as politically risky. Laboratory experiments can conveniently serve as test beds for new market institutions. New institutions can be tried out and refined in the laboratory before they are further tested and implemented in the field. This section discusses some of the test-bed work done so far and uses it to illustrate some of the basic principles and issues in experimental design.

> Laboratory experimentation can facilitate the interplay between the evaluation and modification of proposed new exchange institutions before field implementation.... Laboratory experiments allow one to investigate the incentive and performance properties of alternative exchange institutions, and, with respect to institutional design, they provide a low-cost means of trying, failing, altering, trying, etc. This process uses theory, loose conjecture, intuitions about procedural matters and, most important, repeat testing to understand and improve the features of the institutional rules being examined. (McCabe, Rassenti, and Smith, 1993, p. 309)

Two kinds of work are discernible in test-bed research. When the institutions are reasonably well-specified, an experiment can be designed using classical approaches discussed in this chapter in order to measure and compare their performance characteristics. The studies by Hong and Plott (1982) and by Grether and Plott (1984) described below fall into this *performance testing* branch of test-bed research. On the other hand, when the institution itself has to be designed through an iterative design-test-revise process, classical experimental design techniques usually cannot be applied to the overall process, although they may be useful for some phases of the project. This second branch, *developmental testing* is exemplified in Grether, Isaac, and Plott (1981), Plott and Porter (1989), the McCabe et al. (1993) effort to develop a uniform-price double auction, and the McCabe et al. (1988) effort to develop a "smart" market for natural gas. We shall now briefly touch on both branches of test-bed research.

3.6.1 Performance testing

Grether and Plott (1984) conducted some early test-bed experiments dealing with a controversy about existing market institutions. In May 1979 the U.S. Federal Trade Commission filed an antitrust suit against the four domestic producers of a gasoline additive, tetraethyl lead. The suit claimed that uncompetitive high prices were sustained by three institutional practices: advanced notification of price changes (AN), "most favored nation" guarantees to customers that nobody else will get a lower price (MFN), and "delivered pricing" quotes that include transportation cost (DP). The four lead producers argued that the institutional practices were a convenience to customers and had no anti-competitive effects.

In their laboratory study, Grether and Plott break the AN institution down into three focus variables: price publication with three levels (N = no seller publishes prices, L = the two largest sellers publish, and A = all sellers publish prices), price access with two levels (B = only buyers see published prices, and A = all buyers and all sellers see published prices), and advanced notice per se with two levels (Y = yes, a seller can change price only if it is announced in the previous period, and N = no advanced notice required). They made MFN a single two-level (Y or N) variable and omitted DP from their study. Even so, there are potentially $3 \times 2 \times 2 \times 2 = 24$ institutional treatments (i.e, conjunctions of the four treatment variables).

In order to keep the study within budget, Grether and Plott held constant most other relevant variables including supply–demand parameters (at a level chosen to resemble the field conditions) and the basic exchange institution (bilateral search using telephones). Some conjunctions of treatments are vacuous or uninteresting (e.g., access to prices when no sellers publish prices) and some are especially interesting (e.g.,

AAYY = all disputed practices present, and N-NN = all disputed practices absent). Given the time and budget limitations, Grether and Plott used only 8 of the 24 possible treatments in their 11 laboratory sessions of 16 to 25 periods each. The most interesting treatments were used most often and most sessions use an ABA crossover design.

The data clearly support the conclusion that transaction prices are near competitive equilibrium when the disputed practices are absent (e.g., in treatment N-NN) but are substantially higher when the practices are all present in treatment AAYY.

The authors are cautious about drawing firm conclusions for the U.S. lead additive industry. However, they do convincingly argue that the disputed practices could no longer be presumed to be benign. After the experiments, the defendants lost the case to the government in trial but won on appeal. We conclude that the experimental design was adequate for the authors' purposes and that it provides an example of good exploratory work. A more careful design would be necessary in follow-up work to assess the separate and interactive effects of the institutional practices.

An institutional performance test by Hong and Plott (1982) used an even simpler experimental design. Railroad companies lobbied with the Interstate Commerce Commission to require barges to post rates. Railroads argued that publicly posted rates will make the industry more competitive, and protect the smaller barge companies from being secretly undersold by their larger rivals. While railroads had been required to post prices, the dry bulk cargo market on Mississippi operated largely by telephone between carriers and shippers.

Hong and Plott's (1982) simple design had one treatment variable, market organization, that took two values, posted price and telephone market. Two replications required a total of four market sessions. Identical parameters, based on scaled-down judgments of people in the industry, were used in all four sessions. Posted price markets revealed higher prices, lower efficiencies, and lower profits for smaller sellers. The railroads soon backed down from their efforts to change the prevalent rules for the barge market.

3.6.2 Development testing

Developmental test-bed studies are essentially sequential in nature. Since the design of the institution is being evolved, the factorial and other classical experimental designs described in the preceding sections in this chapter cannot be used to structure the overall study, but the general principles of control and randomization remain as important as ever. In the following paragraphs, we give a few examples of developmental test-bedding.

From 1968 through the mid-1970s, landing rights at major U.S. airports (Washington National, Kennedy, La Guardia, and O'Hare) were allocated among airlines by committees consisting of airlines that had been certified by the Civil Aeronautics Board. With the Airline Deregulation Act of 1976, the possibility that these committees could be used as a barrier to new competition arose. To what extent was the committee process, already in place, compatible with the Airline Deregulation Act?

Grether et al. (1981) conducted demonstration experiments with two kinds of institutions, committees and markets. The primary purpose of this experiment was to demonstrate the consequences of alternative decision-making processes. The authors found that (1) the outcome of the committee process is sensitive to the consequences of the default option resorted to in case of a deadlock in the committee; (2) separate committees for different airports could not efficiently handle the interdependencies between the airports; (3) the committee process is insensitive to the profitability of the individual airlines. In the market experiment they found that (1) speculation in landing slots was not a serious problem; (2) price of landing slots was determined not by their value to large airlines but by their marginal value; and (3) market processes can be designed to efficiently solve certain problems that are not solved efficiently by the committee process. Over the years, airlines have come to favor a market process for allocation of airport landing slots though the Federal Aviation Administration favors an administrative solution.

The U.S. Federal Energy Regulatory Commission funded a series of studies on electric power and natural gas networks (see Alger, O'Neill, and Toman, 1987a, b; Alger, 1988; McCabe et al. 1988; and Plott, 1988). As explained in the *Science* magazine overview, "Smart Computer-Assisted Markets," by McCabe et al. (1991), technological progress now allows markets to be created for goods with important indivisibilities and complementarities. For example, a gas distributor will want to make a purchase from a gas producer only if she can also purchase adequate transmission rights from pipeline owners at sufficiently favorable prices. Existing networks and computerized market programs could support the new markets, which promise substantial efficiency gains over traditional contracting arrangements.

For example, price dispersion disrupts markets for highly complementary goods like gas and gas transmission. Despite its great virtues, the double-auction market institution produces dispersed transaction prices, but some alternative market institutions do not. The call (or clearinghouse) institution, for instance, collects all bids and asks during a trading period, aggregates them respectively into demand and supply curves, and clears the market at a single, uniform price defined by the intersection of supply and demand. For use in markets with the complementary goods, McCabe et al. (1993) design a new market institution, the uniform-price double auction (UPDA) to combine the continuous feedback of the DA with the uniform pricing of the call market. The basic idea (independently explored in Friedman, 1993) is to continually announce the tentative clearing price as bids and asks accumulated during a call market trading period.

McCabe et al. (1993) study 8 variants of UPDA defined by three two-level variables: the call rule (exogenous end to the period at a prespecified time, or endogenous end when some condition holds, say when no new orders arrive for 20 seconds), the update rule (1s or 2s, the distinction involving how much a trader must improve previous offers to transact), and the inform rule (open book = all traders see all tentatively accepted and tentatively rejected bids and asks, and closed book = each trader sees only her own tentatively accepted bids or asks). The authors lay out a $2 \times 2 \times 2$ factorial design with eight replications; the design calls for each UPDA variant to be tested in three sessions using subjects experienced in one of the previous five sessions using that variant. The environment is held constant across sessions; it features a supply–demand configuration that shifts up and down randomly from one market period to the next. The authors find that inexperienced subjects do best with the exogenous close, 1s, closed-book variant, and experienced subjects do best with the endogenous close, 1s, open-book variant, and that efficiencies approach those of the basic double-auction market institution.

McCabe et al. provide a good example of first-stage follow-up experiments, given a large budget. Subsequent follow-up experiments will presumably match the best versions of the UPDA institution against other promising market institutions in a variety of laboratory environments. Appropriate designs again would be factorial, or, if funding becomes tight, fractional factorial. The next step would be field trials. As McCabe et al. explain, Steve Wunsch moved to Arizona in 1991 with his new electronic market system that competes with the major traditional exchanges in New York and Chicago. Thus opportunities for field experiments seem close at hand.

Among other examples of developmental work, Ferejohn, Forsythe, and Noll (1979) used experiments to examine the characteristics of Station Program Cooperative (a method used by noncommercial television stations in the United States to acquire programming), and to develop alternative bidding procedures. In their preliminary report, they found that the "theoretically superior bidding procedure" was dominated in important respects by SPC. Plott and Porter (1989) have conducted extensive work on developing market-like institutions for allocation of resources of U.S. National Aeronautics and Space Administration's proposed space station. The future scope for developmental testing seems unbounded.

4

Human subjects

What makes experiments so different from other methods economists use is the presence of human subjects. This is why doing experiments changes the way you think about economics. Rewarding data and insights arise when human behavior helps cast new light into one of the many corridors of economics that have remained unlit by other methods. Long ago Adam Smith inferred the existence of an "invisible hand" from its consequences. In the laboratory we can observe how real untutored humans are able to operate that hand in specific circumstances. Economic theory has largely bypassed questions about how humans observe, learn, memorize, form expectations, adapt, formulate, and choose strategies and decisions, by making convenient assumptions and leaving the actual discovery of answers to other social scientists. However, answers to these questions about human behavior are crucial to many core areas of economics, including industrial organization, securities markets, and monetary theory. Experimental economists do not seek to answer such questions directly. They do seek, through direct observation of human behavior in appropriately designed economic experiments, to evaluate the ability of competing theories to organize the data, and they provide the data to theoreticians for their use in pushing the theory further.

On the other hand, laboratory experimentation in economics presents a unique set of problems. The most difficult of these problems arise from observing and dealing with real human beings. In conducting experiments, the homogenous abstract agents of economic models and traders/consumers of computerized databases are replaced by flesh-and-blood people with all their infinite diversity, idiosyncrasies, moods, unexpected activity, and free will. Economists are trained to abstract away from this diversity and heterogeneity. Conducting an experiment requires you to make fine judgments about which differences among human beings matter for your purposes, and which differences do not matter.

The first section of this chapter starts out by asking who you should pick for your experiments. This is followed by a section on attitudes of subjects toward risk because this particular dimension of human diversity receives a great deal of attention in economics. How many subjects should you use in your experiment? Competitive models in economics assume atomistic competition, which is unattainable in the laboratory and is not descriptive of most natural markets either. How should you reward the people who participate in your experiments? How should you give them written, computer, or oral instruction? How should you recruit subjects? What are the ethical issues you need to be sensitive to in dealing with your subjects, and in obtaining approval of funding agencies and the human subjects committee on your own campus? We offer our advice on these and other questions, and conclude the chapter with a discussion of recent bargaining experiments.

4.1 Who should your subjects be?

Student versus nonstudent, novice versus expert in the domain of the experimental task, graduate versus undergraduate, volunteers versus draftees, acquaintances versus strangers, and gender have been the main dimensions along which this question of "who" has been addressed (see Ball and Cech, 1990). Your dilemma in selecting the group of people from which you draw your subjects is highlighted in the following questions: Are your subjects insufficiently experienced to really understand the market? Are they bored with your endless repetitions of identical trials?

4.1.1 Students

Most experimental studies to date have used undergraduate or graduate business (MBA) students as subjects for reasons of (1) ready access to the subject pool, (2) convenience in recruiting on university campuses where most of the research is carried out, (3) low opportunity cost of student subjects, (4) relatively steep learning curve, and (5) some lack of exposure to confounding external information. Doctoral students, on the other hand, can be brilliant experimenters but disastrous subjects. You may lose dominance with doctoral students because they often respond more to their understanding of possibly relevant theory than to the direct incentives of your laboratory economy. Doctoral students drawn from economics departments or from business schools are more likely to be aware of your objectives, contrary to Smith's privacy precept. Except in pilot experiments (or experiments specifically focused on the effects of prior knowledge), it is best to avoid recruiting such subjects.

The use of students is occasionally cited as a factor that undermines the external validity or generalizability of experimental research (See Cunningham, Anderson, and Murphy, 1974; Enis et al., 1972). The argument is that students are a narrow and special segment of the total population. The set of economic principles that are applicable to people at large may not coincide with the set that is applicable to this narrowly defined population. In order to effectively address this issue in planning an experiment, you need to analyze characteristics of the college population that may threaten the external validity of the results.

The college population is literate in language, mathematics, and in many cases, in statistics. Economics experiments make demands, sometimes heavy demands, for these skills from the participants. Experimental instructions often compete with apartment lease forms in length and complexity of their fine print. Multistage experiments may require the participants to read and comprehend a great deal of detail in limited time. One might argue that an average consumer or investor is unlikely to have the abilities routinely expected of laboratory subjects. In addition, while laboratory subjects may have several opportunities to gain experience through repeated transactions in the laboratory, the "real" people outside the laboratory may get but one chance to buy a house or choose a college. On the other hand, laboratory subjects in single-session experiments typically have only an hour or two to familiarize themselves with an environment while people in the real world may have years to acclimatize themselves. Ultimately, the desirability of going outside the easily available student subject pool depends on the specific reasons why student subjects might be considered less appropriate for the experiment on hand.

4.1.2 Professionals

The use of business professionals in laboratory experiments may solve some problems but create others. For example, Burns (1985) compared the behavior of professional wool buyers and student buyers in a progressive laboratory auction. She motivated the students by exhorting them to try to maximize their profits. The students were told that trying to maximize their profits will help them gain an understanding of the trading process, and that such understanding would be useful to them in writing an essay on a yet-to-be-announced topic for 10 percent of the course grade. The professionals' "natural competitiveness" was mobilized by a promise to announce the "best" trader at the end of the session. Students proved to be far more adept at maximizing their profits and learning while the professionals concentrated on maximizing the quantity they bought without learning much from prices that fell consistently within each period of the trading session. In their professional environment, wool buyers are said to be used to focusing their skills on detecting the quality differentials among the lots of wool offered for sale. They seemed nonplussed at the absence of this critical feature in the laboratory auction they were invited to participate in. Apparently, learning needed to operate in specific markets is specialized. Burns concluded:

> The wool buyers in this experiment reacted *not* to the opportunities and incentives present in the experimental market but to those present in other situations with which they were familiar. If the object of the experiment therefore is to measure reactions to the *experimental* conditions and objectives, it is unproductive to choose as subjects those whose prior experience is contrary to the current design requirements, for they will have difficulty in adjusting to a new frame of reference with consequent suboptimal behavior. (p. 152).

One author had a similar experience in conducting experiments with traders from Minneapolis Grain Exchange. After sitting through a careful explanation of the rules of trading, and demonstrative examples of double auction, the traders proceeded to trade by the rules of the Minneapolis Exchange that they were used to, completely ignoring what they had been told by way of instruction (Anderson and Sunder, 1989). In other words, salience may be more difficult to establish with experienced professionals.

DeJong, Forsythe, and Uecker (1988) report another experiment comparing the behavior of businessmen and student subjects in sealed-offer markets. Students earned cash varying in amounts from $10 to $25. Anticipating that this much cash may be insufficient to motivate the partners of CPA firms and senior financial officers of corporations, the professional subjects were promised a pewter souvenir if they scored more points than a similarly situated student earned in the student experiment. The mean price, profits, and efficiencies of the two markets were about the same, but the variances of prices and profits were higher for the professional market.

Many studies have reported results from parallel experiments in which students and professionals were given similar incentives. Siegel and Harnett (1964) conducted their bilateral bargaining experiments using General Electric salesmen experienced in bargaining with the customers.

They found the contracts negotiated by students and the professionals to be similar to each other and to the predictions of bargaining theory.

Smith, Suchanek, and Williams (1988) and King et al. (1992) conducted experiments with small business professionals and midlevel executives and even with over-the-counter traders familiar with screen trading. Aside from generally absorbing instructions faster, the professional subjects produced market results similar to the student subjects. Anderson and Sunder (1989) compared the performance of asset markets to detect any differences between the representativeness bias exhibited by student and professional subjects in processing probabilistic information. They found that the professionals were less prone to such biases than the students who participated in similar experiments. Subjects in their experiments received similar sums of money based on their respective performance. In an individual opinion experiment, Alpert (1967) found that students, military personnel, and business managers held different opinions about a manager's method of firing his subordinate. Dyer, Kagel, and Levin (1987) compared the bidding behavior of students and construction workers.

Laboratory experience, measured in number of sessions in which the subject has participated, is usually a controlled treatment variable in most experiments. When you feel that the kinds of skills needed in the experimental task may be difficult to acquire in a few laboratory sessions, it may become necessary to recruit professional subjects. If so, give careful attention to the conditions of recruitment and motivation, and keep in mind Burns's comments:

> The use of businessmen experienced in one set of rules introduces many unknowns which may confuse the issue and make interpretation impossible.
>
> The major role that experienced businessmen or traders can play is in *model development,* or the design of the experimental market itself. Where it is desirable to model a particular market institution, the comparison of the performance of an unbiased subject group, such as the students used here, with the performance of the experienced business group can point up issues of importance to the model that the theoretician may miss. A thorough debriefing or postexperimental discussion is essential to this task. (1985, pp. 152–3).

The advantages of cost and convenience in using student subjects are so large that abandoning student populations as the main subject pool is not justifiable. However, it is prudent to occasionally supplement student experiments with nonstudent experiments, especially when there are strong a priori reasons for divergence in behavior, and when you anticipate criticism (well founded or not) on this score.

4.1.3 Classroom experiments

Should you conduct experiments in your own scheduled classes, or with your own students? Classroom experiments offer the advantages of virtually effortless recruitment and scheduling, and grades can elicit high levels of motivation and effort from subjects without spending money (see Kormendi and Plott, 1982; Williams and Walker, 1993; and Marimon, Spear, and Sunder, 1993). When used appropriately, classroom experiments have great pedagogical value in teaching economics, political science, and management to your students. Besides, large-scale experiments of the type conducted by Williams and Walker would be practically impossible for most people without classroom participation.

Nevertheless, for experiments conducted to gather research data, caution is in order on three accounts. First, the classroom relationship between subjects and the experimenter can create internal and external validity problems. In the classroom, explicit salient rewards in money or grade cannot always be assumed to dominate other incentives such as students' desire to impress their instructor. As instructors many of us bring a personal system of values or point of view to our classes, and seek to imprint it on our students. When using the class for research experiments, we must ask ourselves if this system of values is relevant to the subject behavior or theories sought to be examined in the experiment. If the answer is affirmative, we should either refrain from bringing these values to the class – a questionable course of action because it would undermine the educational process itself – or qualify the reports of such observations by the possibility of interaction with the course instruction. A few benchmark experiments outside the classroom setting can be used to determine if the magnitude of this interaction affects the interpretation of in-class observations in a significant manner.

Second, recruiting subjects from one's own class for experiments conducted *outside* the class also carries some risk of weakening the internal validity of the experiment. The students may be left with the impression that some aspects of their performance in the experiment may be relevant to the course or their grade. Or they may try to impress the instructor in ways that arise from their relationship in the class, not in the laboratory. These problems can be mitigated by taking appropriate care in recruiting and instructions, and by the absence of the instructor from the experimental session.

Third, it is difficult to mesh the pedagogical requirements of sequential learning with the control and replication of treatments demanded by many experimental designs. In addition to these technical reasons, classroom experiments present some ethical pitfalls for social scientists. Our view, apparently shared by most experimentalists in recent years, is that classroom environments are better suited to pilot or perhaps exploratory experiments. Pedagogical value, convenience, and low cost of classroom experiments make them an attractive option for most instructors. We can combine a concern for interests of students with the cautious use of this valuable resource for creating new knowledge. We return to this issue in Section 4.6.

4.1.4 Gender

Economic theory is free of gender and sex. However, there has been a great deal of work in social psychology documenting important differences in behavior by gender and sex (see Maccoby and Jacklin, 1974, and Rhode, 1990, for broad reviews). There have been only a few attempts to examine the effect of gender and sex in economics experiments. Brown-Kruse and Hummels (1990) did not detect any significant difference between the willingness of male and female subjects to contribute toward production of a public good; contrary to the hypothesized direction of the difference, the male subjects contributed a bit more. It remains to be shown that you need to worry about the gender of the subjects in your economics experiments. You may have to be careful about the gender of subjects if the experimental task involves face-to-face adversarial interaction between pairs of subjects (e.g., bargaining). (See Ball and Cech, 1990.)

4.2 Subjects' attitudes toward risk

Preferences, in particular attitudes toward risk, are the most important characteristic that standard economic theory recognizes to be variable across individuals. Reliable demographic data on individual risk attitudes is virtually nonexistent. Yet a great deal of economic theory rests on attitudes towards risk. When dealing with economic environments in which cross-sectional variability of risk attitudes plays an important role, you will be faced with some difficult decisions.

Many models assume that economic agents can be classified by their attitudes toward risk. Most treatments of attitudes toward risk also assume that it is an intrinsic characteristic that may vary across agents but is essentially fixed for an individual. It may well be that an individual's risk attitudes vary with time or context (see Berg, Dickhaut, and McCabe, 1992); but theory and evidence on such variation remain to be incorporated into economics.

Many laboratory procedures are guided by formal models based on highly specific assumptions about risk attitudes. Given the lack of demographic data, experimental economists face a difficult problem in modeling economics of uncertainty in laboratory environments. Three different approaches have emerged.

The first approach is to treat the assumptions about risk attitudes in the relevant formal models as technical assumptions. No effort is made to gain control on the risk attitudes of human subjects who are left free to use their own innate risk preferences in making their decisions. The main advantage of this approach is that it permits the experimenter to obtain evidence for or against the propositions which are more general in the sense of being free of the specific technical assumptions about risk attitudes. For example, the experimental evidence on the effect of futures markets on efficiency of spot prices has been gathered in this manner (Friedman, Harrison, and Salmon, 1983). Being free of specific assumptions about risk attitudes, findings of such experiments are more general than the relevant, risk-specific formal models. By leaving the risk attitudes uncontrolled, you are able to present evidence with plausible generalizability to field situations where the validity of the technical assumptions may be unknown or unknowable. The main disadvantage of this approach is that it cannot be used to gather evidence on propositions where assumptions about risk attitudes are critical, not merely technical. Agency theory and risk-sharing experiments are examples of this type.

A second approach is to directly and independently measure the risk attitudes of the potential participants before conducting the experiment, assign them to various experimental treatments on the basis of this information, and then retest risk attitudes after the experiment. For example, in their test of the effect of risk attitudes on price volatility in asset markets, Ang and Schwartz (1985) used the Jackson Personality Inventory (Jackson (1976) and Jackson, Houdnay, and Vidmar (1972)) tests to isolate subjects with high and low risk aversion. They concluded that, contrary to the theoretical propositions derived by LeRoy and LaCivita (1981) and Grossman and Shiller (1981), markets with more risk-averse subjects exhibit lower price volatility. Tests of such a proposition would not have been possible without some control of subjects' risk aversion. The advantage of Ang and Schwartz approach is that risk attitude, the treatment variable, is measured independently of the behavior being tested, and the measurement is based on a validated test of personality characteristics of individuals. It is possible to question whether the Jackson ordinal measure of risk aversion corresponds closely to personality traits relevant in trading behavior. Construction and validation of alternative instruments for measuring risk aversion in such environments would be an effective way of carrying on a productive argument on this matter. See Van Harlow (1988) for a fascinating example that features five separate measures of risk aversion – two laboratory measures, two psychological inventories, and one blood test!

Becker, DeGroot, and Marschak (1964; abbreviated BDM) introduced the most widely used laboratory method for measuring "home-grown" risk preferences. You give the subject a risky prospect, usually a lottery ticket that pays him y with probability p (and pays 0 with probability $1 - p$). You tell him that you will find a "buyer" whose offer z will be random between 0 and y; the subject must name a selling price x, then you reveal z and he gets z if $z > x$ and otherwise plays the lottery (y,p). It is not hard to show that an expected utility-maximizing subject will name his true home-grown certainty equivalent x^* as the selling price.

The BDM procedure is not foolproof. The expected utility is maximized at $x = x^*$, but moderate deviations of x from x* produce only tiny losses that may not dominate decision costs or other home-grown characteristics. If you use the BDM procedure sequentially, the subject may try to favorably influence your choice of subsequent lotteries by naming high prices x. Even if your lottery sequence is predetermined, he may construct a portfolio of lottery tickets, complicating your inferences. In Section 4.4.2 we describe techniques for mitigating these problems; see also Harrison (1986). These fix-ups will not help if your subject does not maximize expected utility – for example, if she doesn't correctly reduce compound lotteries. But risk preference measurement is not well defined for such subjects in any case.

There is a third category of propositions whose experimental tests cannot ignore attitudes toward risk as mere technical assumption, nor can these attitudes be captured in ordinal measure of more or less risk aversion. These propositions depend on specific functional forms of subject preferences. Precise tests of these propositions require that the subjects have the specified preferences among experimental lotteries, independent of their home-grown preferences for money. Roth and Malouf (1979) had their subjects bargain for the probability of winning a fixed dollar prize, instead of bargaining for money directly. If subjects use expected-utility criterion, this procedure ensures that they would be risk neutral in the object of bargaining – the probability of winning the fixed prize – irrespective of their attitude toward the risk of getting the money. Berg et al. (1986) generalized this procedure by having subjects play for "points," and then using any specified function to convert these points into the probability of winning a fixed dollar prize. Again, under the assumption that all subjects use expected utility as their decision criterion, this procedure allows the experimenter to induce in subjects any desired risk attitude toward experimental points.

This technique for controlling preferences for lotteries in units of experimental exchanges (usually designated "points") brings a large number of models in economics of uncertainty within the range of direct experimental testing. The cost of using the technique is incurred by addition of a layer of transformation of experimental points into probability, and a layer of uncertainty in converting the probability into the realization of the fixed dollar prize. It is built on reduction of compound lotteries axiom, and on the expected-utility criterion. Both these assumptions are contradicted by a significant body of empirical evidence (see Allais's, 1953, and Ellsberg's, 1961, paradoxes and Camerer, 1993, for a recent review).

Empirical evidence on effectiveness of the technique has been mixed. Berg et al. (1986) presented evidence from binary lottery choice and valuation tasks to support the validity of this procedure. O'Brien (1989) applied this technique in an asset market where potential gains from exchange arose from induced attitudes toward risk. Both price and efficiency of these asset markets corresponded closely to the equilibrium predictions conditioned on effective induction of risk attitudes among the subjects. Walker, Smith, and Cox (1990), applied the lottery procedure for inducing risk neutrality in first price sealed-bid auctions and found that the individual bids and winning bids were not well described by the predictions of risk-neutral Nash bidding strategy. Rietz (1990) reports positive results on effectiveness of the risk-inducing technique in sealed-bid auctions, and creation of hysteresis in the behavior of subjects operating under this procedure. Radner and Schotter (1989) report negative results in the context of sealed-bid bargaining.

In summary, the binary lottery procedure appears to push behavior in the right direction, but the magnitude or level of induced risk aversion or neutrality does not consistently jibe with the theory.

4.3 How many subjects?

The atomistic competition of economic theory is rarely an accurate description of markets in the field; certainly it is unattainable in the laboratory. You need practical guidance for determining the number of subjects in laboratory experiments. First, if it is possible to identify a naturally occurring economy whose behavior is sought to be understood, the number of active agents in such an economy could be used as a target. Note that the total number of agents who participate in a natural economy at various times is usually larger than the number who are active at any given time. Given the limitations on availability of human subjects, research budgets, laboratory facilities, and software, this target is likely to serve as an upper limit. A lower limit is obtained from the design of the economy and the relevant theory.

Finally, the shortfall in efficiency of markets from competitive equilibrium theoretically tends to decrease in proportion to the square root of the number of traders (see Gresik and Satterthwaite, 1986, and Satterthwaite and Williams, 1993). This means that the gains in efficiency from increasing the number of agents decline sharply as the number of agents is increased. Most experiments settle for a number close to the minimum. For example, in examining the applicability of the rational expectations model to competitive markets, Plott and Sunder (1982) used three types of traders and two information conditions. To ensure at least some competition in every cell, they had to put at least two traders in each of the six cells for a total of twelve traders. Given the design of the market, it would not have been meaningful to use fewer than twelve traders in this experiment. They used exactly twelve. Most studies suggest that two or three subjects in identical situation (i.e., "clones") are sufficient for attaining competitive results in laboratory markets (Plott, 1982, Smith 1982a). There is also some theoretical justification (Friedman, 1984, Kyle, 1989).

Certainly it makes sense to economize on resources by keeping the number of traders low in laboratory experiments. However, resources permitting, it is desirable to run at least a few experiments with a larger number of subjects as a validation check. Isaac, Walker, and Williams (1992), for example, used 100 subjects in a free-rider experiment. Such massive experiments are rare but may appear more frequently in the future as technology to carry them out is developed.

4.4 Trading commissions and rewards

Cash or other significant salient payment to subjects distinguish economics experiments from survey data. As explained in Chapter 2, the purpose of these payments usually is to provide experimental control over induced characteristics. There is some empirical evidence that the addition of rewards at least makes the results of experiments more reliable and reproducible (Jamal and Sunder, 1991; Smith and Walker, 1992).

4.4.1 Commissions

The early market experiments paid a small (usually a nickel) trading commission to the transacting parties. On the assumption that subjects' effort aversion makes them reluctant to trade the marginal units that may carry small or zero gain, it was thought that the introduction of a trading commission facilitates trading of the marginal units. The trading commission does increase trading volume, but it also shifts the margin itself. Interpretation of the volume data therefore is difficult unless you forbid trading units that would be extramarginal in the absence of a commission. Interpreting price data also has its problems. Even when a unique equilibrium price exists, commissions create an equilibrium price *range* against which the observed data must be evaluated. This is no different from comparing prices observed in a market without commissions against a hypothetical band whose width is equal to the presumed magnitude of frictional forces in the trading process. The gains from employment of trading commissions are ambiguous at best; worse, they may lull the reader or even the experimenter into believing that the frictional forces are absent. The result is that with the exception of experiments in which trading must be induced in order to observe the endogenously generated values traders may attach to the asset (in absence of gains from trading), trading commissions in laboratory are no longer routinely employed.

4.4.2 Rewards

Cash is the most frequently used reward given to subjects in economics experiments, with credit toward course grades a distant second. In addition, an on-time bonus, paid at the time of registration, is often employed for three reasons: to reduce tardiness (which is costly because most experiments cannot start until the last participant arrives), to establish ex ante credibility with the subjects that the rewards being promised to them will be paid to them promptly, and to provide an initial cushion of wealth they can afford to lose in the actual experiment without dipping into their own wallets.

Rewards from participation could be defined directly in terms of dollars. Alternatively, some researchers find it convenient to define experimental rewards in *points* with a conversion rate to U.S. dollars (or local currency) announced in advance. The use of points (or Francs or "PLATO dollars," etc.) makes it easier for the experimenter to retain the privacy of experimental parameters over multiple sessions of an experiment. The conversion rate can be identical or individualized, common knowledge or private information. When saliency of incremental decisions is of concern, dollars per point can be increased by defining conversion only for points earned in excess of a specified level. If you use this device, pick a sufficiently low specified level so you can be reasonably certain that everyone will earn at least that many points; otherwise you face the bankruptcy and convexity problems discussed in Section 4.4.3.

Most economists set the average reward per hour for on-campus experiments about 50 to 100 percent above the typical campus hourly wage for students. You can get a sense of the appropriate reward level by asking subjects (after they have been paid) to indicate on a form whether they would like to be called to participate in another experiment in the future. An 80 to 90 percent affirmative response is a good target.

Estimate the average reward level (or point conversion rate) as follows: (1) calculate the total number of points all subjects in the experiment will earn in each of the candidate equilibrium outcomes; (2) assign your subjective prior probabilities to each experimental outcome; (3) estimate the expected aggregate number of points to be earned by subjects; (4) divide these points by the estimated total hours subjects will spend on the experiment (including instructions) to get points per hour; (5) divide the average hourly dollar rate you wish to pay by points per hour to get the dollars per point conversion rate. Anticipating that it is easier to raise the rates of payment than to lower them, you may be tempted to err on the side of payments that are too low in your pilot experiments. But if you disappoint your subjects early, they may not return for the subsequent sessions to receive the benefit of your generosity.

The next step is to examine the distribution of the expected number of points across individual subjects if their role and endowments are not symmetrical. If significant discrepancies exist, you may wish to compute a separate rate of conversion of points for each class of participants. Alternatively, you can rotate subjects' role assignments during each session and maintain a uniform rate of conversion. If you suspect that the amount of money earned by subjects who are assigned different roles may differ significantly, and there is no convenient way of anticipating or reducing this variation, it is prudent to assign individuals to specific roles by a publicly observable random scheme such as drawing slips of paper from a hat. In this case, we recommend that you announce at the outset the possibility of large differences in earnings that may arise from the random assignment; otherwise subjects may resent the "unfair" setup.

In multisession experiments, you cannot depend on all the subjects who participate in the early sessions to volunteer to return for the subsequent sessions. You can improve your chances of success in such experiments in four ways: (1) use a higher payout rate; (2) recruit subjects for the entire sequence of sessions with specified dates, times, and places; (3) in all but the last session pay subjects in the form of IOUs to be converted into cash at the end of the last session (informing the subjects of this procedure at the time they are recruited); and, if necessary, (4) recruit a few extra hands for early sessions and use them as "helpers" or monitors so they become sufficiently familiar with the environment to be able to step in as substitutes for absentees in the later sessions.

Wealth effects of early-round earnings on late-round behavior can be attenuated by telling subjects that only one or a few rounds, chosen by a specified random device, will count toward reckoning the rewards. This method also helps keep the total cost of the experiment low, even though the contingent rewards in any given round may be large. But be careful how you choose the payment round. One beginning experimentalist we know paid each subject on the basis of her most profitable round in a repeated duopoly experiment. He was surprised to see the duopolists respond to the incentives by implicitly colluding, each conceding large market shares to her opponent in alternate rounds.

Rewards to subjects that depend on the points they earn in relation to the points earned by other subjects in the same experiment are called tournament-type rewards. Such rewards are best avoided, unless such rewards and their consequences are, themselves, the subject of investigation. In asset markets, tournament type rewards generate higher prices and induce risk taking behavior (see Ang and Schwartz, 1985). Offering tournament-type rewards to professional subjects in experiments seems both unnecessary and dysfunctional. Unlike students lured into the laboratory by the prospect of earning the week's rent, professionals volunteer their time out of a sense of service, obligation, or curiosity. They are usually willing to play along, and even get into the game with gusto and enjoy themselves, independent of any rewards. Tournament-type rewards offered by the experimenter may not satisfy either the induced-value theory or the dominance precept in such situations (see Smith, 1976, 1982b). Unless the experimental economy being examined expressly requires payment of tournament-type rewards, such payments are more likely to diminish than to increase experimental control.

4.4.3 The bankruptcy problem

When subjects' earnings become negative (or threaten to become negative) you lose control over induced preferences because negative payments are not credible. In particular, subjects may exhibit risk-seeking behavior in this situation because they believe they have a one-way bet – further negative earnings probably have no actual consequence while positive earnings will actually increase their end-of-session wealth. You don't want to find yourself unexpectedly dealing with such bankrupt subjects.

The best way to deal with the bankruptcy problem is to design the experiment in such a way as to minimize, if possible eliminate, the chances of bankruptcy. However, reducing chances of bankruptcy usually means one or more of the following sacrifices: (1) increasing the cost of the experiment by giving an initial endowment of cash to the subjects; (2) reducing the rate of salient payments in order to create the cushion of initial endowment; (3) reducing the statistical power of the test by allowing the predictions of competing theories to be closer to one another; and (4) placing restrictions (e.g., no short sale, or no transaction at a loss) on permissible behavior of subjects. No matter what you do, you have to pay a price for reducing the chances of bankruptcy in laboratory.

No matter how carefully you design the parameters, an occasional bankruptcy will occur. You should have a well-considered plan of action ready to manage such contingencies in a consistent manner. See the discussion of bankruptcy in Section 6.16 for some suggestions.

4.5 Instructions

Instructions include a broad statement of purpose of the experiment, a clear definition of the resource and information endowments of subjects, the set of choices and actions available to them, and most important, the rules for determining the rewards of individual subjects as a function of the action of various subjects. Instructions may include simple illustrative examples at various steps. Some experimenters also include short quizzes along the way as a test of subjects' comprehension. Unless carefully designed, quizzes run the risk of giving unintended cues about your intentions to your subjects.

An easy way of writing instructions for a new experiment is to start by modifying the instructions for another, similar experiment. Most experimenters go through many drafts before achieving the right balance among precision, clarity, and understandability of instructions and audio-visual aids to accompany them. The principal tradeoff in preparing written instructions is between comprehensiveness (for the record, and the referees) and comprehendability (for your subjects). It is easy to err in favor of the former, making your instructions unintelligible to the subjects. Following are the main elements of written instructions.

4.5.1 Purpose

A statement of purpose of the experiment helps satisfy the subjects' curiosity about why someone is willing to pay them money for playing games that they would gladly play without the additional inducement of cash. A written statement of purpose should be specific enough to satisfy the curiosity of subjects, and yet broad enough to avoid any "demand effects." If subjects are able to form a precise idea of the kind of behavior the experimenter is looking for, this in itself may make such behavior more (or less) likely. The statement of purpose should help preserve the internal validity of the experiment against such demand effects.

4.5.2 Examples

Illustrative examples in the instructions run the risk of contaminating the experiment if subjects read in them implicit suggestions about how they should behave. The risk can be reduced by shifting the scale of numbers used in the examples by one or two orders of magnitude. An occasional experiment would reveal the dangers of this practice when some subjects carry the numbers of the wrong order of magnitude from illustrative examples to the actual experiment. Illustrative examples should be screened so they impart the knowledge of the opportunities and rules to the subjects without giving them behavioral suggestions about the strategies to follow or avoid during the experiment. Some experimenters use balanced pairs or sets of examples to this end.

4.5.3 Privacy

Instructions often include individualized private data pertaining to endowments, information, dividends, and so on. Some experiments are ruined when somebody blurts out this information in the process of asking a clarifying question. When instructions include such information, it must be clearly identified as private, and the subjects warned against revealing it in their own public queries to the experimenter.

4.5.4 Realistic story

Parallelism between laboratory and naturally occurring economies is essential to the former helping us understand the latter. Yet, difficult questions arise when instructions for an experiment are written to make such parallelism explicit for the subjects. For example, should assets traded in the laboratory be given explicit company or industry names and other background color so they will "come alive" to subjects? (See Cohen, Levine, and Plott's, 1978, "chocolate pizza" experiment for an interesting example.)

Bringing color into the laboratory is, at best, a mixed blessing. Increased realism of such a laboratory environment may also bring unknown (to the experimenter) impressions and memories of past experiences over which the experimenter has no control. We know little about this internal versus external validity tradeoff. The current practice appears to compromise by keeping general contextual terms such as buyer, seller, shares, and profit, but avoiding terms with stronger flavor such as opponent, enemy, etc. Color is mostly kept out of the laboratory. In the final analysis, this would appear to be an empirical issue that would have to be thrashed out by comparing data from abstract as well as contextually rich experiments.

4.5.5 Duration of an experimental session

Three hours is close to the upper limit for an experimental session. Sessions of this length may be necessary for gathering long time series without dispersal of the subjects. Dispersal is often undesirable because it inevitably results in communication among subjects. However, sessions of this length do strain the patience of subjects. One method for reducing the length of the session is to impart instruction and conduct a dry run in one session, without revealing the specific parameters, and then conduct the experiment itself in a second session within a few days of the first. Any information that may motivate and enable subjects to form coalitions between the two sessions should be withheld under this arrangement. Provision of food can help keep subjects for longer, but it may create maintenance problems in computerized laboratories.

Increasing numbers of multisession experiments have been reported in recent years. Human subjects committees usually require that the subjects have the option of quitting at any time they wish to, making it difficult to retain the same cohort over multiple sessions. Experiments conducted within the classroom offer a convenient solution to this problem, allowing experiments to extend over several weeks or months.

4.6 Recruitment and maintaining subject history

The percentage of signed-up subjects who present themselves at the laboratory at the appointed hour (the yield rate) varies by campus, weather, and school calendar. Students residing in campus dorms have a higher yield rate than commuters; the yield rate declines before midterms and finals, in unusually bad (or good) weather, and on Friday afternoons. Estimating the yield rate to recruit a sufficient number of students requires the fine art of forecasting and the knowledge of the social calendar and major events in town (e.g., concerts). A knowledgeable research assistant drawn from the appropriate student group is a great help in choosing an experimental schedule likely to maximize the yield rate. After-dinner hours usually work well on residential campuses. Given the high cost of cancellations due to insufficient attendance, most researchers err on the higher side and pay a decent sum to the extra subjects who present themselves on time to avoid alienating them as future recruits.

Keeping a history of participation for individual subjects allows you to recruit experienced subjects later. Avoid mixing novice subjects with experienced subjects, unless the research design specifically calls for such mixing. In that case, ask the experienced subjects to report at a later hour timed to coincide with the completion of instructions for the novice group. In general, experienced subjects should still receive a complete set of written instructions to browse through and refer to as they wish; in addition they should be provided with summary instructions to refresh their memory, highlighting any difference between the current and the prior environments to which they may have been exposed.

An example of announcement for subject recruitment and sign-up is given in Appendix III.

4.7 **Human subject committees and ethics**

Government agencies and virtually all universities in the United States require researchers who work with human subjects to obtain clearance from campus human subjects committees. On most campuses, these committees consist of faculty from medicine, biology, and psychology departments whose research may involve serious potential of harm to their participants. Threat of moral, physical, or financial harm in economics experiments is usually nonexistent, and one would have to conjure up a strained scenario to make a case for psychological harm. With some initial work, many experimental economists have been able to obtain blanket approvals (or even exemptions) from their human subjects committees. For example, the University of Arizona, University of South Carolina, and Washington University either exempt economics experiments or allow wide discretion and judgment to the researchers. You may be able to support your case by citing these examples.

If you use class time or course grades to motivate your students, you may face a conflict between the pedagogical needs of the university's program of instruction, and the research needs of replicating thrice all the cells of your factorial experimental design. Students may not learn anything useful to them from participating in some of your cells. Unless you are lucky enough to have conveniently scheduled multiple sections of a class, replication may be difficult.

In awarding grades based on points earned in an experiment, you must satisfy yourself that such grades measure something that approximates the students' learning objectives in the course. If no such connection can be established, either reveal this fact to the class, or at least keep the experimentally determined component of the grade to a small fraction of the total. The ethical dimension of the classroom experiments will likely receive increased attention from the human subjects committees in years to come.

The most frequently discussed ethical issue in the planning and conduct of economics experiments concerns the possible contamination of subject pools with false information, that may create difficulties for other researchers on the campus. A professor who puts on the researcher's laboratory coat still retains the image of a trusted teacher in the eyes of the student subjects. If an experimenter gives misinformation to subjects (without telling them in advance that they will receive misinformation) and the subjects learn the truth during or after the experiment, subjects may come to distrust any instructions given to them in similar settings. It is difficult, if not impossible, for a researcher to screen out subjects who may have been exposed to such deceptive practices; given the privacy conditions of most economics experiments, it is also difficult to modify the experimental procedures to make even a distrustful subject see the objective conditions of the laboratory economy in the same way as the other subjects do. Failure to pay subjects after a promise or implied promise of payment has been made (the "Just Kidding" gambit) has a similar contaminating effect on the subject pool. Since there is no effective way of monitoring researchers' behavior in this respect, one can only hope that lying to subjects will be widely regarded as unethical in the academic community.

The consequences of misrepresentations made to subjects that cannot be known to them are less clear. The practice of having the subjects play against computer programs without telling them so borders on deceptive. If a researcher presents a carefully chosen predetermined sequence of numbers to subjects as a randomly drawn series, the subjects have no way of finding out, even ex post, that they have been lied to. In such cases, researchers often reveal this procedure in the write-up of the results along with an explanation of why it was deemed necessary. In the absence of financial harm to subjects, some respected experimentalists find such falsehoods to be acceptable price to pay for social science research. Others disagree and oppose deception of all sorts. In any case, if you use any deception in your research design, you had better have a strong justification for polluting the well from which your colleagues draw their own sustenance.

4.8 Application: Bargaining experiments

Laboratory results are joint outcomes of the characteristics of individual subjects, the laboratory institution, and the environment. Some institutions, such as the double auction, powerfully influence individual behavior so that the final outcomes are relatively insensitive to the characteristics and behavior of individuals. Other institutions, such as one-on-one bargaining, are relatively weak in the sense that their final outcomes are influenced substantially by subjects' personal characteristics. Thus, economics experiments can be placed in a broad spectrum defined by the relative importance of institutions and of individual characteristics in determining the final outcomes. Many market, voting, and contractual experiments, driven by economics, political science, and law, tend to the institutional end of the spectrum while individual choice experiments tend to lie at the other end. Bargaining experiments lie toward the individual choice end of the spectrum. They are especially relevant to the concerns of this chapter since the results can be quite sensitive to subjects' personal characteristics, details of instructions, and so on.

The experimental literature on bargaining is large. For a recent survey, we suggest you read Roth (1993). The basic bargaining experiment investigates how two subjects divide a "pie" – for example, $1.00. The institution may vary, allowing free-form face-to-face negotiations, or exchange of a fixed number of rounds of messages, in specified message space, sent through pieces of paper or over a computer network. The bargaining environment may also vary, changing the size of the pie over rounds (e.g., shrinkage to $.90 if the first offer is rejected, to $.80 if the second is rejected, and so on), or specifying that one or both players receive nothing in the event of any disagreement, and so on.

Lawrence Fouraker, an economist, and Sydney Siegel, a psychologist, collaborated on the first reported set of bargaining experiments (Siegel and Fouraker, 1960, Fouraker and Siegel, 1963). In their experiments subject dyads bargained through a structured alternating series of written price-quantity messages until a message from one party was accepted by the other yielding a contract. The theoretical prediction of equal split of the Pareto-optimal (joint maximum) outcome was generally supported by the data. "The dispersion of negotiated quantities around this amount could be decreased by (1) increasing the amount of information possessed by the bargainers, and (2) increasing the payoff increments associated with unit deviations around the Paretian optima" (1960, p. 75). They used information (full, partial, and asymmetric) as a treatment variable and found that bargaining outcomes approached equal split most closely under conditions of full information about payoffs. They established the importance of salient rewards and careful instructions.

Many bargaining experiments in the next two decades were conducted in Germany by Heinz Sauermann, Reinhard Selten, Reinhard Tietz, and Werner Guth. These experiments had a broad interdisciplinary focus, informed by considerations of bounded rationality and fairness norms and other psychological ideas in addition to game theory. A large body of this work has been published in the three volumes edited by Sauermann (1967, 1970, 1972).

Two series of bargaining experiments in the late 1970s revived the interest of English-speaking economists. Alvin Roth and his coauthors studied free-form negotiations over the computer, and varied the payoffs and information in various subtle ways. They induced risk neutrality, assuming that subjects' home-grown preferences are consistent with the expected-utility hypothesis, by having subjects bargain over lottery tickets to cash prizes, rather than bargain directly over cash. They found that popular cooperative-game-theory concepts such as the Nash bargaining solution are unable to account for the sensitivity of outcomes to information conditions. For example, with $5 and $20 prizes at stake for the two bargainers, disagreements are most common when the $5 bargainer knows his partner has $20 at stake but the $20 bargainer does not know his partner's prize and neither knows what the other does or does not know. Such results helped convince economic theorists that noncooperative underpinnings are a practical necessity for cooperative game theory. For experimentalists, this work goes beyond Smith's "privacy" precept and shows how to control subjects' knowledge about others' induced characteristics when it is appropriate to do so.

Elizabeth Hoffman and Matthew Spitzer (1982, 1985) studied single-round, face-to-face bargaining where in the event of a disagreement the pie shrank and was awarded entirely to a predesignated "controller" whose bargaining partner received nothing. They observed remarkably few disagreements (which they interpreted as support of the "Coase theorem"), and remarkably many equal or nearly equal splits of the pie. Later experiments showed that the controller demanded a larger share of the pie when the privilege was "earned" by winning a game of (minimal) skill; when negotiations were over a computer network; and when instructions were phrased appropriately. The outcomes in their experiments also may be sensitive to the gender of the bargainers in face-to-face negotiations.

By the late 1980s a major point of contention had come into focus. In many environments bargainers tend to split the pie more evenly than predicted by Nash equilibrium or more refined notions of noncooperative equilibrium. Psychologists and their allies (including most of the German experimentalists) invoked noneconomic explanations, especially that subjects' home-grown ideas about fairness dominate the results. Other economists argued that in many of these experiments subjects were responding more to social pressure or to demand effects than to the economic incentives: "Ask yourself if you would agree to be very rude to the next stranger you meet at a party if I offer to pay you $5" (Roth, 1988, p. 989).

Kenneth Binmore and his coauthors (1985, 1991) argued that in more structured settings behavior would tend toward Nash equilibrium (NE) predictions. Indeed, they found that Nash equilibrium predicts outcomes rather well in two-round shrinking pie experiments with experienced subjects recruited from economics classes in London. They explicitly instructed their subjects to make as much money as possible, possibly creating demand effects the other way. Later they found similar results using subjects recruited from a wide variety of classes and instructed more circumspectly as follows: "This is not an experiment to find out what sort of person you are. When we see the results we shall neither know nor care who did what. We are only interested in what happens on average. So please do not feel that some particular kind of behavior is expected of you" (Binmore et al., 1991).

Roth et al. (1991) looked for subject pool effects in bargaining and in "market" experiments, the latter being more accurately described as one-sided sealed-bid auctions. They recruited undergraduate subjects (and a few MBAs) from universities in the United States, Yugoslavia (now Slovenia), Israel, and Japan. In essence, they used a 2 × 4 factorial design. The first treatment variable was the institution (auction or one-round bargaining, both computer mediated) and the second was the subject pool. They took careful precautions to hold constant the instructions, payoffs, and other variables across the subject pools. They found that the auction experiments converged toward the same NE outcome for each subject pool, but the bargaining experiments did not. Average offers were higher and disagreements more frequent than in NE in all countries. Subjects made significantly less generous offers in Israel than in Japan and less generous offers in Japan than in the United States or Yugoslavia. Their conclusion, roughly speaking, is that cultural differences in fairness norms have a persistent effect in the bargaining experiments but not in the environmentally similar auction experiments.

Prasnikar and Roth (1992) soften their support for fairness explanations. They use a single subject pool (University of Pittsburgh undergraduates) but examine three institutions that in NE produce unequal ("unfair") payoffs. They find that ultimatum experiments (i.e., one player makes a single offer and neither player gets anything if the other player rejects it) persistently produce approximately equal splits, contrary to NE, but outcomes under the other institutions converge to the unequal NE, even though fairness arguments should apply equally well to all three institutions. They argue that the main difference is the out-of-equilibrium incentives. The other two institutions reward NE play by one player even when his partner deviates, but the ultimatum experiments penalize it: when the first player makes a NE ("unfair") offer, he is more apt to receive the disagreement payoff of $0.00 than if he deviates from NE and makes a more generous offer.

What should you make of all this? Certainly it is grist for theorists. In our opinion, the results point up the need for a learning theory that can predict when behavior will converge to equilibrium and when it will not. Of more immediate relevance to most readers, after thinking about this material for a while, you will be in a better position to anticipate when your experimental results will be sensitive to your choice of subject pool, instructions, and the magnitude and type of rewards.

5

Laboratory facilities

Until the mid-1970s virtually all economics experiments were conducted using little more than paper, pencil, chalkboard, and a watch in standard classrooms or meeting rooms. Since the early 1980s, more and more experiments rely on computers for data entry, communication, and recordkeeping. Computers bring both advantages and disadvantages. While a few experiments absolutely require a computer (and a few preclude their use), in most cases it is up to you to decide whether to conduct your experiment manually or on a computer. We discuss this issue before describing the facilities you will need for conducting experiments in each mode.

5.1 Choosing between manual and computer modes

Manual and computer markets are as different, and as similar, as driving and flying. The choice of transportation is hardly arbitrary; different destinations and objectives of travel call for different choices. Likewise in choosing your experimental mode, you must be clear about the purpose of your experiments.

Paper-and-pencil experiments allow you a great deal of freedom in changing your design, treatments, parameters, and procedures with little effort and delay. In contrast, computer experiments often require the software to be rewritten (and inevitably debugged once again). Unless you are lucky enough to be working with an experimental economics software that already incorporates the variation you wish to make, changing the software can be time consuming. If the software is borrowed, you may not have the source code to make the changes; even if the source code is available, deciphering programs written by others is difficult at best. If the experiment involves pressing of more than a few keys by subjects, the use of computers may also introduce

61

keyboard skills as a nuisance variable. Finally computer facilities are expensive in equipment, maintenance, and support staff time. Funds are needed not only for initial installation, but also for continually updating it in response to fast changing technology. The greatest disadvantage of computer-based experiments is that, given the high cost of developing software, you run the risk of allowing computers and software availability to become the guiding force in your research program. If you stick to pencil and paper, you have a better chance of staying the course with the substantive problems of economics you may wish to address.

Yet, an increasing proportion of experiments being reported today are conducted on computer networks as opposed to the face-to-face, paper-and-pencil and chalkboard mode. This is so because, in spite of their high cost, computers confer distinct advantages.

You can exercise tighter control on the flow of information in computer networks than in a room full of expressive faces, eye contact, body language, and voice inflections. When you study subtle informational issues in a laboratory, computer networks can therefore provide better control and sharper discrimination. However, if your purpose is to understand some aspects of field economics that operate in a manual mode, then you may wish to avoid computer networks, which eliminate important aspects of human cognition and communication. Does mob psychology play a significant role (beyond economic fundamentals) in the futures pits of the Chicago Board of Trade? Computer networks may not be the right vehicle for addressing such questions.

Computer markets also offer the advantages of fast and accurate data capture, fast and individualized communication between you and the subjects as well as among the subjects, and the possibility of offering computerized instruction. To the extent computers permit you to have less interaction with the subjects, the possibility of your contaminating the results through demand effects is also attenuated.

Williams (1980) reports the implementation of the first laboratory software to fully computerize a double auction (PLATO Double Auction). This software has been used for a large number of experimental studies conducted at University of Arizona and Indiana University. The paper documents some early concerns with the nature of differences between the behavior of oral and computerized trading institutions. For example, subjects need more time in the computer mode to learn to trade than in the oral mode. The range of messages traders can and do send in a face-to-face auction can be larger and less controllable by the experimenter.

5.1.1 Partial computerization

Computerization is not an all-or-nothing proposition. Analysis of data is usually computerized even if the data have been captured through manual experiments. A transitional procedure is to have subjects use pencil and paper to record their choices, to gather the pieces of paper, and to enter the data into a notebook computer which computes the outcomes while the subjects wait. If the amount of data is large, the procedure can be awkward and slow. However, considering the huge costs of developing software, it is an attractive option for many experimental projects, especially in the early stages. If partial computerization turns out to be too slow or cumbersome, you can always move on to further software development. A second, and important, advantage of partial computerization is mobility; your lab can go anywhere with you in a briefcase and your friends and colleagues can repeat your experiments themselves without having to build a laboratory. Computerization of instructions is the last step, often omitted.

We recommend that in your first experimental project you work with someone who already does experiments, and use the same facilities and techniques. Like many other skills, techniques of doing experiments are best learned through apprenticeship. Attending meetings of Economic Science Association to network with other researchers has given a good start to many. If you have to start out on your own, we suggest that you try to do your experiments manually at first. Sinking money into computer hardware and software is a risky proposition, especially on your first or second project.

5.2 Manual laboratory facilities

You can conduct manual experiments in a classroom with plenty of blackboard space, one or two overhead projectors and screens, adequate desk space for each subject, and a large table for your own materials. Try to have enough space in the room for the subjects to be seated sufficiently far apart to reduce leakage of information through sight or voice. Easy walking access between the experimenter station and each subject allows individualized attention to subjects during the instruction phase of the experiment. For example, in a manual double auction, it is important for each subject to be able to hear all others, and to see the blackboard and the screens clearly; a horseshoe layout works well. Find adjoining classrooms with a connecting door when you need sight and sound separation between groups of subjects. Most manual experiments can be conducted in ordinary classrooms.

5.3 **Computerized laboratory facilities**

Computerized experiments require greater commitment of space, time, and resources. A computer laboratory can be thought of as a high-fixed-cost, low-marginal-cost production facility. Given sufficient demand and sufficient resources, it is best to have a dedicated computer lab for economics for two reasons. First, the use patterns of an economics laboratory do not mesh well with those of computer classrooms and casual users. Experiments are often scheduled at short notice, subject to availability of participants and completion of prior experiments in a series. This makes it difficult to coordinate the use of shared facilities with classes scheduled months in advance. Second, experimental use of facilities is cross-sectional, requiring many machines for a few hours at a time, while individual use of a lab is longitudinal, often requiring one or a few machines for long periods of time. Closure of the entire lab on short notice for experimental use may alienate other users of shared facilities. However, only a few schools have sufficient demand to justify dedicated facilities, and most researchers today share them to varying degrees with other computer users on their campus.

Planning aspects of a computerized economics laboratory are discussed under the headings of space, hardware, software, and maintenance and management.

5.3.1 Space

Fifty square feet per workstation is a rule of thumb for planning economics lab facilities – about 35 square feet per station in a single room for laying out subject workstations, 5 square feet for equipment and storage, and 10 for the experimenter's work space. The subject room can be separated from the experimenter's room by a door and a glass partition (no need for one-way mirrors) to permit conversation in the experimenter's room while an experiment is in progress. You should have partitions that block subjects' view of others' screens, but subjects should be able to look over the screens to see common information on a chalkboard or projection screen. Since natural light interferes with screen visibility, laboratories can be built in a basement level when the needed ceiling height is available.

5.3.2 Layout

Workstation layouts depend on four main considerations: control of subjects' view, convenience of imparting group and individualized instructions, cost and safety of wiring the workstations, and monitoring of subject behavior (especially unauthorized conversation). Some laboratories seek these advantages by placing workstations on casters, which permit flexibility in arranging the workstations in convenient patterns according to the needs of specific experiments. A false floor that permits wiring of alternative workstation placements is an additional convenience.

5.3.3 Furniture

Besides comfort, two conflicting factors are important in choosing workstation furniture. Effective blocking of impermissible or unmonitored communication among subjects (e.g., through voice, keyboard sound, eye contact, view of others' screens) also makes it difficult to impart group instruction and common information, and to monitor subject behavior. Recently available (and relatively costly) workstation furniture in which the screen is placed under a glass window in the desk surface eliminates the need for visual partitions in the lab room. However, this option may sacrifice comfort, flexibility, and control of other forms of impermissible communication. A more popular option is to use lightweight, removable desktop partitions.

5.3.4 Hardware and communications

Hardware and communications planning for an economics lab involves considerations of experimental need, cost, compatibility with software, and flexibility. Hardware configurations in existing laboratories vary from remote mainframes with Internet or leased phone lines (NOVANET at Arizona and Indiana), to local workstations or minicomputers and dumb terminals (Colorado, Iowa, and University of California at Santa Cruz), to IBM-compatible PCs connected by Token Ring or other local area networks (Bonn, Cal Tech, Carnegie Mellon, University of Pittsburgh, Pennsylvania, Chicago, South Carolina, and Washington University). It is cumbersome to develop applications software for the Apple Macintosh, but Rick Wilson at Rice University and perhaps a few others have managed to do so. NeXT is easier to write for but does not yet have much software to go with it. Unix workstations (e.g., Sun Sparcstations and IBM Riscstations) are beginning to make some inroads (e.g., at the new University of Arizona lab) but are still expensive for the relatively minor amounts of local computing power utilized in most laboratory experiments.

Laboratories are likely to be upgraded to faster machines every few years. This is so because hardware prices continue to decline, laboratory implementations of economics experiments become more complex and sophisticated, with graphic display of real-time data and intelligent decision support for traders. It seems fair to assume that lab equipment will have to be changed every five to seven years. It is therefore important to design facilities that will readily accommodate newer types of hardware without major remodeling.

Wiring of workstations includes not only power and connections to other workstations and the monitor machine, but also connections to larger networks at the university, national, or international level. NO-VANET (formerly called PLATO) labs in many universities have been used to conduct large coordinated experiments across campuses. With the availability of Internet and other high-speed networks that join computers at virtually all universities in the United States and many universities abroad, it is now becoming possible to conduct much larger experiments (see Williams and Walker, 1993) than had been possible on any single campus. Again flexibility seems to be the key requirement of lab design so that the experimenter can exploit new technology as it becomes available.

5.3.5 Software

Software is the key resource in a computerized economics laboratory in terms of both the time and money it takes to develop and maintain. All too often, researchers who set out to develop their own software seriously underestimate the cost and time of developing laboratory software, even after being reminded of the popular software maxim: It is the last 5 percent of the work on software development that takes up 95 percent of the effort.

There is no mass market for laboratory software. Commercially available statistical, graphics, worksheet, communications, and database programs can be used for analysis of results, but rarely for conducting experiments. Excellent software has been developed in several labs for conducting economics experiments. Arlington Williams's PLATO double auction, Charles Plott's Multiple Unit Double Auction, Thomas Copeland and Daniel Friedman's Double Auction Asset Market, Shyam Sunder and Dan Gode's MARKET-2001, Srivastava and O'Brien's SI-MULAB are examples of software being used to conduct economics experiments. Much of this software has been shared across labs. However, these packages have been developed by economists to meet the needs of their respective research programs. Consequently, few of them have the generality, transportability, and documentation of commercial software, though Plott's MUDA comes close. Borrowed software usually requires high levels of author support, which is difficult for even the most willing and cooperative of the authors to provide. Plott and his lab staff have been exceptional not only in distributing their software and documentation, but also in providing generous user support.

A second problem is that most of the available software has not been written by trained software engineers and lacks the flexibility needed for varied use in different research programs. Given researchers' tendency to invent new features of economics institutions and theories, you probably soon will want to modify any software you borrow. In most cases, labs who share their software do not share the source code. Even when the source code is available, it is not easy to modify someone else's software especially if it is not well structured and documented.

This sad state of affairs seems likely to persist because there is no coordinating agency and no market to support commercial development of highly generalized software for conducting experiments. A large market is emerging for instructional software, but such software is unlikely to support a broad range of research applications. In principle the problem could be solved by a central funding agency such as the U.S. National Science Foundation. So far, however, the NSF has restricted itself to making grants for substantive economics applications and has not recognized the need to support general instrument development or to coordinate local initiatives.

Since mutual compatibility of hardware and software is crucial, a beginning experimentalist who locates suitable software is often better off conducting her experiments in the lab where the software was developed rather than importing it to her own lab. This strategy can save time and money, though it also precludes the pedagogical by-product of experimental research, which may, in the long run, turn out to be more important. A second possibility is to get experience by visiting an existing laboratory, modifying the set up on-site to your own needs, and then transporting it back to your home institution or rewriting it.

You can get up-to-date information on laboratory hardware and software at professional meetings, especially the meetings of the Economic Science Association. and on an electronic bulletin board maintained by the Economic Science Laboratory at Arizona.

5.4 Random number generation

Many experiments require the generation of random numbers. The researcher must choose devices for production of random numbers and decide whether these numbers should be generated ahead of time, and if they are, whether it is permissible to "make them look random."

Coin toss, poker chips in a bag, roulette wheels, and bingo cages are frequently employed devices to generate random numbers in the laboratory. A bingo cage, being visible, also has a certain drama and suspense as the participants watch the balls tumble inside the cage until one falls into the bucket. Visible physical devices enhance credibility and therefore are the best choice, other things being equal.

In manual experiments, other things may not be equal for three reasons. First, the desired distribution of the random variable may be difficult to obtain from a physical device. Second, and more frequently, an experimenter may worry that the production of random numbers from a physical device under the watchful eye of the subjects may produce an "unusual" sequence that does not *appear* to be random. Instances such as ten heads in a row from coin tosses may, it is feared, destroy the credibility of the experiment, or may yield little usable data from the precious money and time spent on the experiment. Third, and most important, the experimenter may want to increase the statistical power of the tests by conducting matched pairs of experiments that differ in a specified treatment but otherwise are identical in all respects, including the realization of random variables. The first of these problems is usually addressed using computer-generated pseudorandom numbers, suitably transformed where appropriate; the second and third concerns are usually addressed by using a predetermined and screened sequence of numbers and by informing the subjects that this sequence was generated by using a specified random-number–generating device. Pseudorandom numbers generated by computer routines are a deterministic sequence that depends on the initial seed chosen. Thus, to someone with sufficient knowledge of the random-number–generating computer algorithm and its seed, computer-generated numbers may not be random. Further, there is no way for experimental subjects to know whether the supposedly random numbers being presented to them in the lab have not been predetermined by the experimenter. Even worse, participants may suspect that the experimenter is engaged in an active game against the participants by choosing each number in the supposedly random sequence after observing the results up to that point in the market.

Credibility is the main issue in choosing between physical devices on the one hand and predetermined sequences or computer-generated random numbers on the other. As a practical guide, you should ask yourself the following question: If I were a subject in this experiment, would I have any reason to suspect that the choice of random numbers might be used strategically by the experimenter? If the answer is yes, then you should stick with a visible physical device if at all feasible.

5.5 Application: Experiments with monetary overlapping generations economies

The difficulty of conducting experiments at macroeconomic scale lies at the heart of skepticism about development of economics as an experimental science. While conduct of economic experiments at macro scale is indeed difficult if not impossible, experiments do not have to be at macro scale in order to erect an experimental base for macroeconomics. Fortunately, the development of micro foundations of macroeconomics in the recent decades provided an opening for experiments to make a contribution. Lucas (1986) suggested that the indeterminacy of equilibria in overlapping generations models of fiat money is a behavioral issue that could probably be resolved with the help of observations from appropriately designed laboratory economies. In this application section, we briefly describe a series of experiments on monetary overlapping generations economies carried out over a period of eight years, starting from completely manual and ending with highly computerized environments. These experiments provide an interesting example of complex interaction that occurs between laboratory modeling on one hand, and field observations and mathematical modeling of the same phenomena on the other.

5.5.1 Equilibrium selection in a simple OLG economy

Lim, Prescott, and Sunder (1994) designed an overlapping-generations (OLG) economy consisting of three or four two-period lived agents in each generation. The model yields a stationary equilibrium, as well as a continuum of nonstationary equilibria. Following Lucas's suggestion, this experiment was intended to discover if some subset of these equilibria would dominate the rest in organizing the observations.

Laboratory modeling of such economies presented two challenges. First, the overlapping-generations model requires each agent to live only once, but experimental experience suggests that convergence to equilibria in even simpler laboratory economics, when it occurs, takes several periods of repeat experience. Second, the overlapping-generations model has no termination, a condition that cannot be replicated in a finite laboratory session.

The first problem was solved by recruiting and training $N > 3n$ subjects for an experimental economy with generations of size n. While n subjects played the "young" generation (each endowed with 7 "chips," the consumption good) and n subjects played the "old" generation (each endowed with 100 "francs," the fiat money), the remaining subjects waited and watched as "outsiders." At the end of the period, n subjects were randomly chosen from this pool of outsiders to enter the economy as young of the next period as the young became old and the old exited to join the pool of outsiders. This procedure permitted the individual subjects to gain experience with the economy through repeated participation in the economy for two periods at a time. At the same time, waiting in the pool of outsiders for a random number of periods ensured that, every time subjects entered the economy, their decision-making horizon did not extend beyond their exit from the economy.

The second problem is that whenever you terminate an overlapping-generations economy in laboratory, you will face young agents who have sold a part of their endowment of consumption goods for fiat money with the expectation of using the money to buy consumption goods in their old age. Proper experimental implementation of an overlapping-generations economy requires that the laboratory session be terminated in such a manner that agents are indifferent to its termination at any time. In order to terminate the laboratory economy without inducing end-of-the-session effects the authors had the "outsider" subjects play a forecasting game. At the beginning of each period, each outsider was asked to submit a price forecast. In order to elicit their best forecasts, a cash prize was given each period to the subject whose forecast came closest to the (average) observed price during the period. As a part of initial instructions, they were also told that if the economy is terminated at the beginning of period $N + 1$, the fiat money balances will be converted into consumption good at the average forecast price for period $N + 1$. Within a few periods, subjects' price forecasts were quite close to the actual prices, and succeeded in making the subjects indifferent to the period of termination.

The market between the "young" and the "old" generations was organized as an oral double auction in which the young could sell their chips to the old for their francs. Each transaction was for one chip at a time, except the last transaction of each member of the old generations was permitted to be a fractional transaction so they could exhaust their holding of fiat money before exiting the economy. The first two sessions revealed that in the oral double auction, the old had persistent difficulty in using up all their money before the end of the period, with the result that the total supply of money in the economy declined each period, as did the theoretical equilibria of the economy.

Since holding the money supply at a constant level was important in these economies, and it was not convenient to do so with oral double auction, this auction form was abandoned in favor of a partially computerized alternative. Each member of the young generation was asked to submit a discrete eight-point supply function for chips (i.e., the unit prices at which she was willing to sell up to 0, 1, 2, . . . 7 chips, respectively) to the experimenter on a slip of paper. These data were entered into a portable computer. The computer program interpolated continuous individual supply functions, aggregated them into a market supply function, constructed the market demand function assuming all the money of the old is spent on chips, and calculated the market clearing prices and allocations. Computer output was distributed to the subjects.

The results of the experiment lend strong support to the stationary solution to OLG model. Nonstationary solutions are not supported by data from any of the four economies of this experiment.

5.5.2 Hyperinflationary monetary economies

Marimon and Sunder (1993a,b) examined OLG economies in which government finances a fixed real deficit through seigniorage. These economies have two stationary and a continuum of nonstationary rational-expectations equilibria. Since mathematical analysis or econometric analysis of field data has not helped select from this large set of equilibria, macroeconomic prescriptions of the theory for price-stabilization policy remain ambiguous. Laboratory experiments were designed to see if such observations could help solve this important indeterminacy problem.

After starting with the partially computerized economies, the authors invested considerable time and money in computerizing the system. This enabled them to approximately double the number of periods of data they could gather in a single session. The new experiments retained the laboratory market institution with the discrete eight-point individual supply function and programs for calculating the market clearing price and allocation.

The results of the experiment suggest that the Low Inflation Stationary State, one of the two stationary equilibria, is the best candidate for organizing the data. This equilibrium is consistent with the classical prescription that it is possible to reduce inflation by reducing the seigniorage. The results do not support the High Inflation Stationary State or the continuum of nonstationary equilibria. The data suggest that agents learn adaptively, and underline the need to develop models of learning to close important gaps in the theory.

5.5.3 "Sunspot" economies

Marimon, Spear, and Sunder (1993) further modified the software to examine the effects of expectationally driven uncertainty in overlapping-generations economies. The theoretical "sunspot" models postulate that agents believe that a variable (which is in fact unrelated to the economy) has real effects, and show that such beliefs can induce the agents to behave in a manner that vindicates the postulated beliefs. Empirical exploration of this idea through field observation has remained beyond the grasp of economists. Even a laboratory implementation of a sunspot model presents a difficult challenge because it requires subjects to conjecture a specific functional relationship that does not exist a priori. The model also requires the subjects to solve a difficult optimization problem. In the following paragraphs we describe various attempts to implement "sunspots" in laboratory. None of these implementations would have been feasible without full computerization of the overlapping-generations economies.

5.5.3.1 Computer-assisted decision for subjects: The overlapping-generations model requires agents to solve their consumption-saving problem in the "young" period in light of their expectations about market price in their "old" period. Early pilot experiments, and the Marimon and Sunder (1993,a,b) experiments suggested that it is a difficult problem to solve. Subjects' announced supply functions typically deviate significantly from the supply functions that would be optimal given their revealed beliefs about the price expected in the "old" age. Since the essence of the sunspot model lies in agents learning to form and modify their beliefs about the future, Marimon et al. (1993) decided to further abstract away from the market mechanism. They solicited the "young" agents for their single-point price expectations about their "old" period, and let the computer solve for their optimal chip supply functions. Thus the role of the computer as an optimizing decision aid was increased in order to reduce the noise associated with intuitive optimization. This change enabled the authors to focus the experiment on expectations formation, the heart of the problem of sunspot equilibria.

5.5.3.2 Introducing sunspots in the laboratory: The first attempt to introduce sunspot beliefs, based on Woodford's (1990) suggestion, involved a blinking red or yellow square on each subject's computer screen. The color of the square changed each period according to a first-order Markov process known to the subjects. In addition to other salient payments, subjects received a dollar amount X_c depending on the color c of the square in the period, in order to focus their attention on the blinking square. In addition, the historical data about each period of the economy was displayed on computer screens in the same color as the color of the square for the period. These devices failed to produce sunspot equilibria; apparently the possibility of spontaneously generated conjectures is insufficient to create coordinated beliefs necessary for sunspot equilibria.

A second attempt to implement sunspots in laboratory was based on the assumption that subjects may develop coordinated beliefs in a functional relationship through common experience, and may continue to hold such beliefs even after the intrinsic cause of such a relationship disappears. Instead of making additional payments on the basis of the color of the square, the chip endowment of the young was set at Y_c depending on color c. Changing chip endowment of the young created a real shock to the economy that was perfectly correlated with the color. These real shocks created fluctuations in price and the historical record of prices was displayed on the computer screens in the respective colors. This gave subjects the opportunity to learn to associate the two colors with the high and low prices respectively. After operating the economy for a specified number of periods, the real shock was withdrawn without making a public announcement of its withdrawal. Contrary to the predictions of the sunspot model, price fluctuations were not sustained in the absence of the real shock. Since the "young" subjects could observe their endowment of chips, the withdrawal of the real shock was transparent to them, making it a faulty implementation of the sunspot idea.

In their third attempt, Marimon et al. (1993) found a more subtle way to deliver a real shock to the economy in the early periods. Instead of changing the chip endowment of the young they changed the size of the young generation that entered the economy to N_c depending on the color c of the blinking square. When the real shock was withdrawn (generation size held constant irrespective of the color for the period) individual subjects could not know that any change had taken place. In this implementation, it was possible for them to continue to believe in the price-color relationship they had observed during the periods in which the real shock was in effect.

This experiment provided the first empirical data suggesting that if agents expect sunspots to matter, they can matter. As to why and how should the agents come to have such beliefs, the experiment reveals no evidence for emergence of such beliefs unless subjects have shared a common experience with cyclical phenomena of this nature. This laboratory evidence takes the sunspot phenomena beyond the realm of mathematical economics to the possibility of being triggered and coordinated in complex economies with media, politics, and thousands of sources of information and decisions.

6

Conducting an experiment

Learning to conduct economics experiments is like learning to swim or bike; no amount of reading will substitute for giving it a try. You will find it more efficient to learn lab practice by offering to assist someone who does experiments. It is also easy to pick up good as well as bad habits from others. This chapter is intended as a helpful checklist for a beginner. As you learn to conduct experiments yourself, you will develop your own more detailed checklist of do's and don't's.

6.1 Lab log

It is a good lab practice to record all experiments in a bound log book by date, purpose, subjects, software, and parameter values. Also note any unusual events (e.g., "Ran with 8 subjects instead of the planned 10 due to no-shows.") It is amazing how soon we forget what we did, when, and why. A log book is a permanent record of great value.

6.2 Pilot experiments

Conducting pilots is usually the *only* sensible way of developing the design and procedures of new experiments. In conducting pilots, you will discover many things, including ambiguities in the instructions, missing information, unintended leakages of information, too much time for some activities and too little for others, weaknesses or malfunctions in software or random-number–generating devices, insufficiency of assistants, and lack of coordination and timing of your tasks. Some pilot experiments are planned as such, but quite often this designation is applied ex post to experiments in which procedural glitches arise.

Should you record, analyze, and report data from pilot experiments? We believe that all data should be saved; you never know when you might want to take another look at it, if only to remember exactly what went wrong. Pilots add to accumulated knowledge of laboratory technique and instrumentation. Experimenters seldom spend much time analyzing or reporting data from pilots that are intended to work out procedural glitches. On the other hand, if you use pilot experiments to explore how behavior changes as you vary theoretically relevant parameters, say the number of bargainers or the number of rounds of bargaining, then you should report the results to avoid a selection bias in your published results. See Roth (1990) for amplification of this point.

6.3 Lab setup

Reserved lab time should start about thirty minutes before and extend to thirty minutes after the scheduled presence of subjects in the lab. At the front end, time is needed to set up and test the equipment, computers, and software; to write instructions on the chalkboard; to set up subject stations with instructions, identification numbers, forms, and so forth; and to set up cameras, and projectors as needed and to make arrangements for registration. Supplies (e.g., chalk, pencils, writing tablets, overhead pens, blank slides, calculators, and computer storage disks) should be arranged in advance. Shared-use computer laboratories need extra time to check and reset machine configurations as necessary. (Remember the computer lab version of Murphy's Law: If there exists a default setting at which your software does not work, lab machines revert to this setting whenever you take a coffee break.) After the conclusion of the experiment, time is needed to pay and debrief the subjects, download – or at least back up – data from computers, projectors, or chalkboards, and to return borrowed equipment.

6.4 Registration

Recognize and register each subject on arrival. If the human subjects committee so requires, give your subjects a written statement of their rights and ask them to sign a release form (see Appendix III for an example). If applicable, pay out the prompt arrival bonus, or at least let the subjects know that they will receive it for sure at the end of the session. Some subjects may bring friends who were not recruited for the experiment. If they are acceptable substitutes for possible no-shows, invite them to stand by until the scheduled starting time.

It is good practice to assign seats by drawing lots because it helps break up any groups of friends who may be inclined to talk to one another during the experiment, without making you appear to discriminate. Do not engage in experiment-related small talk with the waiting subjects; such informal comments may end up dominating anything else you might tell them later in the instruction phase of the experiment. If the number of subjects who show up exceeds the number needed for the experiment, some may be retained as helpers or monitors, with the promise of a fixed payment or payment of the average amount earned by the participants. Some experimenters (including the authors) sometimes use such helpers as stand-by replacements in multisession experiments, but not everyone approves of the practice.

6.5 Conductors

Who should conduct the sessions? The investigator who designs and plans the experiment is not necessarily the best person to conduct the sessions, especially if in manual mode. You can reduce the possibility of demand effects by having your sessions conducted by an independent person who is informed of the procedures but innocent of the relevant theories or purpose of the experiment. This would be a step toward the "double-blind" practice of medical and other forms of experimental research. Since replicability of findings by other investigators has not yet become a major issue in experimental economics, it may be difficult to justify the additional cost and effort involved in such arrangements at the present time. However, with expansion of this branch of economics, conflicts will arise, and this question may have to be revisited.

Your presence during pilots and exploratory sessions is valuable. Direct observation may suggest procedural improvements that would not occur to you given only secondhand accounts of the session.

6.6 Monitors

Sometimes, in implementing state uncertainty and information asymmetry, in asset market experiments for instance, you may have to ask subjects to accept your unverified assertions at face value. Most subjects are quite willing to do so, but some may quietly harbor doubts, especially if they have experienced or heard about deceptive experimentation. You can deal with this problem by having the subjects themselves randomly pick a subject as a nonplaying monitor. The monitor is expected to watch all that the experimenter does, including activities beyond the view of the participating subjects (e.g., drawing of random numbers) and to report to the subjects and the experimenter if any activity violates the announced rules and procedures. Monitors can be paid at a fixed rate, or (if they can't really affect subjects' earnings) receive an amount equal to the average earned by the participants during the session.

6.7 Instruction

Instruction is the first order of business after the subjects are seated. If leakage of information is irrelevant or unlikely, it is even better to let the subjects have written instructions to read before coming to the session. The purpose of oral instruction is to take advantage of the fact that it is easier for most people to understand the rules of a game from personal explanation and illustration than from reading. In addition, oral instruction to subjects who sit in the same room helps make the instructions common knowledge (or at least common information) among the subjects. In manual experiments, you may read out written instructions, while subjects are asked to read along in their own copies. This allows you to emphasize procedural points on a chalkboard, or give illustrative examples of complicated steps. A certain number of clarifying questions can also be entertained at this stage. In deviating from the written text, you must be sensitive to the replicability issue – being reasonably sure that another experimenter would provide a similar interpretation of the written instructions. Otherwise, such interpretations should be made a part of the written instructions, because it is the written instructions that constitute the experimental record to be transmitted to readers and other researchers.

In computerized experiments, all or a part of the instructions may be provided through computer screens. Hypercard on Apple computers and Windows-related software on IBM-compatibles are a convenient way of generating instructions that subjects can browse through at their own pace. However, instruction through private computer screens is not an effective way of imparting common information to the subjects.

When participation requires comprehension of complicated steps, some experimenters choose to divide the instructions into several steps. Each step is followed by an illustrative (or actual) game that requires and reinforces the understanding of that step. Subjects may earn money in these intermediate steps. When a subject does not seem to understand the instructions for the step, the experimenter faces the delicate task of deciding whether it is appropriate to provide a special explanation to that individual. If the observed behavior of the subject arises from a misunderstanding of the instructions, the experimenter may reread the relevant part of the instructions or go through an example. Paying special attention to individuals, unless they ask, runs the risk of giving them undocumented messages, a possible threat to replicability.

6.8 Handling queries from subjects

Even the most careful instruction and illustration are rarely enough; invariably, there are queries from subjects. We have four suggestions. First, handle queries publicly, or at least publicly within the appropriate subset of subjects, to avoid giving other subjects the feeling that they might be missing something. Second, remind subjects to phrase their queries so as not to reveal their private information (if any), and remind yourself to be careful not to reveal anyone's private information (or their status in the experiment, if it is supposed to be private) in answering these queries. Third, phrase your answers so as to avoid guiding subjects' choice of actions in the experiment. Fourth, recognize that you may have to defer answers to some questions; otherwise you may not be able to maintain privacy about the specific behavior or theories being investigated.

6.9 Dry-run periods

Many experimenters use the first two to four periods of a session as a dry run in which no payments are made for the performance. In these periods subjects' queries can be handled, even permitting the private information of subjects to leak out when it will not be relevant to later periods. The first few periods are special: They generate virtually all the queries; subjects need more time; experimenters make mistakes of procedure; and subjects make serious errors (e.g., carrying numbers used for illustration during the instruction phase into the actual experiment). Of course, you should announce dry-run periods in advance. If you are kind and supportive of the subjects' mistakes during early periods, they will be more inclined to forgive your mistakes in good humor. Admit the errors, start over, and report such incidents in footnotes to the research reports.

6.10 Manual conduct of markets

Manual-market experiments give rise to some additional logistical problems. You should remind the subjects that it is important (1) to keep accurate records according to instructions, and (2) not to engage in unauthorized communication. In manual markets, the experimenter may lose track of time, so a separate timekeeper is helpful. The experimenter should not give encouragement or discouragement to the submission of bids or offers, and should maintain a neutral voice and stance. In manual auctions the action may become too hectic for the auctioneer to handle. Increasing the length of the period does not necessarily solve the problem because all traders may want to trade in the early or late part of the period. It may help to use the following rule: The first person to speak up after the auctioneer finishes repeating the bid, ask, or transaction is recognized. If you are conducting the experiment by yourself, you may have trouble recognizing traders in the order that they raise their hands because you may be looking at the chalkboard or at a slide when hands go up. Unless subjects face a wall clock with a second hand, a thirty-second or fifteen-second warning helps subjects wrap up the transactions before the period ends. Ask your subjects to update their written record at the end of each period; do not allow them to defer the entries until the end of the session.

6.11 Recording the data

Data are all you get from an experiment, so whatever you do, don't mess up or lose the data. You should plan in advance how to capture your data into a permanent record. In computerized experiments, the software should automatically capture the data, but you should also make backup copies of the data files at the end of the session, and record the file names, size, and so on in your logbook.

In manual experiments, data are captured in recording sheets filled out by subjects and the experimenter. Well-designed recording sheets make it easier to make correct entries. Common information (e.g., bids, asks, prices in a double auction) is recorded on the blackboard or slides. Slides are better because they already constitute a permanent record, while blackboard data must be transcribed to something more permanent. You can photograph the chalkboard and the seating arrangement, or even videotape the whole session if voice and other behavior in the session are important.

In addition to performance data, you must also accurately record experimental treatments, conditions, and parameters. Write down a description of why you decided to conduct your session. It will come in handy a few months later when you get around to analyzing the data from all your sessions.

6.12 Termination

Many economics experiments are repeated for an indefinite number of trials (usually as many as will fit into the designated length of the session) in order to maximize subject experience, learning, and the chances of behavior settling down into a stable pattern. If you let the subjects know in advance that the nth period will be the last of the session, some subjects may try "something different" in that last period. In some experiments – such as the iterated prisoner's dilemma – there is an economic rationale for behaving differently in the last period; in other cases, one can only speculate about the motivations behind such behavior – perhaps the curiosity about "what will happen if?" dominates other incentives in the last period. Since the learning argument implies that the data from the last period are most important for inference about equilibrium, it is best to avoid identifying the final period until it has ended. If you have promised a 2:00 P.M. end to your experimental session, terminate some time earlier to avoid this problem.

At the end of the final period, remind your subjects to perform any remaining steps needed such as transferring data from the computer screen, completing their records and calculations of profits, filling out debriefing forms and cash receipts, gathering and arranging their papers, recording sheets, and so on in the folder provided, and presenting themselves with the folder at the payment station.

6.13 Laboratory termination of infinite-period economies

Many laboratory economies are designed to explore situations in which there is no defined final period. Special attention then is in order to avoid end-of-the-session artifacts of the laboratory. One termination technique, introduced by Lim, Prescott, and Sunder (1994) and discussed previously in Section 5.5.1, used a forecasting game with payments that made subjects indifferent about the timing of the last period.

Camerer and Weigelt (1990) use a probabilistic mechanism to terminate markets for indefinitely lived assets. If subjects have an indefinitely lived asset that pays a dividend of 1 and terminates with probability π at the end of each period, its expected present value is $1/\pi$. The expected present value of an infinitely lived asset that pays a dividend of 1 at the end of each period and has a discount rate of π is also $1/\pi$. Since you can, as the experimenter, control and announce the value of π, this equivalence permits you to interpret the observations from a market for indefinitely lived, stochastically terminated assets as if they were obtained from a market for infinitely lived assets.

6.14 Debriefing

Experimental psychology has an elaborate tradition of debriefing and manipulation checks. By contrast, many experimenters in economics provide no formal debriefing. The fear is that asking specific questions about the experiment or subject behavior may influence behavior when subjects return for a subsequent session, or may contaminate the subject pool through dormitory talk about what the experimenter may be looking for. To the extent that economists rely on learning and experience of subjects who participate in repeat experiments, this concern has some basis. On the other hand, experimental economists attribute a large role to institutions in determining behavior; how reliable are experimental results that are highly sensitive to subjects' speculations about the motivations of the experimenter? Manipulation checks and debriefing may give you important information and insight about whether the subjects understand the instructions, about the attitudes they bring into the lab, and about their strategies and thought processes. In our opinion, you should not discard this opportunity to learn, except with good reason. We recommend a blank sheet with the request, "Write any comments you may have on this experiment, and your participation in it" as in Appendix III, especially in the pilot or exploratory phases of your investigation.

6.15 Payment

Subjects prefer to be paid in cash. The experimenter may wish to avoid the hassle of handling cash and making change by writing checks instead. Keep private the exact amount you pay each subject because otherwise you may create a trophy mentality of "who won the most money" and undermine the saliency of your marginal rewards. Whenever possible, call subjects individually to an isolated location or a separate room to be paid. They may yet exchange information about what they earned. There is not much you can do about that. Have the subjects fill out a cash receipt similar to the one illustrated in Appendix III before making the payment. If it is a multisession experiment in which the same subjects are to attend multiple sessions, it is better to fill out an IOU form (again see Appendix III) as a tangible evidence of what the subjects have earned during the first session, encouraging them to return for the subsequent sessions.

6.16 Bankruptcy

In spite of our advice in Section 4.4.3 and despite your best efforts to minimize the chances of a subject going bankrupt, on occasion you may be confronted with a subject with negative final earnings. Usually it is impractical to ask the hapless subject to make a net payment to you, and such payments might imperil your standing with the human subjects committee. What should you do?

You should have a well-defined plan to deal with bankruptcies, and not wait to make a spur-of-the-moment decision. The easiest option is to let bankrupt subjects go with zero payment. Unfortunately, as mentioned in Section 4.4.3, this tends to induce risk-seeking behavior in subjects with low (or negative) earnings. Moreover, if you don't announce this option in advance, it becomes an ex post violation of the payment schedule and may contaminate subjects' expectations for your own or your colleagues' experiments. It is not an attractive option. A more common practice is to announce in advance that subjects whose earnings fall below some threshold will immediately be dismissed from the experiment. This procedure maintains your credibility, but the endogenous change in the number of subjects (and again, in their induced risk preferences) may undermine the validity of your experiment.

A third option, successfully employed at CalTech, is to have the subjects agree before beginning of the session that they will reimburse the experimenter for any negative net earnings from the experiment in the form of assistantship work at a specified hourly rate.

6.17 Bailout plan

Every experimenter has days when nothing seems to go right. Not enough subjects turn up, or they turn up late, leaving insufficient time to complete the experiment. Computers or other equipment breaks down or software errors crash the experiment. The experimenter forgets to bring instructions, forms, slides, experimenter parameters, or cash, or brings the wrong items. The bingo cage spews out a red ball eight times in a row, and the subjects begin to mumble about what is really going on. When disasters strike and adrenalin runs high, it helps to remember that these things happen to everybody. You can try to salvage the session as an instruction session, apologize for the unexpected termination of the session, pay a fixed bonus payment to the subjects for their trouble, and ask them to sign up for another date. Most people will understand and cooperate.

6.18 Application: Committee decisions under majority rule

Decision making in committees is a core concern in political science. Political theory developed from the tradition of philosophy, sociology, history, and field observation, but in recent decades Kenneth Arrow, Duncan Black, Anthony Downs, James Buchanan, and others built public choice theory on foundations of mathematics and economics. The theoretical results about committee behavior by these and later authors were rarely verified or applied by sociologists or political scientists. Fiorina and Plott (1978) report the first laboratory experiment designed to compare the explanatory power of competing theoretical models of committee behavior. This work sparked a new subdiscipline of experimental political economy, so we will describe in more than our usual detail how they conducted their first experiments. See Palfrey (1991) for a collection of more recent political economy experiments.

Fiorina and Plott began by narrowing the class of committee processes to investigate by applying four conditions: (a) members know and understand the personal consequences of committee decisions; (b) members have well-defined preferences over the committee decisions; (c) there is no previously fixed parliamentary procedure other than minimal rules of order and majority rule; and (d) no private conversations, agreements, payments, or understandings are permissible among subsets of committee members. In each of the sixty-five sessions (divided into Series 1, 2, and 3) subjects were assigned to five-member committees that chose a point on a blackboard by majority rule. All points on the board were assigned rectangular coordinates between (0, 0) and (200, 150). Each subject was privately assigned an ideal or maximum payoff point on the board (i.e., this point was the peak of his or her personal hill of preference contours). Iso-payoff contours were circular for Series 1 and 3, and elliptical for Series 2. The greater the distance between a subject's ideal point and the point chosen by the committee, the smaller the payoff to the subject.

All committees started from the northeast corner of the blackboard (200, 150). Any member of the committee could make a motion to move to a specified point on the board, and the status quo would shift to that point if the motion was carried by a majority vote. The process could be terminated at any time by a majority vote. The payoff to individual subjects was determined only by the final point chosen by the committee.

In order to predict the outcome of the committee sessions, Fiorina and Plott (1978) conducted an exhaustive search of the literature for both egoistic as well as nonegoistic models. The twelve egoistic models they considered included two game-theoretic (1 = the core and 2 = the von Neumann–Morgenstern solution), three vote-theoretic (3 = the voting equilibrium, 4 = the min-max set, and 5 = the voting equilibrium under a city-block metric), four agenda-based voting-theoretic (6 = the obvious agenda, 7 = the median along coordinates, 8 = the binary amendment, and 9 = agenda manipulation), and three coalition-theoretic (10 = minimum winning, 11 = resource coalition, and 12 = minimum winning coalition of maximum value) models. The four nonegoistic models considered were 13 = the maximum group return, 14 = the fair point, 15 = the dominant personality, and 16 = the obvious point.

The first series of sessions was designed to isolate models 1–8 and 16 (all of which made an identical prediction) from the remaining 7 models (each of which made its own unique prediction). Other treatments in this series included high versus low payoffs, and full versus no communication among the committee members. In the full-communication condition subjects could discuss any proposal openly; in the no-communication condition, they could only make a motion and vote on it. The low-payoff sessions showed high variance in outcomes, and were discontinued in the following series of sessions. The communication treatment seemed to make little difference in Series 1, and the subsequent sessions were conducted under conditions of full communication.

The results of Series 1 clustered around the common prediction of models 1–8, and 16 and seem to decisively reject models 9–15 for this committee institution and environment. Series 2 was designed to isolate models 5 and 7 from 1–4, 6, and 16. The results did not support models 5 and 7 and clustered around the common prediction of the other models. Series 3 sessions were designed so core and voting equilibrium did not exist; only the obvious point (model 16) and min-max set (model 4) were defined. The committee outcomes were dispersed around the min-max set, though the explanatory power of the set was not high. On the other hand, absence of the core did not result in complete dispersion of the outcomes over the blackboard as some theories have predicted.

Fiorina and Plott (1978) is a good example of a seminal experiment conducted with little more than paper, pencil, and chalkboard for equipment and facilities. In this, as in any other good experiment, most of the work goes into defining the critical issues, identifying the relevant theories and facts, and designing critical experiments before any subjects are recruited. The published paper includes detailed instructions and parameters to enable the reader to replicate their research. Instructions have been reproduced in Appendix II.

7

Data analysis

Imagine that you have just assembled the raw data from your recent experiments on market efficiency. You gaze at sheets of paper covered with numbers specifying which subjects did what and when they did it. Do the data support the efficient-markets hypothesis or not? You could stare at the raw data for hours and be none the wiser. It is time to begin your *data analysis*. You will transform and process the raw data in various ways to find out what they have to say. Think of data analysis as a form of interrogation. But be gentle – coax the data to tell their own story. You will learn very little if you torture the data until they confess.

This chapter introduces the basic tools for analyzing experimental data. Many experimentalists prefer a two-phase approach. The first phase is qualitative or descriptive and is intended to give an overview of what the data have to say. The tools are graphs and summary statistics. The second phase is more quantitative and is intended to give specific answers to specific questions. Here the tools are inferential statistics.

Experimental data and happenstance data raise the same general issues and require mostly the same analytical techniques, but there are notable differences in emphasis. Experimental data often come from newly created environments and are unlikely to be familiar to most readers, so the descriptive phase is particularly important. In most respects, statistical inference is quite straightforward for data obtained in well-designed experiments. Some subtleties do arise, which we discuss in Section 7.2. Section 7.3 should provide helpful perspectives on statistical tests of experimental data and a quick review of several specific tests, but for systematic training you will have to consult texts such as Box et al. (1978), Conover (1980), or Kirk (1982). Finally, after summarizing our advice on data analysis, we illustrate the main ideas while reviewing some of the literature on first price auctions.

7.1 Graphs and summary statistics

Day 18 of session Das2 was about as simple and straightforward as a trading period can be in a double-auction asset-market experiment. There were 8 traders divided equally into two types, each trader initially endowed with three shares. At the beginning of each 2-minute trading period ("Day"), all traders were notified of their per share payouts for the Day; for Day 18 the payouts were 25 cents for type 1 traders and 75 cents for type 2 traders. (Some Days type 1 traders get a payout of $1.95 and some Days type 2 traders get a payout of $1.65 in this session.) You might like to know whether all shares were acquired by the traders who valued them most highly (type 2), whether prices approached the fundamental value of 75 cents, whether prices were volatile, whether convergence was fast or slow or nonexistent, and so on.

Table 7.1 provides a complete record of all activity in the trading period, about 100 events (bids, asks, etc) in all. Look at Table 7.1 for a minute or two. Do these raw data answer your questions clearly? Now look at Figure 7.1, where the same data are plotted. (The upper step function is the best ask price, the lower step function is the best bid price, and stars indicate transaction prices. The horizontal dashed line is the equilibrium price, $0.75 per share. The realized payouts (1B, 2B) for the two trader types are indicated in the upper left corner, and the final allocation of shares is indicated in the lower right corner.) You can see at a glance in Figure 7.1 exactly what happened on Day 18 of session Das1. After about 10 seconds the traders had begun to digest the bad news (the low payouts to type 1 and 2 traders are indicated in the upper left corner of the graph by the notation 1B, 2B). Bids rose quickly to near the fundamental value of 75 cents and asks gradually declined toward that value, taking about 60 seconds to converge. By this time traders transacted 6 times, all accepted bids. Accepted asks were common in the 8 later transactions. Except in the first 30 seconds, the pace of trade was quite steady and all transactions prices were between 70 and 75 cents per share. By the end of the trading period, all 24 shares were held by the right type (2) of traders.

Summary statistics can be very useful in conjunction with graphs or even on their own. The final allocations shown in the lower right corner of the graph are summary statistics. Another example not shown explicitly is the mean transaction price. It is $0.725, a -2.5 cent deviation from equilibrium. This single number summarizes much of the information in Table 7.1 relevant to testing equilibrium theory.

Table 7.1 *Data from trading period Day 18 of double-auction asset market Das2*

period	subper	time	id	cpid	event	price	qty	bbid	qty	bask	qty
18	1	81	5	-	ASK	1.65	1.00	0.00	1.00	1.65	1.00
18	1	87	6	-	ASK	2.00	1.00	0.00	1.00	1.65	1.00
18	1	98	2	-	BID	0.70	1.00	0.70	1.00	1.65	1.00
18	1	104	3	-	ASK	2.00	1.00	0.70	1.00	1.65	1.00
18	1	107	0	-	ASK	1.50	1.00	0.70	1.00	1.50	1.00
18	1	120	7	-	ASK	1.70	1.00	0.70	1.00	1.50	1.00
18	1	126	6	-	ASK	1.55	1.00	0.70	1.00	1.50	1.00
18	1	133	0	-	BID	0.70	1.00	0.70	1.00	1.50	1.00
18	1	166	7	-	ASK	1.80	1.00	0.70	1.00	1.50	1.00
18	1	175	0	-	BID	0.74	1.00	0.74	1.00	1.50	1.00
18	1	189	5	-	ASK	1.45	1.00	0.74	1.00	1.45	1.00
18	1	217	2	-	ASK	1.49	1.00	0.74	1.00	1.45	1.00
18	1	235	4	-	ASK	1.00	1.00	0.74	1.00	1.00	1.00
18	1	240	0	-	ASK	1.40	1.00	0.74	1.00	1.00	1.00
18	1	248	6	-	ASK	2.00	1.00	0.74	1.00	1.00	1.00
18	1	254	3	-	BID	0.74	1.00	0.74	1.00	1.00	1.00
18	1	259	2	-	ASK	1.45	1.00	0.74	1.00	1.00	1.00
18	1	289	0	-	ASK	0.95	1.00	0.74	1.00	0.95	1.00
18	1	292	5	0	SOLD	0.74	1.00	0.74	1.00	0.95	1.00
18	1	296	0	-	CANBID	0.74	--	0.74	1.00	0.95	1.00
18	1	301	6	-	ASK	0.99	1.00	0.74	1.00	0.95	1.00
18	1	306	5	3	SOLD	0.74	1.00	0.74	1.00	0.95	1.00
18	1	311	3	-	CANBID	0.74	--	0.70	1.00	0.95	1.00
18	1	317	2	-	BID	0.74	1.00	0.74	1.00	0.95	1.00
18	1	337	0	-	BID	0.74	1.00	0.74	1.00	0.95	1.00
18	1	345	2	-	BID	0.70	1.00	0.74	1.00	0.95	1.00
18	1	375	4	-	BID	0.20	1.00	0.74	1.00	0.95	1.00
18	1	380	2	-	BID	0.74	1.00	0.74	1.00	0.95	1.00
18	1	395	6	-	ASK	0.94	1.00	0.74	1.00	0.94	1.00
18	1	415	4	-	CANASK	1.00	--	0.74	1.00	0.94	1.00
18	1	427	1	-	BID	0.65	1.00	0.74	1.00	0.94	1.00
18	1	457	2	-	ASK	0.93	1.00	0.74	1.00	0.93	1.00
18	1	468	0	-	CANBID	0.74	--	0.74	1.00	0.93	1.00
18	1	473	4	-	CANASK	0.70	--	0.74	1.00	0.93	1.00
18	1	473	4	0	SOLD	0.74	1.00	0.74	1.00	0.93	1.00
18	1	491	5	2	SOLD	0.74	1.00	0.74	1.00	0.93	1.00
18	1	494	2	-	CANBID	0.74	--	0.65	1.00	0.93	1.00
18	1	495	5	-	CANASK	1.45	--	0.65	1.00	0.93	1.00
18	1	506	0	-	BID	0.74	1.00	0.74	1.00	0.93	1.00
18	1	510	6	-	ASK	0.90	1.00	0.74	1.00	0.90	1.00
18	1	531	2	-	ASK	0.91	1.00	0.74	1.00	0.90	1.00
18	1	538	0	-	ASK	0.85	1.00	0.74	1.00	0.85	1.00
18	1	547	0	-	CANBID	0.74	--	0.65	1.00	0.85	1.00
18	1	552	4	-	CANASK	0.72	--	0.65	1.00	0.85	1.00
18	1	552	4	0	SOLD	0.74	1.00	0.65	1.00	0.85	1.00
18	1	571	2	-	ASK	0.88	1.00	0.65	1.00	0.85	1.00
18	1	582	0	-	BID	0.74	1.00	0.74	1.00	0.85	1.00
18	1	609	0	-	CANBID	0.74	--	0.65	1.00	0.85	1.00

Table 7.1 (*cont.*)

period	subper	time	id	cpid	event	price	qty	bbid	qty	bask	qty
18	1	614	6	-	CANASK	0.74	--	0.65	1.00	0.85	1.00
18	1	614	6	0	SOLD	0.74	1.00	0.65	1.00	0.85	1.00
18	1	620	4	-	ASK	0.74	1.00	0.65	1.00	0.74	1.00
18	1	624	2	-	BID	0.70	1.00	0.70	1.00	0.74	1.00
18	2	655	2	-	BID	0.66	1.00	0.66	1.00	0.74	1.00
18	2	674	0	-	BID	0.73	1.00	0.73	1.00	0.74	1.00
18	2	683	7	-	ASK	0.80	1.00	0.73	1.00	0.74	1.00
18	2	692	6	-	ASK	0.74	1.00	0.73	1.00	0.74	1.00
18	2	735	0	-	CANBID	0.73	--	0.66	1.00	0.74	1.00
18	2	739	7	-	CANASK	0.70	--	0.66	1.00	0.74	1.00
18	2	739	7	0	SOLD	0.73	1.00	0.66	1.00	0.74	1.00
18	2	745	4	-	CANASK	0.74	--	0.66	1.00	0.74	1.00
18	2	751	2	-	BID	0.67	1.00	0.67	1.00	0.74	1.00
18	2	764	6	-	ASK	0.70	1.00	0.67	1.00	0.70	1.00
18	2	772	0	-	CANBID	0.74	--	0.67	1.00	0.70	1.00
18	2	777	6	-	CANASK	0.70	--	0.67	1.00	0.85	1.00
18	2	777	0	6	BOUGHT	0.70	1.00	0.67	1.00	0.85	1.00
18	2	787	4	-	ASK	0.71	1.00	0.67	1.00	0.71	1.00
18	2	816	0	-	CANBID	0.74	--	0.67	1.00	0.71	1.00
18	2	824	4	-	CANASK	0.71	--	0.67	1.00	0.85	1.00
18	2	824	0	4	BOUGHT	0.71	1.00	0.67	1.00	0.85	1.00
18	2	830	7	-	ASK	0.70	1.00	0.67	1.00	0.70	1.00
18	2	870	0	-	CANBID	0.74	--	0.67	1.00	0.70	1.00
18	2	872	7	-	CANASK	0.70	--	0.67	1.00	0.85	1.00
18	2	873	0	7	BOUGHT	0.70	1.00	0.67	1.00	0.85	1.00
18	2	878	6	-	ASK	0.75	1.00	0.67	1.00	0.75	1.00
18	2	911	2	-	ASK	0.73	1.00	0.67	1.00	0.73	1.00
18	2	915	7	-	ASK	0.80	1.00	0.67	1.00	0.73	1.00
18	2	917	6	-	ASK	0.74	1.00	0.67	1.00	0.73	1.00
18	2	932	0	-	CANBID	0.74	--	0.67	1.00	0.73	1.00
18	2	938	2	-	CANASK	0.73	--	0.67	1.00	0.74	1.00
18	2	938	0	2	BOUGHT	0.73	1.00	0.67	1.00	0.74	1.00
18	2	946	6	-	ASK	0.72	1.00	0.67	1.00	0.72	1.00
18	2	962	0	-	BID	0.70	1.00	0.70	1.00	0.72	1.00
18	2	973	0	-	CANBID	0.70	--	0.67	1.00	0.70	1.00
18	2	974	7	-	CANASK	0.70	--	0.67	1.00	0.72	1.00
18	2	974	7	0	SOLD	0.70	1.00	0.67	1.00	0.72	1.00
18	2	991	2	-	BID	0.71	1.00	0.71	1.00	0.72	1.00
18	2	1005	1	-	BID	0.70	1.00	0.71	1.00	0.72	1.00
18	2	1028	0	-	BID	0.70	1.00	0.71	1.00	0.72	1.00
18	2	1049	2	-	ASK	0.72	1.00	0.71	1.00	0.72	1.00
18	2	1076	0	-	CANBID	0.74	--	0.71	1.00	0.72	1.00
18	2	1079	6	-	CANASK	0.72	--	0.71	1.00	0.72	1.00
18	2	1079	0	6	BOUGHT	0.72	1.00	0.71	1.00	0.72	1.00
18	2	1086	2	-	ASK	0.73	1.00	0.71	1.00	0.73	1.00
18	2	1129	0	-	CANBID	0.74	--	0.71	1.00	0.73	1.00
18	2	1131	2	-	CANASK	0.73	--	0.71	1.00	0.85	1.00
18	2	1131	0	2	BOUGHT	0.73	1.00	0.71	1.00	0.85	1.00
18	2	1165	0	-	BID	0.73	1.00	0.73	1.00	0.85	1.00
18	2	1196	2	-	ASK	0.84	1.00	0.73	1.00	0.84	1.00

Time is measured in tenths of a second from the beginning of the trading period. Traders with I.D.'s 0–3 are type 1 and have payout $0.25 per share on Day18. Traders with I.D.'s 4–7 are type 2 and have payout $0.75. The counterparty in a transaction appears in the cpid column. In this session the quantity traded (qty) is always 1.0, i.e., trades are for single indivisible shares. The best bid and best ask are denoted bbid and bask.

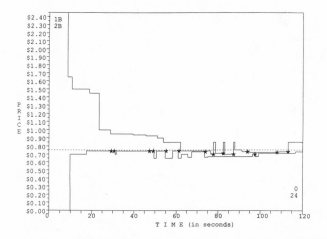

Fig. 7.1 Time graph for Day 18 of Das2. The upper step function is the best ask price, the lower step function is the best bid price, and stars indicate transaction prices. The horizontal dashed line is the equilibrium price, $0.75 per share. The realized payouts (1B, 2B) for the two trader types are indicated in the upper left corner, and the final allocation of shares is indicated in the lower right corner.

For another example, consider the risky choice experiments reported in Kachelmeier and Shehata (1992). Their raw data are certainty equivalents (selling prices elicited via the Becker-DeGroot-Marschak procedure mentioned in Section 4.2) from various subjects for various lotteries with differing probabilities of winning a fixed cash prize. With 50 trials for each of 20 subjects in their first session, the raw data consists of 1,000 numbers. Their main summary statistic is called CE ratio, the ratio of the certainty equivalent to the expected value, usually averaged over subjects. Figure 7.2 reproduces their Figure 1. You can see at a glance that subjects demanded a substantial premium before they were willing to sell the low-probability lotteries, but the premium decreased as the win probability increased and when a high cash prize was substituted for the low cash prize.

How can you choose a good summary description of your data? Perhaps the best advice is to look at past work for an effective presentation, and modify it to deal with special features of your own data. The tradition behind Figure 7.1, for example, goes back at least to Smith (1962). But

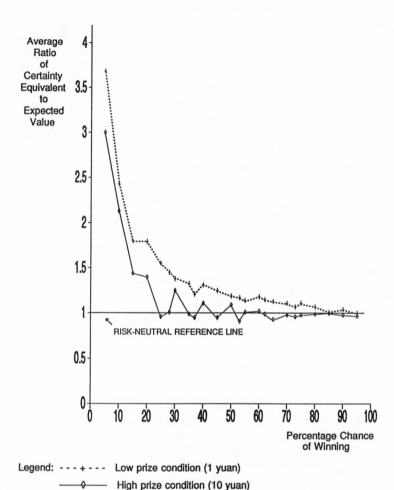

Fig. 7.2 Certainty equivalents and expected values.

the display was modified to show bids, asks, and transactions in clock time, rather than just the traditional transaction sequences, because an important goal for the experiment was to see how bids and asks adjust over time.

A good summary of your data accomplishes several goals. First, it allows you to see regularities (or irregularities) in the data that require further investigation. Graphs are a remarkably efficient means of screening for erroneous data. It is equally important to spot correct but anomalous data. For example, summary data might show that one subject in a risky choice experiment has a much lower CE ratio at low win probabilities than the other subjects. Further investigation might disclose that the low average is due to selling prices of zero. You should then check whether the prices were correctly recorded, whether the subject received proper instructions, and so forth. If the data are in fact correct, you might wish to see whether other subjects indulge in zero selling prices. The upshot might be a modified theory in which subjects with very low expected winnings and high subjective computational costs will bid zero, with implications that go to the foundations of decision theory! If you hadn't worked out the data summary, you probably wouldn't have spotted the zero bids and you would have missed the opportunity to correct your data or to extend the theory.

A second goal of qualitative data analysis is to guide subsequent quantitative analysis. For example, you may wish to analyze discrepancies between theoretical equilibrium prices and actual prices in a double-auction market. But what is the appropriate "actual price"? Is it the average transaction price in a trading period? The last transaction price? The midpoint of the bid-ask price interval? A summary graph like Figure 7.1 gives you a basis for making an appropriate choice and indicates whether other choices are likely to give different answers. Your formal statistical inferences will be more reliable if they are grounded in a good descriptive analysis.

A third goal is pedagogical. A good graphical display or set of descriptive statistics gives your reader an easily accessible overview of your data. The reader will then be encouraged to read on to your conclusions and will be in a better position to assess their credibility.

Data summaries are less important for well-known happenstance data, such as financial market data or national income accounts data compiled by government agencies. The econometrician analyzing such data probably already has an adequate perspective on the data and is aware of its main features. Her readers will want to get quickly to her contribution, perhaps a more subtle inferential statistic, and may be impatient with a lot of familiar descriptive statistics. By contrast, experimental data usually are new and in some respects unfamiliar, so a descriptive summary is essential.

Sometimes the main question addressed in an experiment can be answered directly from the summary statistics or graphs. For example, the issue in a set of recent market experiments was whether a theoretically inefficient market institution called CHQ was less efficient in practice than a theoretically more efficient institution called CH. Figure 7.3

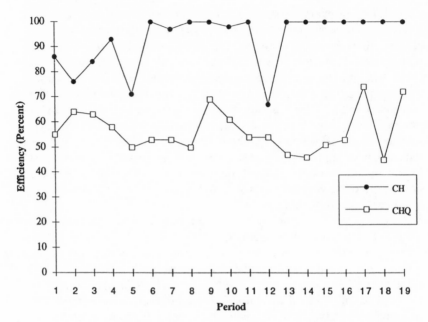

Fig. 7.3 Efficiency under the clearinghouse (CH) and quantity-only clearinghouse (CHQ) institutions. Efficiency is defined as trading profits paid as a percentage of maximum possible trading profits. The data come from all 19 CH periods and the first 19 CHQ periods of two sessions (Chq1–Ch4a and Chq2–Ch4b) reported in Friedman and Ostroy (1993).

graphs efficiency in the two sessions using both institutions. (Efficiency is defined as trading profits paid as a percentage of maximum possible trading profits. The data come from all 19 CH periods and the first 19 CHQ periods of two sessions, Chq1-Ch4a and Chq2-Ch4b, reported in Friedman and Ostroy, 1993.) The answer is obvious from the graphs – it immediately strikes your eye that efficiency is always higher in the CH markets, irrespective of the group of subjects or other nuisances. Leonard J. Savage referred to the pratice of drawing conclusions from such blindingly obvious graphs or summary statistics as the "interocular trauma test."

Is any other test really necessary? Experimental physicists usually rely on Savage's test and seldom resort to formal hypothesis testing. Some of our respected colleagues say privately that economists should follow the physicists' example. If the interocular trauma test is inconclusive, they argue, then you should rethink your experimental design or your presentation of the data. Some other economists (anonymous referees for the most part) insist on hypothesis tests even when the Savage test seems conclusive. They argue that your clever graphical presentation may overstate the weight of the evidence and that the discipline of conducting hypothesis tests will help keep you honest.

Most practicing experimental economists, including both of us, take an intermediate position. Occasionally the Savage test should convince even the most skeptical, and then it is sufficient. More often it will not suffice. Experimental economists, unlike physicists, usually have to deal with many nuisance variables and relatively few observations, so even clever designs and large budgets can not always produce transparent results. When in doubt (or in doubt about referees) we recommend that you conduct routine hypothesis tests.

7.2 Statistical inference: Preliminaries

Suppose that your graphs and descriptive statistics do not give crystal clear answers to some of your questions, even though your experimental design and descriptive statistics are well chosen. At this point you turn to the second phase of the data analysis: formal statistical tests, or inferences. The formal tests are generally meant to provide specific answers to questions of the form "Does treatment X affect outcome Y?" For example, does the double auction market institution (treatment $X =$ DA) increase market efficiency (outcome Y) relative to an alternative institution (treatment $X =$ CH)? Sometimes you ask questions of the form "Is outcome Y better predicted by model M1 or by model M2?"

The most obvious way to answer the first sort of question is to compare the effects $\{y_{DA}\}$ associated with one treatment $X =$ DA to the effects $\{y_{CH}\}$ associated an alternative treatment $X =$ CH. If the y_{DA}'s are larger on average you might be tempted to conclude that the DA institution is more efficient. Likewise, you would be tempted to conclude that model M1 is better than M2 if on average its forecasts are more accurate. But your conclusion might be incorrect because of experimental error. The rest of this section will equip you with the conceptual tools for understanding the sources and consequences of experimental error. Later sections introduce statistical techniques for making correct inferences even when some experimental error is unavoidable.

7.2.1 Basic concepts

Statistical procedures begin with a collection of *observations*. A single observation is often called a run or experimental trial. A trial will include measurements of the treatments X and the outcomes Y. For example, a trial (or unit of observation) in a sealed-bid auction experiment might consist of the value v_t and the bid b_t of a single bidder in a given period, together with block data such as the number of bidders, the distribution parameters for v, and the auction rules.

The appropriate unit of observation is not always clear. For instance, in market experiments, is it a single transaction? A single market period? A subset of market periods? Or perhaps a single experimental session or even a whole set of sessions? The answer depends on the theoretical framework and the purpose of the experiment. For example, the market period is the natural unit when your purpose is to test theories of market equilibrium. If you were interested in the microdynamics of information acquisition, by contrast, the natural unit of observation would be transactions or even individual trader bids and asks. At the other extreme, someone interested in the asymptotics of group learning behavior would legitimately regard an entire experimental session as a single trial.

Suppose you have picked an appropriate definition of trial and now have a set of observations to analyze. The fundamental problem you now must deal with is the imperfections of your set of observations. To the extent that you get different results on replication – that is, to the extent that outcomes differ when you (or another experimenter) run the experiments again with exactly the same set of treatments – your analysis must deal with *experimental error*.

Experimental error has two sources: measurement and sampling. Measurement error is conceptually straightforward. The values in your recorded observations may not be exactly the actual values. Perhaps you misheard a bid in an oral auction, or perhaps you made a mistake in writing it down. Even more serious, you might have lost experimental control and not been aware of it at the time. For example, you might have inadvertently given role A information to a role B subject. Or in a game-theory experiment you may have transposed the intended payoff matrix on every player's screen (as did one of us recently).

Careful choice of laboratory procedures, automating data capture and transmission where possible, and building in redundancy should minimize the amount of erroneous data. You should always take a second precaution: Using your data summaries, check the raw data for large outliers and other anomalies, and check whether the anomalies are actually measurement errors. When you detect erroneous data you should throw them out before you run statistical tests, because even a few bad data points (say, due to a misplaced decimal point) can affect your results.

Sometimes failure of experimental controls produces data that still are interesting (e.g., the transposed matrix may induce a new coordination game instead of the intended coordination game) and you may want to retain it. Such reparametrization is permissible as long as your analysis recognizes the inadvertent change in experimental design (e.g., you have a randomized block but not strict factorial) and you acknowledge the problem in your write-up, perhaps in a footnote.

The rest of this chapter will presume that you have chosen effective laboratory procedures and descriptive data summaries, so that the measurement error consists mainly of minor round-off errors.

Sampling error requires a more extensive discussion. Perhaps the best way to think about it is to consider the collection of all possible trial outcomes given your treatments. Since the time of Galton's classical studies of physical characteristics in human populations, this hypothetical collection is called the *population* of outcomes. There is always some variability in the population because of uncontrolled nuisances such as subjects' attention to the task. You may prefer to think of the variability as "random fluctuations." For any given set of treatments, the variability induces some distribution for the possible outcomes. Logically enough, the induced distribution is called the *population distribution*. If you knew the population distribution, your inferential task would be trivial. For example, if the population mean for DA efficiencies were larger than the population mean for CH efficiencies, then you would correctly conclude that the DA institution is on average more efficient.

Nontrivial statistics are necessary because the population distribution can never be known precisely. Your budget and patience, however large, will allow you to run only a finite number of experiments; you can never observe outcomes of *all possible* trials. Nevertheless you do have useful information about the population distribution because you have actually run a subset of all possible trials and have recorded the outcomes. Thus your actual data constitute a finite *sample* from the population distribution. Sampling error, the second source of experimental error, arises to the extent that your sample is not representative of the underlying population. In the DA versus CH example, the mean of your DA-efficiency sample will almost always differ from the true mean of the DA population, and similarly for the CH sample. These sampling errors could be large enough to lead you to the wrong conclusion about which institution is more efficient.

7.2.2 Good samples and bad samples

You cannot expect to get a perfect sample, whose distribution exactly reproduces the population distribution. But with some care you can minimize sampling error within the bounds of your finite resources. That is, you can take steps to avoid bad samples and to get good samples.

There are two main ways of getting good samples. The first is to make the sample as close as possible to a classic *random sample,* in which each observation is independently selected from the population distribution. That is, in a random sample, each point in the population has an equal chance of being selected in each observation. The other way is to try to take a "stratified" or *balanced sample,* in which you subdivide the population into several segments and draw observations from each segment with frequency proportional to the weight of the segment in the population distribution. For example, in a voter survey (a field experiment) each interviewee could be drawn from the voter population by some random device such as throwing a dart at a printout of registered voters. This procedure could give you a truly random sample. Professional interviewers usually prefer a balanced sample, in which they segment the population by age, sex, education, location of residence, or other observable variables, and then select a proportionate number of interviewees from each segment. A balanced sample will tend to produce smaller sample errors than a random sample of the same size to the extent that outcomes differ across segments, the segments are observable, and their weights in the population are known. Otherwise, random samples are preferable.

Finding procedures that give you good (random or balanced) samples is not always easy. The general problem is that there may be unrecognized relationships among relevant variables in your experiment so that your data represent a small and atypical portion of the population rather than the population as a whole. For example, suppose an experimenter wants to measure the degree of altruism in individual subjects. If he selects subjects in the usual way, advertising the opportunity to earn "substantial cash rewards" in undergraduate economics classes and signing up volunteers, his altruism measurements probably will not be typical of the population of U.S. residents. He failed to recognize the possible relationship between the variables [attends economics class] and [responds to advertisement promising cash] and the outcome [measured altruism]. As a result, he probably collected an unbalanced, nonrandom *biased* sample.

Perhaps the most important advantage of experimental data is that it can provide better samples than happenstance data. Two examples of bad samples of happenstance data may help drive this point home.

Bad Happenstance Sample 1. A bank analyst wants to estimate his bank's profitability in its major loan categories: real estate, commercial/industrial, and consumer. When he regresses historical bank profits on quantities (amounts outstanding in each loan category) he gets unstable coefficient estimates – the magnitude and even the sign change when he varies the beginning or ending dates of the historical data or when he switches from monthly to quarterly data. The underlying problem turns out to be that the bank's policy has been to keep tight bounds on the portfolio composition. For example from 1970 to 1985 real estate loans were not allowed to exceed 30 percent of the loan portfolio and never fell below 27 percent. The historical data therefore all come from a thin slice of the hypothetical profitability population, and as a result the separate effects of the explanatory variables (the loan categories) can't reliably be estimated from this unbalanced and nonrandom sample. Perhaps the analyst will have better luck with his statistical analysis if he can find similar banks with different portfolio policies and can construct a balanced sample from the combined data.

An econometrician would call Sample 1 a case of insufficient variation or multicollinearity. The problem need not arise from deliberate policy. For example, the historical capital/labor ratio and the factor price ratio might be almost constant in an industry, precluding good estimates of the elasticity of substitution from historical data. Since focus variables generally are controllable in the laboratory, you can avoid bad samples of this sort by choosing good experimental designs. Factorial and related designs covered in Chapter 3 ensure that the focus variables vary independently and over a sufficient range so that you can assess their effects.

Bad Happenstance Sample 2. An antitrust analyst studies the relationship between concentration and price over time in several narrowly defined industries. To her surprise she finds several industries for which periods of lower prices seem to go with periods of greater concentration (i.e., fewer competing firms). Further investigation discloses that in most of these cases both price and concentration were driven by a third variable, the price of related goods. For example, in the slide rule industry, price decreases and increasing concentration were both consequences of dramatic reductions in the price of electronic calculators.

An econometrician probably would call this an omitted-variables problem or an identification problem, and could provide a long list of related examples. The historical price data for slide rules were a biased sample of their concentration-segmented population distribution because the demand-side relationship with the electronic calculator price (or at least its impact on slide-rule quantity demanded) was not recognized. The sample suggests an incorrect inference because the price observations for high concentration were taken from the part of the population distribution associated with low demand.

Good experimental technique can prevent most problems of this sort. The experimental analog of the antitrust study would vary the focus variable (concentration) independently of the other controllable variables, including most variables which could shift demand. Randomization would neutralize the effects of other nuisance variables on the measured outcome (price). The result would be a good sample from which valid inferences could be drawn.

Despite the tremendous advantages laboratory techniques provide in creating good samples, some serious problems remain, arising particularly from learning effects and group effects. Human subjects usually learn from experience. The action a subject takes in a particular trial of an experiment may be affected by her experience in previous trials. To the extent that this sort of learning affects your measured outcomes, your sample is not random. Specifically, the trials in a single experimental session are not independent.

Group effects can also produce samples drawn disproportionately from a small subset of the population distribution. For example, in two recent double-auction market sessions with inexperienced subjects, the group of subjects in one session consistently produced more bids and fewer asks than the outwardly identical group in the other session.

In principle, the proper way to deal with these problems is to characterize the nature of sample dependence and to adjust the statistic accordingly. Beginning econometrics students learn how to deal with serially correlated time series data in just this way. Unfortunately learning and group effects have not yet been characterized with any precision, so no valid statistical correction presently is available.

Some experimentalists recently have dealt with the problem by adopting a very conservative definition of a trial – for example, count only the last (or next-to-last) period in a market session. This may be the only practical thing to do when learning effects are extreme, but we do not recommend the practice in general. The approach ignores a lot of potentially informative data, and doesn't completely cure the problem anyway–there may be group effects (or subject pool or protocol effects) that extend across sessions conducted in a given laboratory. Rassenti, Reynolds, and Smith (1988) (and some older unpublished work) deals with the problem by assuming learning effects take the form of exponential decay toward a behavioral equilibrium. We regard this approach as promising but unproven.

We have three recommendations. First, encourage your econometrically inclined colleagues to work on the problem; it probably is important in some of their favorite field data as well as in most laboratory data. Second, include appropriate caveats when you report formal statistical tests. For example, in an ABA crossover design, learning and group effects may tend to drive the observed A mean toward the observed B mean, so conventional confidence levels then would represent a lower bound on the true confidence level associated with your hypothesis test. In the bid/ask example given previously, the conventional confidence level for rejecting the null hypothesis (equal bid/ask ratios across the experiments) would represent an upper bound on the true confidence level. We recommend that you think through the uncontrolled nonrandomized nuisances in your experiment and, if you consider them significant, tell your readers the direction of probable bias in formal test statistics.

Our third recommendation is to extend your randomization scheme to different subject pools, different laboratories, and so on, whenever feasible. The folk wisdom among experimental economists is that an empirical regularity becomes credible when it is replicated with three different groups of subjects, preferably from different pools and in different laboratories. While we see no magic in the number 3, we endorse any procedures that broaden your sample of the population distribution.

7.3 Reference distributions and hypothesis tests

Hypothesis tests assess the probability that differences in observed outcomes across treatments are due to sampling error rather than due to differences in the underlying population distributions. Such an assessment requires a *reference distribution,* an empirical counterpart or proxy for the population distribution. You may construct a reference distribution directly from the samples themselves or from some external data source. Whether your source is internal or external, you may or may not decide to impose a parametric structure on the reference distribution. Your choice of reference distribution largely determines your choice of test statistic, and therefore the power and robustness of your results.

7.3.1 Internal reference distributions

The most common choice is an internal parametric distribution, usually the normal or the Student t. For example, suppose you wish to see whether subjects in a game theory experiment are equally likely to choose each of their two available pure strategies, $x = 0$ or 1. You can impose the parametric structure that the mean choice $\bar{x}$ is normally distributed with unknown population mean μ and known variance s^2/n, where n is the sample size and $s^2 = \Sigma_{i=1}^n (x_i - \bar{x})^2/(n-1)$ is the usual variance estimate. Under the null hypothesis that the population mean is 0.5, the normalized sample mean $z = n^{1/2}(\bar{x} - 0.5)/s$ has the unit normal distribution. An observed $\bar{x} = 0.6$ from a sample of size $n = 36$ with $s = 0.2$ yields $z = 6(0.1)/0.2 = 3.0$. Tables show that the probability of drawing an observation $|z| \geq 3.0$ from the unit normal distribution is only about 0.0026 (a two-tailed test) and the probability of drawing a $z \geq 3.0$ is about 0.0013 (a one-tailed test). It is better to use the more powerful one-tailed test whenever you can specify the direction of the effect of treatment. Here you can confidently reject the hypothesis that the true population mean is 0.5 and that the observed sample mean of 0.6 was due solely to sampling error.

Of course, the test just described assumes you know the population variance. In practice, you usually only know the sample estimate s^2. The internal parametric reference distribution based on a normal population with unknown mean and unknown variance is called Student t, after the pseudonym adopted by the statistician William S. Gossett (1876–1937). In a t-test you compare the same normalized sample mean $n^{1/2}(\bar{x} - 0.5)/s$ to tabulated values for the Student t distribution with $\nu = n - 1$ degrees of freedom. In the example with $t = 3.0$ and $\nu = 35$, we get one- and two-tailed probabilities of about 0.0025 and 0.005. The probabilities are about twice as large as with the normal reference distribution, but they are still small enough for you to reject confidently the null hypothesis.

You can use more elaborate formulas but the same logic to test hypotheses of the form "treatment A promotes higher performance than treatment B." Assume that measured performance is normally distributed with unknown mean μ_A (μ_B) under treatment A (B) and that the unknown variance is the same under both treatments. Then the "pooled t" statistic

$$t_p = (\bar{x}_A - \bar{x}_B) / (s (1/n_A + 1/n_B)^{1/2}),$$

where the sample sizes are n_A and n_B, and the combined sample variance is s^2, has the Student t distribution with $\nu = n_A + n_B - 2$ degrees of freedom.

If you designed your experiment so that A and B trials occur in n

matched pairs, you can sharpen the test. Form the matched pair differences $x_D = x_A - x_B$, and compute their mean $\bar{x}_D$ and variance s_D^2. Then form the "matched t" statistic, $t_m = n^{1/2}(\bar{x}_D)/s_D$. For sufficiently large values of either t_m or t_p you can confidently reject the null hypothesis that the A and B populations have the same distribution.

A numerical illustration may be in order. Recall the boys' shoes example of Section 3.3, in which we want to know whether the new sole material A wears more slowly than the old material B. The data reported in Box et al. (1978, p. 100) give sample sizes of $n_A = n_B = 10$, sample means of measured wear of $\bar{x}_A = 10.63$, $\bar{x}_B = 11.04$ (so $\bar{x}_D = -0.41$), with $s = 2.43$, and $s_D = 0.386$. Then $t_p = (10.63 - 11.04/(2.43/5^{1/2}) = -0.41/1.09 = -0.38$, while $t_m = (10^{1/2})(-0.41)/0.386 = -3.36$. Tables of the Student t distribution give one-sided 1 percent critical values of 2.25 for the pooled t ($\alpha = 0.01$, $\nu = 18$) and 2.82 for the matched pair t ($\alpha = 0.01$, $\nu = 9$). Since the absolute value of t_m exceeds the critical value, we conclude that the new material A wears significantly more slowly.

Why did we pose "no effect" as the null hypothesis and the effect we were looking for as the alternative hypothesis? This is the customary way to do it. Although you can find an occasional counterexample in the literature (e.g., Schotter and Braunstein, 1981; De Long and Lang, 1992), it usually is considered bad form to reach a conclusion by failing to reject the null hypothesis. Perhaps you failed to reject because the data are sparse or noisy, not because the null hypothesis really is correct. Your readers will probably find it more satisfying if you reach your conclusion by rejecting a boring null hypothesis in favor of your desired (often one-sided) alternative hypothesis, as in the example. Why use a 1 percent confidence level? Custom again. Smaller confidence levels are better, since we are talking about the probability of mistakenly rejecting a true null hypothesis. Economists often will settle for a 5 percent or even 10 percent confidence level when working with a small or noisy data set, but everyone prefers a 2 percent or 1 percent confidence level when the data are reasonably good.

Why were we able to reject the null using the matched t but not the pooled t statistic in the example? Recall that the matched-pair design, assigning materials A and B randomly (to left and right or right and left) shoe soles, is intended to eliminate experimental error due to nuisance variables. The sharp decrease in s_D relative to s, and therefore the sharp increase in t_m relative to t_p, demonstrates the success of the matched-pair design in this example.

The reference distributions discussed so far assume that the underlying populations are normally distributed. The Central Limit Theorem provides some justification for assuming that the mean of a random sample is normally distributed, even when the observations themselves are not drawn from a normally distributed population. Nevertheless, the normality assumption remains unattractive in some cases. For example, the period-by-period market efficiency data in Figure 7.3 certainly are not even approximately normal. More extreme examples occur when your equilibrium occurs at a corner, so deviations can't even be symmetric. (See Chapter 9 for an example called Bernoulli-choice experiments.) In such cases you may prefer to use a free-form (or *nonparametric*) reference distribution in testing the null hypothesis that treatments A and B yield the same population distribution of outcomes. The idea is that if the null hypothesis is true, then each assignment to A or B trials of the measured outcomes is equally likely. The reference distribution then consists of all possible assignments of the data to the treatments, and the test statistics give the probability that a difference between the A and B trials at least as extreme as observed could have come from a random assignment.

The Wilcoxon (or Mann-Whitney U) statistic is perhaps the most popular example of a nonparametric test. You (or preferably your computer programs) rank-order the data from lowest measured efficiency to highest, keeping track of whether each trial was an A or B treatment. Then you sum the ranks S for the (say) A trials. The statistic S has known mean and variance under the null hypothesis of no differential effect when there are an equal number n of observations under the A and B treatments, so the distribution of the statistic $T = \text{mean/variance}^{1/2}$ is approximately unit normal in large samples. Good statistical programs can compute the exact probabilities (confidence levels) for any T-value even in moderate-sized samples, and in samples of unequal sizes. A useful variation of this Wilcoxon test, explained on p. 226 of Conover, allows you to test the null hypothesis of equal variances instead of the usual null hypothesis of equal means.

Another popular statistic, called the binomial or signs test, uses a nonparametric reference distribution which is especially useful for matched-pair data. You (or the computer programs) count the number r of paired differences that are positive and the number w that are negative. Under the null hypothesis that positive and negative differences are equally likely, r has a binomial distribution with mean $0.5n$ and variance $n(0.5)(1 - 0.5)$, where $n = r + w$. A little algebra then shows that normalized sample mean is $z = (r - w)/(r + w)^{1/2}$. This statistic is approximately unit normal in large samples; its exact binomial distribution can be calculated precisely in small samples. (It is customary in small samples to subtract the "continuity correction" 0.5 from the numerator.) Once again, you can reject the null hypothesis of no differential effect in favor of the hypothesis that A leads to larger observations than B if z is sufficiently large.

The Wilcoxon test is computationally simple and the binomial test is even simpler. But the Wilcoxon test keeps track only of ordinal relationships and ignores quantitative sample information, and the binomial test ignores all sample information except the signs of the matched-pair differences. Ignoring information reduces power of the test. In the present era of cheap computing power it is worth considering nonparametric procedures that are computationally demanding but use all sample information. The prime example is called the *bootstrap*. To illustrate, suppose your data consists of five matched pairs (x_{Ai}, x_{Bi}), $i = 1, \ldots,$ 5. Construct an internal reference distribution of hypothetical data by taking all permutations of the actual data. Thus you have $2^5 = 32$ hypothetical sets of matched pairs, one of which is the actual data. For each hypothetical data set h, compute the difference of means $\bar{x}_A^h - \bar{x}_B^h$; these thirty-two differences form the reference distribution for the actual difference $\bar{x}_A - \bar{x}_B$. The fraction of the hypothetical differences that exceed the actual difference is the confidence level with which you can reject the null hypothesis of no difference in favor of the alternative hypothesis that $\bar{x}_A > \bar{x}_B$.

You can also bootstrap unmatched data. Given n A-observations and m B-observations, there are $(n+m)!/(n!m!)$ hypothetical assignments of the $n+m$ actual observations to the two treatment levels with n assigned to A and m to B. Under the null hypothesis of no effect, the set of hypothetical A-means (B-means) defines a reference distribution for the observed A-mean (B-mean). (See Box et al., 1978, p. 97, for a numerical example.) The bootstrap reference distribution converges to the t-distribution as the sample size increases, but gives more accurate confidence levels in small samples.

7.3.2 External reference distributions

Sometimes theory prescribes a specific reference distribution. For example, you may conduct a k player game experiment where the payoff function has a unique mixed-strategy Nash equilibrium $p_1, \ldots,$ p_k. Then you probably want to test the hypothesis that observed strategy frequencies $n_1, \ldots, n_k$ represent $N = n_1 + \ldots + n_k$ independent draws from the reference distribution $p_1, \ldots, p_k$ – that is, that your subjects all play the Nash-equilibrium strategy. A standard test is to compute the normalized sum of squared deviations

$$C = \sum_i \frac{(\frac{n_i}{N} - p_i)^2}{p_i} .$$

It turns out that C has the Chi-squared distribution with $k - 1$ degrees of freedom, so you locate your computed value in a standard table to determine the confidence with which you can reject the null hypothesis.

The origin of external reference distributions can be empirical rather than theoretical. Suppose, for example, you run experiments parallel to the extensive published work of Professor Jones. Using her published data (request raw data from her directly if the published data are inadequate), you can estimate the parameters of an appropriate distribution (e.g., normal or binomial) and use that fitted distribution as your reference distribution. Then go ahead and see if you can reject the usual sort of null hypothesis–for example, that the mean of your data is the same as the mean of her data (the reference mean). Alternatively, if your software permits, you can use the exact empirical distribution of her data as your reference distribution. Then you can run the usual nonparametric tests, such as the Wilcoxon and the bootstrap, to see whether you can reject the usual null hypothesis. Failure to reject the null hypothesis in this case is evidence that you successfully replicated Professor Jones's results.

7.3.3 More statistical tests

The test statistics mentioned so far – the normalized sample mean, the pooled t and matched t, the Wilcoxon T, the binomial z, and the Chi-squared statistics – are not the only ones useful for hypothesis testing. To begin with, the Chi-squared statistic is handy even in the absence of a theoretical reference distribution. For example, you may want to see whether treatments such as instructions or feedback information affect the strategy frequencies in your game-theory experiment. The standard approach is to write out a contingency table (columns defined by treatments and rows by strategies) and calculate a Chi-squared statistic analogous to C for the entire table; large values allow you to reject the null hypothesis that the treatment had no effect.

There are many other statistical tests associated with contingency tables. Perhaps the best known is Fisher's exact test. It is appropriate for contingency tables where both row totals and column totals are constrained by your design and/or by the nature of the task. See Chapter 4 of Conover (1980) for a clear exposition.

There are several general-purpose test statistics that compare an empirical distribution to a reference distribution. The Kolmogorov-Smirnoff statistic measures the maximum distance between the two cumulative distribution functions; you can reject the null hypothesis that the underlying population distributions are the same for sufficiently large values of the test statistic (Conover, ch. 6).

The tests mentioned so far deal only with a single treatment variable. Suppose your experiment features several treatment variables and you are satisfied with a (multivariate) normal reference distribution. Then you can use the classical analysis of variance (ANOVA) procedures. ANOVA allocates the variance in your data to each treatment variable and to residual variance. Appropriate variance ratios have the F-distribution (discovered by R. A. Fisher, of course) under the null hypothesis that the treatment variable has no effect. Thus, you can get ratios for each treatment variable and compare them all to tabulated critical values of the F-distribution to determine which of your treatment effects are significant. For details see any statistics text used by social scientists other than economists.

Most economists are more familiar with multiple regression than with ANOVA. Fortunately, you can get equivalent test statistics from multiple regression because ANOVA is a special case of the general linear model (see Kirk, 1982, ch. 5). The regression for two-level treatment variables is simple. Just define a 0-1 dummy variable for each treatment variable, and regress your data on a constant and the dummies. The estimated coefficient for each dummy is the mean effect of the corresponding treatment, and its t-statistic is the standard t test statistic for the null hypothesis that the treatment variable has no effect. If your design kept the treatment variables orthogonal, then these t tests are independent and the results will not be affected when you omit or include other treatment variables in the regression.

The discussions in this section focus on hypothesis testing for treatment variables. The ideas apply equally well to comparing alternative models, say models A and B. Let x_{Ai} and x_{Bi} be the forecast errors of the two models for predicting observation i. Then you can use all the matched-pair tests as well as the more general tests to try to reject the null hypothesis that the A-errors have the same distribution as the B-errors.

A final remark on statistical technique. This chapter has emphasized classical hypothesis testing and estimation because these are widely used by economists and better suited to experimental data than to happenstance data. You should also be aware that there are numerous Bayesian techniques. Roughly speaking, these techniques summarize the empirical evidence by mapping prior beliefs (before exposure to the data) into posterior beliefs (after digesting the data). Bayesian techniques generally are more consistent with decision theory and eventually may replace classical statistical techniques, but at present are not standardized for experimental (or even happenstance) data. Therefore we omit coverage, and refer the interested reader to Leamer (1978) for a general position statement and to Boylan and El-Gamal (1992) for a recent application to experimental data.

7.4 **Practical advice**

Data analysis interacts with experimental design, and you should think through both before you start conducting your experiments. Specifically,

1. Choose your laboratory protocols to reduce measurement error – automate data capture where possible, build in redundancy, and so forth. In manual experiments, have two persons record the data independently. See Section 6.11 for further suggestions.
2. Choose your treatments to produce good samples. Pay special attention to possible learning effects and group effects, since these nuisances are difficult to control or randomize. Remember that fancy statistical procedures are a poor substitute for good samples.
3. Choose experimental designs that will allow you to employ efficient statistics, such as designs that produce matched-pair data, or designs with orthogonal treatment variables.

Once you have conducted your experiments and have gathered the data, you should begin with a qualitative data analysis. We recommend that you

4. Search published literature and use your imagination to find effective graphical displays and summary statistics. Try out several possibilities before making your final choices. Popular worksheet software (Lotus, Quattro, Excel, Wingz, etc.) are well suited for this task.
5. Look for outliers and other irregularities in the data. Eliminate those due to measurement error, and think about possible causes of the correctly reported irregularities (and regularities).

If skeptical colleagues find your conclusions obvious from your qualitative analysis, then you are ready to get on to your final write-up. Usually you will run some formal statistical tests to better understand what your data have to say. If so,

6. Look for appropriate external reference distributions, arising from theory or from existing data. If external reference distributions are unavailable or insufficient, use standard parametric and nonparametric internal reference distributions.
7. Conduct the relevant hypothesis tests or equivalent parameter estimation procedures (regressions). Include a caveat if you suspect your design hasn't fully controlled for or randomized out group or learning effects.

7.5 Application: First-price auctions

The practice of selling an object to the highest bidder in an auction goes back to ancient times, but no satisfying theoretical analysis of this practice appeared until Vickrey (1961). His approach was to postulate what is now known as independent private values: Each bidder i knows her own value v_i and regards the unknown values of the other $n - 1$ bidders as if drawn independently from some specific distribution. Vickrey then used what now is called Bayesian Nash equilibrium to predict the bids and the outcome of an auction. Assuming that traders are risk neutral and that the specific distribution is uniform on an interval $[0, \bar{v}]$, Vickrey predicted that anyone with a value of v_i would bid $b(v_i) = (n - 1)v_i /n$. This result applies to first price-sealed bid auctions (once-and-for-all bids are submitted privately and the highest bidder pays his bid price for the object) and some other outwardly different auctions such as the Dutch auction (the first bidder to stop a declining price clock gets the object at the indicated price).

After a gestation period of a decade or two, Vickrey's model spawned a large body of theoretical literature, surveyed in McAfee and McMillan (1987). Experimentalists quickly noticed that this theory had sharp predictions and important applications but was difficult to test in the field. Building on Coppinger, Smith, and Titus (1980), the study by Cox, Roberson, and Smith (1982) analyzes bidding behavior in first price and other auction institutions. The treatment variables also include the number n of bidders and the upper endpoint $\bar{v}$ on the uniform distribution of private values. For each subject, the authors separately regress the bids b_i on a constant and the values v_i, and they tabulate mean price and price variance. To compare the price data to theoretical predictions, the authors rely on a Kolmogorov-Smirnoff test; the only graph in the paper illustrates the K-S test. They also use a binomial test to compare behavior across auction institutions. The authors conclude that the first-price auction data are not consistent with the original Vickrey (1961) model, which assumes risk-neutral bidders, but generally are consistent with extensions of the model that assume uniformly risk-averse subjects.

Follow-up studies extend the environment and institutions in various ways. The most thorough report on first-price auction experiments is Cox, Smith, and Walker (1988). In one short table they summarize the outcomes of 690 auctions from 47 previous experiments. The table segments the sample into 8 subsamples according to the number of bidders and other design features (such as whether the session involved an alternative auction institution in an ABA crossover design.) For each subsample the summary statistics are the mean observed price and its deviation from the Vickrey prediction. The table also reports the *t*-statistic for the null hypothesis that the mean deviation is zero. The null is rejected in 7 of the 8 subsamples in favor of the alternative that price exceeds the Vickrey prediction, a result consistent with risk-averse bidding.

The authors then pursue the risk-averse bidding hypothesis by examining individual behavior. Relying on a Wilcoxon test to compare each subject's bids to the Vickrey predictions, they reject risk-neutral bidding in favor of risk averse bidding for a majority of subjects. Graphs of the points (v_t, b_t) for individual subjects suggest that subjects differ in their apparent degree of risk aversion. To pursue this possibility, the authors regress bids b_t on a constant and value v_t separately for each subject, and tabulate the estimated slope coefficients and intercepts. They also graph cumulative distribution functions for the regressions' R^2 and for F statistics across pairs of regressions. The results support the view that behavior differs significantly across subjects.

Preexisting theory did not consider heterogeneously risk-averse bidders, so the authors construct a Bayesian Nash equilibrium bidding model called CRRAM (for constant relative risk aversion model) that covers this case. They find that the existing data are generally consistent with CRRAM. Since the model was constructed to explain the existing data, the authors conduct new experiments to test the model further. CRRAM correctly predicts that tripling monetary rewards has no significant effect on the bid functions. It is less successful in predicting changes in bid functions when rewards are nonlinearly transformed. CRRAM also fails to account for nonzero intercepts in bid functions in the original data. In a final iteration of theory and experiment, the authors construct modified versions of CRRAM which allow nonzero intercepts. One version, called CRRAM*, is generally consistent with the existing data as well as with data from new experiments designed to test it.

Surely this is an impressive body of scientific research. Nevertheless it is under attack on two fronts. Skeptics can question whether the departures from Vickrey behavior really are significant and, if they are, whether alternatives other than risk aversion have received adequate consideration. Harrison (1989) forcefully argues that departures from Vickrey behavior are negligible and therefore the dominance precept is not satisfied. To make his case, Harrison presents several diagrams showing that unilateral deviations from the Vickrey bid function typically result in rather small expected losses. He points out that the deviations are highly non-normal and so he relies mainly on nonparametric statistical techniques. He finds that the (true, population) median expected loss is very likely to be less than 8 cents per bid. Other critics disagree with Harrison's emphasis on median losses and point out that even a robust statistic may not capture key features of the data (i.e., a moderate number of large losses would not be detected by the median if there are enough small losses). Some critics argue that learning explanations may improve on the risk-aversion explanations. Readers interested in the substantive issues raised by first price auction experiments should read the Kagel (1993) survey and the December 1992 *American Economic Review* interchange on Harrison (1989).

8

Reporting your results

You have thought through some important economic issue, found a way to examine it in the laboratory, designed an appropriate set of experiments, run them, and analyzed the data. You have learned a lot through the whole process, and it appears that the results may interest, even surprise others. Time to kick back and congratulate yourself on a job well done? Well, don't relax quite yet. You still have to present your results to your peers. If your write-up is sloppy or confusing, all your hard work probably will have no impact on others. If you report your results effectively, you may help people change how they think about the issue. You already have had the personal satisfaction of learning something new. Now by effectively communicating this learning to others, you can amplify the social benefit of your work as well as your personal satisfaction.

This chapter offers suggestions on how to report the results of your experiments effectively. We emphasize the preparation of articles for academic journals, but most of the suggestions apply equally well to seminar presentations, consulting reports, or book chapters. The first section discusses the scope of research you should try to cover in a single paper. Next we present customary ways of organizing the paper, and offer advice on polishing your prose, tables, and figures. The rest of the chapter discusses current standards for documenting your work and offers advice on how to schedule various stages of your project. We illustrate many of our points in a discussion of asset-market experiments.

8.1 Coverage

Every essayist, whether an economist, or journalist (or physicist for that matter) must decide *what material* to cover and at *what depth* to cover it. Coverage decisions can be particularly difficult for experimental economists. Usually you will get some puzzling results in your initial laboratory sessions, so you conduct follow-up sessions. Often the new results create as many puzzles as they solve, so you conduct more follow-up sessions, creating new puzzles, and so on. The process eventually terminates, either because you resolve all the important puzzles or (more likely) because you run out of time, money, or patience. At this point you may have far more material than you can fit into a single paper, but the scope of this material is probably too narrow for a publishable book. Somehow you will have to select a subset of your material.

In choosing which data to report you must balance two conflicting objectives. First, to keep your readers' attention and to aid their retention, you want to focus on a single issue or a small set of closely related issues. Therefore you want to select only the most directly relevant data. Second, you want to present an accurate and complete picture of your results. In particular, you want to avoid selection biases.

Roth (1990), taking a cue from Leamer (1983), warns that experimentalists too are susceptible to selection biases in reporting their results. He argues forcefully in favor of treating the entire set of trials in an investigation as a single experiment. If the designation of "experiment" were reserved for various subsets of trials, he argues, investigators might be tempted to report selectively from the trials they have conducted, with dysfunctional consequences for the discipline as a whole. However, Roth acknowledges the other side to the argument by quoting the example of Robert Millikan and Felix Ehrenhaft from a report by the National Academy of Science's Committee on the Conduct of Science (1989). Ehrenhaft reported all his data and concluded, incorrectly, that there is no lower limit on the magnitude of electrical charge found in nature. Millikan, on the other hand, used only what he regarded as his "best" data sets to demonstrate the unitary charge of electron, and went on to win the Nobel Prize for this landmark discovery.

How should you resolve the data-selection dilemma? We believe that within your budget and time constraints you should vary treatments and replicate sufficiently to obtain a reasonably broad base of valid data, and you should analyze all of it until you understand its main characteristics. Then you should select the most relevant portion of the data for closer analysis, after satisfying yourself that your selection does not distort the conclusions. In your written report you should briefly but carefully *describe your selection process* and then devote most of your report to analyzing the data selected. That way your readers can judge the relevance of your data for themselves, and know where to go for additional evidence. Our advice admittedly places a heavy burden on you, the experimentalist, but we think the burden is justified because the scientific validity of your results is at stake.

The decision regarding depth of coverage also must balance conflicting needs. First again, you want to be brief and not tax your readers' patience with dispensable details. But second, you want to be sufficiently complete so readers understand what you have done and how you reached your conclusions. Many of your readers probably are not as familiar with your procedures as they are with standard econometric procedures for field data. Consequently, they may misinterpret what you did if you omit too many details.

With some extra work, you can resolve this conflict satisfactorily. In the text of your paper, try to convey the main features of your procedures and omit most of the details. But in an appendix, write up your procedures in sufficient detail that any competent experimentalist could fully replicate your work, and make the appendix available on request. In doing so, you will assist your fellow experimentalists, depersonalize the empirical basis of economics, and strengthen its scientific foundations. To drive the point home, we reprint the *Econometrica* guidelines in Appendix IV. These guidelines should generally be followed even if you have no intention of submitting your work to that journal.

8.2 Organization

Your experimental paper should be organized generally in the same manner as other empirical economics papers. In recent decades, empirical papers in economics usually have the following organizational plan:

> Part A Introduction. Statement of issues, background information, literature survey, overview of the paper and results.
>
> Part B Relevant theory. A brief summary often suffices.
>
> Part C Data and results.
>
> Part D Conclusions and discussion.

Experimentalists face some expositional issues that other empirical economists usually can ignore. If you present theory before describing your laboratory environment, you are left to defend the gaps between the two. You may prefer to describe your laboratory environment, institutions, and treatments first, before specifying the theoretical models that may be relevant to understanding the outcomes of such economies. This is especially useful if the relevant theory is poorly developed. Presentation of data and results also requires careful exposition because typically your data are new and in some respects unfamiliar to most of your readers.

Experimental economists generally deal with these expositional problems by modifying the basic organizational plan as follows.

Part A	Introduction. Statement of issues, background information, literature survey (may go elsewhere), overview of the paper and results.
Part B1	Laboratory procedures. Basic environment and institutions, treatments, design, subject pool, etc.
Part B2	Relevant theory. Can precede B1 if relevance is clear from introduction. May conclude with a list of testable hypotheses.
Part C1	Descriptive data analysis. Graphs and summary statistics.
Part C2	Inferential data analysis. Hypothesis tests or the like. May be omitted if conclusions are evident in the descriptive data analysis.
Part D	Conclusions and discussion.
Appendices	Instructions to subjects, raw data, mathematical derivations, procedural and statistical details, etc. To be published if the editors desire, otherwise available on request.

This outline is for pedagogical purposes only. It is best to think about our outline and to look at the organization of good published articles that are relevant to your work. Then choose a tentative organization and modify it in response to colleagues' comments that make sense to you.

8.3 Prose, tables, and figures

For reasons we do not fully understand, wordsmithing standards seem higher in economics than in most other experimental disciplines such as psychology and biology, and most economists spend a lot of time polishing their prose. Unless you don't care about publication, or unless you are a gifted writer, you also will devote a large fraction of your research time to prose polishing. Remember that if better writing makes your work accessible to even 10 percent more readers, the return is well worth the investment. You should expect to rewrite your paper several times before you are done with it. It may help to ask yourself the following questions as you work on your prose.

Did I leave out any information my readers need to understand this sentence or result?

Have I repeated myself too often on this point?

Is there a way to rearrange the paragraphs or sentences to make the material easier to absorb?

Can I recast this sentence to make its meaning clearer on first reading? Did I slow the reader down by making gratuitous backward or forward references (e.g., "See Section 8.4 below")?

Is there a more apt or vivid way to make this point?

Good writing is an art. It does not come naturally to most economists (ourselves included), but we all improve with practice. You can increase your rate of improvement by reading Strunk and White (1979), McCloskey (1985, 1987), and Hamermesh (1992), and by taking their advice to heart.

Many readers will skim your article, pausing to look more closely at diagrams, graphs, and tables. Even careful readers usually depend heavily on figures and tables. Therefore the success of your paper depends disproportionately on the quality of your figures and tables, and you can get a high payoff from polishing them so they are easy to understand. As you polish, ask yourself the same kind of questions as for your prose. For example, do lines 5 and 6 of this table convey any useful information? Would a separate diagram help clarify this fundamental point? Do I have too many lines in this graph?

The *Journal of Finance* and a few other academic journals require that each table and figure be completely self-contained, suitable for reproduction in a textbook without your surrounding prose. In our view this standard is a bit extreme, but the general idea is a good one. Ask yourself: Will my readers remember the meaning of this acronym used as a column head? When in doubt, make the column heading self-explanatory or define it in a caption or note. And so forth. Good published work on related issues is the best source of ideas for improving your tables and figures. You may find Tufte (1983, 1990) useful as general references.

8.4 Documentation and replicability

Philosophers of science assign a central role to replicability. More specifically, in the opening paragraphs of the *New Palgrave Dictionary* entry on experimental economics, Smith (1987) explains why progress in our discipline depends on experimentalists being able to replicate one anothers' work. As an experimental economist, you have the responsibility of documenting your work so that it is replicable. Given your documentation and other necessary resources such as access to subjects or special software, another competent experimentalist should be able to conduct an experiment that you would regard as essentially the same as your own. Further, she should be able to process your raw data in the same way you did.

To meet this replicability standard, four types of documentation are necessary:

> *Subjects* Maintain printed or electronic copies of instructions to subjects. Also, maintain records of how, when, and where you recruited and trained subjects. Your institution probably also requires you to maintain records of cash payments to subjects.
>
> *Laboratory environments* Maintain copies of software and special materials, and descriptions (at least) of hardware you used, in sufficient detail that your laboratory environments could be recreated.
>
> *Raw data* Keep electronic or hard copies of all your valid data. Include records of time and circumstance, such as a lab log.
>
> *Data processing* Keep records of your specific procedures, such as the SAS (a popular statistical software) procedures used to produce Table 3 of your paper.

When you have finished your project, you should consider sending your data to a public archive. Some funding agencies, such as the National Science Foundation, require this. Many use the U.S. national archive of social science data maintained by the Inter-university Consortium for Political and Social Science Research (ICPSR). The mailing address is PO Box 1248, Ann Arbor, Michigan 48106-1248.

8.5 **Project management**

Unless you have previous experience, you probably feel a bit uncertain about how to combine planning, experimentation, data analysis, oral and written presentations, and documentation. You probably will begin and end these tasks more or less in the order listed, but there will be considerable overlap. We offer our advice on project management in the form of answers to several questions that may be on your mind.

When should I begin presenting my results? As soon as you have a reasonably broad set of valid data (i.e., without important glitches), you should begin to analyze it, and when you obtain an interesting result you should think about presenting it. Initial oral presentations usually are best made to an informal and friendly audience at the time you are finishing the first complete draft of your paper. Don't wait until you have highly polished results because then you would miss the opportunity to act on your colleagues' good suggestions.

Should I write up my results in one long paper or several shorter papers? Both of us tend to err on the side of putting too much material into a single paper, but we've certainly seen the opposite error as well. Remember that the scope of a paper is defined by the issues addressed, not the number of experiments. Basically, it is a judgment call. If you are unsure, ask your colleagues for advice.

When should I submit a paper for publication? Journal standards for experimental economics are the same for other kinds of empirical economics. Read Hamermesh (1992) and consult trusted colleagues if you are unsure whether your paper is ready for submission.

When should I make my documentation available to other experimentalists? The current custom is to offer all documentation except raw data on request as soon as you begin to circulate a draft or working paper version of your results. There is no consensus as yet on raw data; some experimentalists have delayed sending it for as long as two years from the time of initial publication of results. Others honor requests for raw data before publishing anything. You incurred the costs of producing the data so you deserve the right of first access. On the other hand, the full social benefits will be realized only when the data are available for cross validation, new tests by other investigators, and student training. We hope that it becomes customary to release data upon acceptance for publication or within a year of completion of the main experiments, whichever comes first.

8.6 Application: Asset-market experiments

Field data are exceptionally plentiful and accurate for asset markets. Every day there is a new mountain of precise price data for stocks, bonds, commodity futures, options, and foreign-currency markets. Despite their impressive mass and precision, the field data have some weaknesses. Trading volume data are reasonably good, but accurate allocation data are much harder to obtain. More important, traders' preferences, endowments, and information are not observable in field settings. Hence you can't directly measure allocational efficiency or the fundamental value (i.e., the value incorporating and aggregating all current information) for an asset market in the field. You can measure price volatility for field assets, but you can't determine how much of it is efficient response to new information and how much of it is excessive and inefficient.

Laboratory asset market data have complementary strengths and weaknesses. Budgetary considerations dictate that only a few traders will participate in laboratory markets over relatively short periods of time. However, traders' preferences and information can be controlled, so you can measure efficiency directly. If you are interested in the effects of the trading institutions, you can systematically vary them in the laboratory. Experimental studies of asset markets were initiated to examine the abilities of markets to disseminate information and to allocate resources efficiently when the initial distribution of information is asymmetric. We shall describe only the main features of a few studies here. For a detailed survey, see Sunder (1993).

Plott and Sunder (1982) initially designed their experiment in 1980 to learn how large a fraction of traders must have information in order for the market to behave as if all traders are informed. The authors expected the results to show that, as the number of traders who have information at the outset increases, the allocative efficiency of the market will rise. This sort of quantitative link between initial information dissemination and market efficiency cannot be confirmed from field data because the researcher cannot know the information conditions of the individual traders.

Plott and Sunder (1982) made important abstractions and borrowed from the prior experimental studies in creating their laboratory model of the stock market for the purpose of testing the efficiency hypothesis. First, stocks have indefinite lives and pay periodic dividends whose amounts are uncertain. They abstracted away from indefinite lives to a single dividend because multiperiod lives were not critical to the principle of information dissemination in markets. Second, exploration of the issues of information efficiency needed uncertainty of payments, and they borrowed the design of uncertainty in their first market session from Plott and Wilde's (1982) experiment on professional diagnosis versus self-diagnosis. When this information structure proved to be too complicated, they simplified it in the subsequent market sessions. Third, an experimental model of the stock market had to permit each participant to be a buyer as well as a seller. This feature was borrowed from Forsythe, Palfrey, and Plott (1982). Each trader was given an initial endowment of two assets and a large working capital loan. The working capital loan enabled each trader to buy and sell freely within a trading period, though the net short sale within a period had been restricted to the initial endowment of two assets in order to limit the risk of subjects' bankruptcy. Fourth, the per unit dividends were specified so as to hold the rational-expectations equilibrium price to a constant level within each period. Fifth, dividends were varied across the three classes of traders in order to generate gains from trading and to enable a measure of allocative efficiency of the market to be defined and examined. Finally, information about the realized state of the world that determined the dividends was withheld from some traders in order to examine if these traders are able to learn the information through the market process itself.

Thus the focus variable in Plott and Sunder's (1982) experiment is information (i.e., prior notification of the realized state) with three levels: none, insiders (e.g., two of the four traders of each type are notified), and all. Nuisance treatment variables include the state probabilities and the state-contingent valuation schedules, and whether or not the number and identities of insiders are announced. Basically the design is randomized block, each block consisting of two to nine trading periods. The results supported the rational-expectations (RE) model, as prices and allocations converged to efficient levels and insiders' excess profits became insignificant.

While Plott and Sunder reported the results of all five market sessions, they also selectively used information from their early sessions to guide their exploration. Their results can be used to illustrate the critical and controversial nature of the issues discussed in Section 8.1. Only one out of a total of nine private-information periods of the first two market sessions betray any hint of information dissemination. Using the statistical averages, the null hypothesis of no-dissemination would not have been rejected. Yet, the behavior of market in period 9 of market 2 suggested that, under appropriate conditions, such dissemination might occur. The authors then conducted a third market session with experienced traders that yielded firm evidence in favor of information dissemination. Millikan's use of his "best data" can be an excellent example to follow if you apprise your reader of all the facts of the case.

Clear evidence of market efficiency from the third market session led the authors to seek replication in a fourth session with a fresh set of subjects. Having replicated, they wrote the first draft of the paper and presented the results at two workshops. Comments received at the workshops led to a fifth market session in which the number of states of the world was increased to three. Design, conduct, and presentation of the experiment took only six weeks, much less than the authors' other work.

Do the striking efficiency results stand up in more difficult environments? Having observed dissemination of information from the informed to the uninformed, Plott and Sunder (1988) designed an experiment to examine if, and under what conditions, the markets can perform the more difficult task of aggregating diverse information in possession of individual traders. Can markets behave as if everybody has all the information? They took the three-state design of the fifth session of their 1982 paper and altered the information structure. If state X was realized, half the traders were told that the state is "Not Y" while the other half were told that it was "Not Z." Would the market behave as if every trader knows for sure that the state is X? Results of their initial sessions revealed the answer to be negative, and shifted the focus of research to finding market environments in which such aggregation can occur. The subsequent sessions revealed that information is aggregated in markets that fulfill either of the two conditions: (1) homogenous preferences (same dividend distribution for all traders) or (2) trading a set of securities that span the state space. In further work, Forsythe and Lundholm (1990) found that even in incomplete markets with heterogenous preferences, additional trading experience can lead to information aggregation.

Unlike their 1982 paper, market sessions for Plott and Sunder (1988) were conducted over a span of three years at geographically dispersed locations. The first market session was found to aggregate information only because, it was later discovered, one subject was inadvertently given information she should not have had. This session was excluded from the published work. The working versions of both papers included complete raw data appendixes which were later analyzed in published articles by other authors.

Copeland and Friedman (1987) report the first computerized asset-market experiments. (See Williams, 1980, and Anderson et al., 1989, for evidence that computerized asset markets are more difficult than oral.) Their environments had several dimensions of additional complexity including news (i.e., information regarding the realized state arriving during the trading period), and possibly heterogeneous states. To cope with the large number of potentially important nuisances they employed a 2^4 half-factorial design with the fourth variable confounded with the three-way interaction of the other variables. In this and later work, the authors found that the rational-expectations model continues to outperform alternative simple models in most dimensions, although there are some interesting anomalies. Two follow-up papers by the same authors examine the interaction of an information market with the asset market, and examine an empirically oriented model of partial information aggregation. After several rejections and numerous revisions, the papers eventually were published in 1991 and 1992.

Smith, Suchanek, and Williams (1988) draw quite different conclusions from a different environment examined in dozens of experimental sessions over several years. They report frequent large bubbles – episodes where the asset price rises far above the fundamental value for an extended period of time, usually ending in a sudden price crash to or below the fundamental value. The environment differs from most previous asset-market studies in at least two respects: They generally have only one trader type (so there are no induced gains from trade), and they use long-lived assets with little stationary repetition. Despite some useful follow-up work by Porter and Smith (1990) that systematically tests several hypotheses regarding bubble formation, it is not yet clear which design differences are responsible for the inefficient prices. Follow-up work continues in several laboratories around the United States.

9

The Emergence of experimental economics

Why has the experimental tradition been so late to emerge in economics? In Chapter 1 we argued that a discipline becomes experimental when innovators develop techniques for conducting relevant experiments. However, development of experimental technology is only a part of the story and raises as many questions as it answers. Why were innovators able to develop new techniques in the 1960s and 70s and not before? Why did mainstream economists begin to acknowledge the relevance of laboratory experiments in the 1980s and not even later? To answer such questions we must look at the development of the economics discipline as a whole.

In this chapter we offer a brief historical account of the emergence of an experimental tradition in economics, and our own tentative explanation of its timing. We are not historians and do not try to be complete and definitive; our goals are more modest. Now that you are familiar with the techniques of experimental economics, you should understand how they arose and how they relate to other experimental traditions in the social sciences. Our historical account may provide useful perspectives. You may also find the story of some interest in its own right.

We begin with some ideas about the evolution of scientific thought, mostly drawn from Kuhn (1970) and Lakatos (1978), and apply these ideas to economic theory. The historical narrative in the next several sections is based on Smith (1991) as well as on personal conversations and correspondence with Charles Plott and several of the other people involved. We trace the development of experimental economics up to early 1980s when it found increasing acceptance into mainstream economics. After a quick geographical sketch of activity in experimental economics in the early 1990s, we discuss the divergence of the discipline

121

from contemporary experimental psychology. The chapter concludes with a discussion of some classic and contemporary game theory experiments.

9.1 Economics as an experimental science

In any discipline, meaningful experiments are possible only when some of the key variables recognized by the discipline are amenable to experimental control. But the set of key variables is not constant; it changes over time as the received theory changes. Paradigms shift when a complicated set of explanations based on many variables are replaced by a simple explanation based on fewer variables. Some variables that were believed to be crucial in the old paradigm may be absent from the new. If the lack of controllability of such variables prevented the discipline from being experimental in the old paradigm, the discipline may become experimental in the new paradigm. The double helix model of DNA and the plate tectonics theory in geology are recent examples of new paradigms that opened new avenues of experimentation in the disciplines of molecular biology and geology.

The amenability of a discipline to experiments is not inherent in the discipline; it depends on the current state of the underlying theory. Although Aristotle recognized the value of field observation, he and the other ancient Greek academicians discounted the value of physics experiments because his theoretical conception of the discipline (natural philosophy) allowed no scope for experimentation (Lloyd, 1984). Experimentation in physics became routine only after Newton and others created theoretical concepts (such as force, mass, etc.) suitable for controlled manipulation.

The ruling paradigms in economics until the 1960s had little room for laboratory experiments. At that time there was a sharp division between microeconomics and macroeconomics. The scale of macroeconomic phenomena precludes most kinds of controlled experimentation. By the same criterion, astronomy too might be regarded as a nonexperimental science. Because of their inability to manipulate the planets, stars, or galaxies, astronomers had to devise ingenious, sometimes spectacular, quasi-experiments on naturally occurring phenomena to adduce convincing evidence to reject or support contending theories (e.g., a quasi-experiment with the 1914 solar eclipse verified Einstein's prediction about the curvature of space in the neighborhood of large masses). It would be politically and ethically difficult, if not impossible, to conduct macroeconomic experiments that manipulate monetary and fiscal policies in order to gather observations to verify or reject various macroeconomic theories. It is hardly surprising, then, that Paul Samuelson,

Milton Friedman, and most of their contemporaries at midcentury regarded economics as inherently nonexperimental.

But these arguments do not apply to microeconomics, just as the arguments about the nonexperimental nature of astronomy are inapplicable to most terrestrial physics and chemistry. Why didn't mainstream microeconomists seek experimental approaches by the 1950s? It seems to us that the reasons here are more subtle and go to the heart of economic theory.

Among all social sciences, (micro)economics has achieved an extraordinary degree of coherence and power because of its willingness to abstract from reality and to use the mathematical techniques of optimization and the concept of equilibrium. Thus mainstream economists were not (and mostly still are not) interested in testing whether human beings actually maximize utility or firms maximize profit, or in testing literally whether markets clear. They were (and still are) interested in testing the *consequences* of assuming these things, for example testing the comparative statics of competitive equilibrium. It is virtually impossible to ensure that the abstract assumptions of optimization and equilibrium are met in the laboratory, so it was easy for microeconomists to ignore, even reject, the possibility that laboratory experiments may contribute anything useful to their discipline.

In our view experimental economics became viable mainly because changes in the ruling paradigms of microeconomics (and then macroeconomics) from the 1960s created openings for meaningful experimentation. General equilibrium theory, social choice theory, industrial organization theory, game theory, and voting theory matured to the point that they could provide serious alternatives to one another as a foundation for understanding economic phenomena. Microeconomists by the late 1960s often had to choose among alternative equilibrium concepts (e.g., competitive equilibrium, Nash equilibrium, and the core) before they could begin to interpret field data. Sometimes they had to choose among multiple equilibria even given a single equilibrium concept (e.g., three Nash equilibria).

At this point the need for a method of choosing among competing economic principles became recognized. The question "Which of these models best predicts what is observed in the simple experimental economies?" (Plott, 1991, p. 906) becomes pivotal when each of the alternatives has some a priori plausibility. When there is only a single plausible theory, the experimentalist is reduced to examining theoretical propositions of the form "If x then y." Typically x includes unobservables such as beliefs, preferences, or strategies and the "if" part of the conditional cannot be shown to be satisfied in the laboratory. Experiments tell economists little about whether such theories are "true." The point is that the presence of alternative theories changes what is meant by testing a theory and gives greater scope to laboratory experiments.

For these reasons, experimental techniques began to make inroads into microeconomics, game theory, public choice theory, and industrial organization theory in the early 1970s. At about the same time microeconomic theory began to be used to build a new information economics, macroeconomic theory, and financial economics. Experimental techniques followed microeconomics into the new fields to examine substantive empirical propositions, for example about expectation formation. Experimentalists were able to seize the opportunities created by progress in economic theory because of earlier laboratory work, especially in decision theory and game theory. Let us now take a closer look at that prior work.

9.2 Games and decisions up to 1952

There is a long tradition in psychology of studying choice behavior in the laboratory. Specific laboratory-testable propositions arise from utility theory as developed by von Neumann and Morgenstern (1944/1947) as an adjunct to game theory and as further developed in its own right by Savage (1954), Arrow (1971), and others. Game theory from the beginning was recognized as incomplete, requiring empirical evidence to identify the relevant equilibrium concepts and to select among multiple equilibria.

By 1950 a circle of talented mathematicians at Princeton (including John Nash, Lloyd Shapley, and John Milnor) began an empirical tradition they called "gaming" – participatory exercises that draw on or illustrate game-theoretical points, for teaching, operational, or entertainment purposes. An overlapping group of mathematicians and psychologists at RAND corporation in Santa Monica, and other groups around the country, began about this time to conduct experiments informed by the emerging theories of decisions and games.

In 1952, a proposal from University of Michigan, with the support of the Ford Foundation, the Office of Naval Research, and RAND Corporation, resulted in an interdisciplinary conference at Santa Monica, California. One participant, Herbert Simon, describes the background:

> I believe that the 1952 Santa Monica conference came out of the general stir about the whole range of things that was then sometimes put under the label of cybernetics. RAND was at the center of that stir, and just about everyone involved had close connections with the RAND group and/or the Cowles

Commission. This was a response not only to the vN&M [von Neumann and Morgenstern, 1944] (which was itself a response to these developments), but to the whole postwar interest in the applications of mathematics to human affairs – which encompassed computers, servomechanism theory, information theory, mathematical economics, mathematical learning theory, game theory, brain architecture, robots, and operations research (I am sure I have omitted some items). To the extent that some of the people interested in these matters had backgrounds in various areas of empirical science, they brought empirical techniques, including experimentation, into the picture. (Quoted in Smith, 1991, p. 21– 22).

The proceedings of this conference had a major influence, both on the participants' work as well as on many others through the papers published in a volume edited by Thrall, Coombs, and Davis (1954). The integrating theme of the conference was the use of mathematics in social sciences, but five of nineteen papers and a good part of the discussion at the conference had to do with the reporting and interpreting results of experiments.

Several conference participants subsequently had major influence on development of game theory and experimental economics – Jacob Marschak, Roy Radner, and Herbert Simon, to name just three. Simon (1955, 1956) used results presented at the conference to develop the contrast between his concepts of substantive and procedural rationality; what is rational to the experimenter, given all that she knows, may be quite different from what is rational to the subject in an experiment, given his typically highly incomplete knowledge of the environment in which he is expected to act.

9.3 Two pioneers

One of the controversies at the 1952 conference was interpretation of William Estes's (1954) results for "Bernoulli-choice" experiments. His subjects were asked to guess which of two lights would appear next, the actual sequence being random in the sense of independent Bernoulli trials. While the observed results of these experiments were consistent with psychologists' asymptotic learning theory (the relative frequency with which subjects predict each state converges to the true probability of that state), decision and game theorists found such behavior quite irrational because the expected reward could be maximized by *always* predicting the state that had the higher probability. Subjects' payoffs in Estes's experiments were not salient; they were asked to "do your best to make a correct prediction."

Sidney Siegel, a young Stanford experimental psychologist, reflected on Simon's distinction between substantive and procedural rationality and its implications for Estes's results. Siegel conjectured that the boredom arising out of repeated, almost mindless, responses causes subjects in Bernoulli learning experiments to deviate from rational behavior. If so, he reasoned, the amount of this deviation can be increased or decreased by manipulating the monetary rewards and punishments associated with the prediction task, and by introducing cognitive and kinesthetic variability in the task. Siegel (1959) presents convincing empirical support of this hypothesis.

Siegel also became interested in group decisions and joined with Lawrence Fouraker, a Pennsylvania State University economist specializing in oligopoly theory, for laboratory investigations of bargaining in bilateral monopoly, duopoly, and triopoly settings. They documented the dramatic effects of changing the salient payoffs and the information conditions (Siegel and Fouraker, 1960; Fouraker and Siegel, 1963). Ever since then, experimental economists have paid close attention to these variables. Siegel's other legacy to experimental economics is his insistence on careful instructions and inclusion of instructions in research reports. Indeed, experimentalists today may be surprised to find so many familiar phrases in the instructions published as an appendix in Fouraker and Siegel (1963).

Although he was not a participant in the 1952 conference, Martin Shubik worked in the circle of Princeton and RAND mathematicians, and enthusiastically promoted "gaming" and experimentation in the 1950s and beyond. Fouraker, Shubik, and Siegel (1961) was intended as the opening of an ambitious laboratory research program, but the collaboration was interrupted by Siegel's untimely death in 1961. Shubik was also interested in free-form "gaming," including role-playing business-simulation games developed jointly with Richard Bellman (later famous for his theoretical work in dynamic programming) and others. Shubik's dollar auction is a simple example of gaming, used to illustrate escalation or addiction. A classroom instructor usually conducts the auction with the following rules: (1) bidding starts at 5 cents, (2) bidding increases in steps of 5 cents, (3) the highest bidder gets the dollar bill and pays the amount bid, (4) the second highest bidder pays the amount bid but receives nothing, and (5) no conversation or collusion is permitted among the participants.

Shubik envisioned a large-scale computerized laboratory for conducting experiments and for gaming, an idea that Austin Hoggatt first brought to reality, at the University of California at Berkeley in the 1960s. (One of us – Sunder – recalls Professor Hoggatt proudly showing him, a faculty recruit, around the lab during his visit to Berkeley in early 1973; Daniel Friedman also met Hoggatt, about 10 years later). Shubik served as James Friedman's thesis advisor and kindled his interest in game theory and laboratory oligopoly experiments. Friedman (1967) and Friedman and Hoggatt (1980) are examples of 1960s experimental economics at its best. They patiently pursued the implications of the game theory available at that time. Experiments of the 1970s followed a different path. The importance of these early game theory experiments became apparent with the resurgence of game theory in the 1980s.

9.4 Experimental economics in Germany

The German movement in experimental economics started with Reinhard Selten, best known to game theorists for his path-breaking theoretical work on refinements of Nash equilibrium. Selten's interest in laboratory experiments arose early in his career in the mid-1950s from his exposure to the gestalt psychologist Rausch at Frankfurt and to two U.S. publications: the Thrall, Coombs, and Davis volume on the 1952 Santa Monica conference, especially the paper by Kalish et al., on characteristic function experiments, and the American Management Association's book on computerized business games designed by Richard Bellman et al. (1957). Selten convinced Sauermann, his economics teacher, of the appropriateness of experiments and published his first paper with him, "Ein Oligopolexperiment," in 1960. In addition to Selten and Sauermann, the German group also included other students of Sauermann such as Becker, Berg, Haselbarth, Tietz, and others. Sauermann collected, edited, and published three volumes of this work in a book series, *Beitrage zur experimentellen Wirtschaftsforschung* (Contributions to Experimental Economics) (1967, 1970, and 1972). Another volume edited by Tietz (1982) appeared ten years later.

Experimental economics in Germany developed steadily and, until the mid 1980s, rather separately from the United States. Most of the German work has dealt with games and decisions (including bargaining) and has been informed mainly by the ideas of bounded rationality. Little of the work was published in English. See Tietz (1990) for a fairly recent position statement. In the last few years, experimental economics has become more globally integrated, due in part to efforts such as Selten's 1991 two-week summer workshop at the University of Bonn, and the annual meetings of Economic Science Association. However, it still seems fair to say that most work in the United States has retained the outcome orientation of economic theory, while most work in Germany is oriented toward understanding behavioral processes. Much of the German research continues to pursue the goal of building a theory of bounded rationality.

9.5 Early classroom markets

The roots of the U.S. orientation toward outcomes, rather than processes, and toward tests of explicit equilibrium theory, can be traced back to market experiments beginning with Edward Chamberlin (1948). Quite separately from the contemporaneous activity at Princeton (and later at RAND and Stanford and Berkeley), Chamberlin conducted classroom markets at Harvard University in the 1940s. You may recall from Section 2.6 that Chamberlin was the first to assign value and cost parameters to subjects to create supply and demand curves. However, the classroom experiments used a rather weak market institution (a form of bilateral search), no stationary repetition, and no salient rewards. Chamberlin was a leading proponent of monopolistic competition as a theoretical alternative to competitive equilibrium, and unabashedly promoted his theoretical position by emphasizing the discrepancies between outcomes in his classroom markets and the predictions of competitive equilibrium. Given the lack of a preexisting experimental tradition in economics and given the emergence at this time of competitive equilibrium as the centerpiece of economic theory, it is not surprising that few (if any) of Chamberlin's students and colleagues saw scientific value in these classroom experiments.

As a Harvard graduate student in the late 1940s, Vernon L. Smith participated in one of Chamberlin's classroom markets, and at first his response was also dismissive. However, as an assistant professor at Purdue a few years later, Smith reconsidered the matter and concluded that the idea of subjecting propositions derived from economic theory to experimental tests was a sound one. He ran a few classroom markets of his own. However, he modified Chamberlin's procedures in two important respects in order to give competitive equilibrium a better shot. First, all bids and offers were immediately made public, because this public information better captures the idea behind perfect competition than the localized price information in Chamberlin's markets. This centralized market institution, which Smith called a double auction after Farwell (1963), more closely resembles the trading institutions used in modern financial and commodity markets. Second, instead of expecting the competitive equilibrium to be attained instantaneously at all times, Smith relied on Marshallian hypothesis that markets tend to approach equilibrium over time when supply and demand remains stationary. He therefore specified the individual (and market) supply and demand functions in units per trading session, and replenished the endowments of traders at the beginning of each of several consecutive periods. This procedure, later known as stationary repetition, allowed subjects the opportunity to get used to the environment in which they traded.

Smith's first experimental economics article, published in the *Journal of Political Economy* in 1962, presented results of eleven classroom experiments conducted over a span of six years. Subjects in these experiments were not paid any tangible rewards and were only asked to try to make as many points as they could. Yet, the transaction prices and final allocations converged closely to competitive equilibrium predictions when bids, offers, and transaction prices were publicized. Controlled shifts in supply and demand conditions led to changes in price and volume that, except in the transient phase, corresponded closely to the comparative static predictions of competitive equilibrium theory. Smith also made two observations that pointed away from and beyond the extant theory: (1) convergence to competitive equilibrium may be influenced by the shapes of the supply and demand functions as well as by their point of intersection, so the Walrasian process model of tatonnement (or excess demand) is an inadequate explanation, and (2) the rules of the trading institution (such as single versus double auction) may affect the market outcomes. These observations continue to influence economics experiments to the present day.

9.6 Building theoretical foundations, 1960–76

After completing most of the work reported in his first experimental article, Vernon Smith visited Stanford in 1961. Influenced by Siegel's methodology and technique, Smith began to think systematically about conditions that could ensure meaningful economic experiments. He returned to Purdue and in 1963 began teaching a seminar that covered individual and group decision making and utility and matrix game experiments in addition to what little was available on experimental markets. In the summers of 1964 and 1965 Richard Cyert, Lester Lave, and Smith organized Faculty Research Workshops in Experimental Economics at Carnegie Tech with support from Ford Foundation. The workshops attracted most interested researchers in the United States, but the organizers could not find a publisher for a volume of refereed papers from this effort. Another effort, by James Friedman and Vernon Smith, to publish a collection of experimental reprints in 1969, also failed for the same reason, though *The Review of Economic Studies* published a symposium on the subject in 1969.

In the 1960s and well into the 1970s there simply was no market for experimental economics. It was alright to do experiments provided that you did something else that was more respectable. Smith, for example, worked in investment and capital theory, and later in natural resource economics and the theory of uncertainty and information. Workshop presentations of experimental research raised mostly methodological queries about its validity: How can you get competitive outcomes without complete information? What can you learn from students playing for low stakes? Economists examining "If x then y" propositions questioned whether the "if x" could be implemented in the laboratory. Lack of professional interest, and the skeptical nature of the little interest there was, forced Smith to rethink the basis of experimental economics.

Charles Plott in the late 1960s was a young theorist at Purdue interested in political economy, and a fishing partner of Smith. When they discussed experiments Plott became intrigued with the idea that some kind of Bayesian game could provide a better model of the equilibration process than the competitive equilibrium based on demand and supply. Although tractable models proved elusive (they still are), Plott encouraged Harvey Reed, his graduate student, to conduct experiments to explore the potential of Bayesian games.

In 1971 Plott moved to California Institute of Technology, and frequently found himself forced to give examples of simple economics experiments to explain what economists do to his colleagues in natural sciences and engineering. A fishing trip with Smith to Lake Powell that year led to the realization that experimental techniques are relevant not only to economics but also to social choice theory, public economics, and much of political science (Plott, 1979).

Plott joined a young Caltech political scientist, Morris Fiorina, who had previously conducted experiments with William Riker. In 1973–4, Plott helped Smith arrange a year-long visit to Caltech. Their joint seminar gave a boost to several research projects and to laboratory methodology. In a project financed by a National Science Foundation grant, Fiorina and Plott (1978) found that game-theoretic equilibrium could predict the outcome of committee processes for allocating public goods. (This result came as a shock to the authors who, along with most social psychologists of the day, had tended to dismiss game theory as having little to do with actual behavior.) As we noted in Section 6.18, Fiorina and Plott (1978) was a breath of fresh empirical air for theoretical political economy. Plott and Levine (1978) demonstrated the influence agenda can have on the outcome of a public choice mechanism.

These papers helped nail down three important planks to the emerging methodological platform of experimental economics: (1) a focus on competition among theories to explain data, (2) the "special case" argument (if a theory claims to be general, then it should work in special cases, including the special case of simple laboratory economies), and (3) extension of laboratory methods to field phenomena and policy issues. Plott and Smith (1978) also turned out to be quite influential in its focus on the impact of economic institutions, and in measuring efficiency as the fraction of potential consumer and producer surplus actually extracted.

9.7 Joining the economics mainstream

Vernon Smith moved to the University of Arizona in 1975. With Arlington Williams he developed the first computerized double auction market, and with James Cox began to investigate sealed-bid auctions using noncooperative game theory. With his new colleagues, Smith launched sustained research programs in experimental economics and began to analyze the data from experiments he had conducted in the early sixties. He finally wrote up his core methodological ideas in Smith (1976), and in the more comprehensive manifesto Smith (1982b). Likewise, Plott maintained and expanded the ongoing research at Caltech and wrote his influential 1982 survey. For reasons we discussed earlier, mainstream economics became potentially receptive to experimental methods by the early 1980s, and these articles and ongoing research programs became the foundation of the success experimental work has enjoyed in mainstream economics.

Many economists, including both of us, first heard about experimental economics around 1980 and began to think of new laboratory projects. The numbers of new investigators, new projects, and new publications in mainstream economics journals grew explosively in the early 1980s. Growth slowed to a more sustainable rate by the end of the decade.

In the 1990s, Arizona, Caltech, and Bonn remain the leading centers of experimental economics, each with numerous ongoing laboratory research programs and many permanent and visiting researchers. The Economic Research Laboratory at Arizona, the Laboratory for Experimental Economics and Political Science at Caltech, and the Experimental Economics Laboratory at Bonn are modern computerized facilities for wholesale laboratory research. Nevertheless, the bulk of experimental economic research now comes from the many other centers that have appeared in the last decade or two.

For almost two decades Raymond Battalio at Texas A&M and his colleagues there and at neighboring institutions have produced a steady stream of laboratory research. Indiana University has also been a major center since Smith's students, Arlington Williams and James Walker, joined others there in 1979. The University of Iowa has produced a lot of important experimental work since Robert Forsythe moved there from Caltech in 1982. Pittsburgh has also become a major center of experimental economics since Alvin Roth and John Kagel moved to University of Pittsburgh to join Jack Ochs, and Shyam Sunder moved to Carnegie Mellon University to join Howard Rosenthal and Sanjay Srivastava. Other major centers, involving more than one experienced experimental economist and more than one research program, have taken root more recently in Virginia (Charles Holt) and Virginia Commonwealth (Douglas Davis), Minnesota (John Dickaut and Kevin McCabe), and Colorado (William Schultze). Perhaps the greatest growth recently has been in mid-sized and smaller centers, often with a single research program and a single investigator, such as University of California at Santa Cruz since 1985. Chicago, Cincinnati, Michigan, New York, Northwestern, Pennsylvania, South Carolina, Southern California, Texas at Austin, Washington at St. Louis, and Wisconsin are some important examples. Conspicuous by their absence in this list are most of the leading centers of the 1950s and 60s: Pennsylvania State, Purdue, Harvard, Stanford, and University of California at Berkeley. Outside the United States, most experimental economics programs are in Europe, with a few in Asia. See Appendix V for a partial list of universities where experimental economics research is in progress.

9.8 Divergence from experimental psychology

In the 1950s experimental economics, as exemplified in the work of Merrill Flood and Sidney Siegel, was a branch of experimental psychology that dealt with issues of potential interest to economists. Since then experimental psychology and experimental economics have followed divergent evolutionary paths. If you are an economist who interacts at all with other social scientists, you should be aware of the differences between the experimental traditions.

What are the current differences between experimental psychology and experimental economics? To begin with, there are substantive differences in the issues of interest. The cognitive branch of experimental psychology attempts to identify and describe the internal processes that underlie mental activities such as remembering and categorizing objects or making inferences and decisions. The social psychology branch attempts to identify and describe the basic processes of human interaction. Economic decisions by individuals and economic interactions, market or otherwise, are part of psychologists' territory so there is an overlap with economists of substantive interests. But economists for the most part focus on behavior in specific institutions, such as markets, that often tightly constrain behavior. Psychologists generally prefer to study behavior in the absence of such institutions, apparently in the belief that they will observe the fundamental human cognitive or social processes more clearly in less constrained laboratory environments. Thus there is a significant difference in disciplinary focus.

Second, and perhaps more important, is a stylistic difference. Economics for the last forty years and more is strongly theory-based. Acceptable economic theories must be fully developed from preestablished first principles, and must relate specifically to the core micro theory. Quite the contrary in psychology: New theories with new conceptual underpinnings (e.g., recent connectionist/neural net theories) gain a serious hearing if they appear to offer a better explanation of some body of data, irrespective of their relation to preestablished theory. Moreover, the theory relevant to most of the laboratory experiments performed so far, at least in the United States, is some sort of static equilibrium theory. The actual process by which the equilibrium is achieved (or not achieved) is a nuisance in such economic experiments. For psychologists, of course, the process itself is the main theoretical interest.

A third point of divergence is related to the first two. For experimental economists, salience is an essential and self-evident precept. In order to tie the experiment to relevant theory, we take great pains to establish a clear incentive structure within an institutional framework. Psychologists are more casual about defining their subjects' incentives in the experimental tasks. In particular, most psychologists feel no necessity to offer salient rewards; the admonition to subjects to "do their best" is acceptable. Subjects are often required to participate in experiments in order to qualify for credit in courses.

An example may clarify the point. Recall Estes's (1954) Bernoulli-choice experiments. Subjects trying to do their best might pursue one of the following goals: (1) maximize the fraction of all responses that are correct, (2) produce a sequence of responses that statistically resembles the sequence of outcomes as closely as possible, or (3) maximize the probability of outperforming all other subjects in terms of the fraction of correct responses. Psychologists think of themselves as observing fundamental behavioral processes, so the simple "do your best" admonition seems to them to contain no important ambiguity. An economist would see that these three goals imply different optimal behavior, and would use a specific reward structure to implement a specific goal, or would compare behavior under reward structures implementing the different goals.

The differing attitudes toward deliberate deception spring from the same sources. Economists' personal ethical standards are probably about the same as psychologists', but their tolerance of deceptive instructions is less. Economists recognize that deception undermines salience, both directly and indirectly. Psychologists presume that fundamental processes will be unaffected by deception and so (as scientists) they take a more casual view of the matter. The limits psychologists place on deception spring mainly from personal ethics or societal pressure and human subjects committees, not from scientific principles.

When two disciplines have so much in common, it is natural to speculate on the prospects for synthesis. It seems to us that methodological synthesis is possible and desirable. We hope to see psychologists take salience more seriously, and readopt the Sidney Siegel tradition. On the other hand, economists should become more sophisticated in design of their experiments. Eventually the methodological gap may be spanned.

But a methodological synthesis in itself will not bridge the theoretical gulf and create a seamless tradition of experimentation in social science. It is possible (and personally we believe it desirable) that economists and psychologists with common interests develop a boundary discipline focused on process theories to undergird the equilibrium theories. The German experimentalists have sought such theories for decades with no clear breakthroughs as yet; so we do not expect to see truly successful process theories soon. Even if economists and psychologists eventually come to share common theories about learning and adjustment processes, the substantive differences in focus will remain, with economists emphasizing how institutions shape behavior and psychologists emphasizing intrinsic regularities in behavior. But at that point, should we live to see it, the divergence between experimental economics and experimental psychology will be much smaller than it is today.

9.9 Application: Laboratory games

Game theory is the formal analysis of decisions by interdependent agents. The theory assumes that all agents are fully rational and that they correctly perceive their interdependencies. Since its first general formulation by the mathematician John von Neumann and the economist Oscar Morgenstern in 1944, game theory has been blessed (or cursed) by multiplicity of equilibria. There are several alternative approaches (e.g., cooperative or characteristic form versus noncooperative extensive or normal forms), numerous equilibrium or solution concepts for each approach, and often numerous equilibria for a given solution concept and approach.

Despite valiant attempts (most recently by Harsanyi and Selten, 1988), game theorists have not been able to find a compelling way of selecting the relevant equilibria. Thus there is a normative sense in which game theory is incomplete. Of course, there is also the positive issue of whether humans have adequate perceptual and cognitive abilities to make the theory descriptively accurate.

Both positive and normative issues have encouraged game theorists (and the overlapping group of economists studying oligopoly, imperfect competition, industrial organization, and bargaining) to seek empirical evidence. Consequently game theorists have been among the most consistent consumers of experimental economics. Several of them, notably Martin Shubik, James Friedman, and Reinhard Selten, have also been major producers of experimental economics. We illustrate the interplay between laboratory experiments and game theory by discussing some specific laboratory games conducted around 1950 and some others conducted around 1990.

Kalisch et al. (1954) report experiments motivated by n-person cooperative game theory. Game theorists of the day agreed that the cooperative approach was important but disagreed on the appropriate solution concept. The authors saw an opportunity to test a new concept, the Shapley value, against the older von Neumann-Morgenstern solution (the core was not yet invented). Cooperative game theory, like many other theories, is incomplete in another sense – it does not explicitly (or even implicitly) define the protocols for player interaction.

The authors' first experiment used a free-form face-to-face bargaining protocol among four or five players. The characteristic function, that is the schedule of payments assigned to each possible coalition of players, was publicly announced at the beginning of the experiment. Subjects were rotated across the different player roles, and received salient cash payments at the end of the experiment.

Relying entirely on graphs of actual versus theoretical payoffs for each role, the authors argue that there is "a reasonably good fit between the observed data and the Shapley value" (p. 309) and a poor fit to the von Neumann-Morgenstern solution. The authors note persistent effects of personality traits such as "talkativeness" and acknowledge repeated game effects when they recommend that in future work "the same set of players [subjects] should not be together repeatedly since there is too much of a tendency to regard a run of plays as a single play of a more complicated game" (pp. 326–7). The authors also reported protocols for other experiments but did not analyze the data. For example, the protocol in a second experiment involved a strict sequence for written offers and acceptance/rejection/counteroffers, a protocol that survives in simplified form in the two-person bargaining experiments described in Section 4.8.

The Kalisch et al. (1954) work was influential, especially in Germany, but it was not typical of contemporary work. Anatol Rappoport and

Carol Orwandt (1962) survey dozens of 1950's era game experiments, most of which were either zero-sum games or repeated prisoner's dilemma games. Subjects mostly were undergraduates, often with no salient rewards. (For example, "Payoffs were in imaginary money; however each matrix entry is assumed to be valued in dollars for purposes of the experiment" p. 15.) The work surveyed varied considerably in the attention paid to information and communications issues. Few of the studies used anything beyond descriptive statistics to analyze the data. Most of the papers on zero-sum games concluded that players do not immediately find the relevant (saddlepoint) equilibrium but they do eventually converge to it when the saddlepoint is in pure strategies.

The only study to obtain convergence to a mixed strategy equilibrium, Kaufman and Becker (1961), used robot opponents and strategy allocations. That is, players do not choose a single strategy (perhaps randomly) but rather allocate 100 choices to their alternative pure strategies each period. This allocation device has been rediscovered several times since.

Repeated prisoner's dilemma experiments remained popular in the 1960s and after, in part because the results seemed so sensitive to the number of periods and to details of protocol regarding information and communication. Sometimes players would cooperate; sometimes they would not. James Friedman and others developed the theory of supergames (or repeated games) in the 1960s and 70s partly in response to these puzzling results. Puzzles still remained, though. For example, subjects generally are less sensitive than game theorists to the difference between finite repetition and infinite or probabilistic repetition.

Experiments explicitly motivated by game theory became less common by the mid-1970s. Implicit game experiments survived and prospered in the form of market, political economy and auction experiments. Indeed, with the exception of individual choice experiments, each subject in any economics experiment gets a payoff that depends on others' choices as well as her own, and so is a game in the sense of game theory. However, most economics experiments during the next decade focused on specific economic institutions (and on broader issues in industrial organization, public choice, information economics, and so forth) rather than on general game-theoretic issues.

Experimentalists renewed their interest in explicit game theory as the theory unfolded over the 1980s. Reinhard Selten's Nash equilibrium refinements of subgame and trembling-hand perfection and John Harsanyi's (1967, 1968a, b) concept of Bayesian Nash equilibrium opened the way to new applications in micro and macroeconomics. Meanwhile game theorists invented ever more Nash equilibrium refinements. Inspired by these developments, experimentalists at Iowa and Texas A&M and at Arizona and Caltech and elsewhere launched new research programs in game theory in the late 1980s.

Cooper et al. (1990) exemplifies the work at Iowa. The authors examine some symmetric two-player three-strategy matrix games with multiple Nash equilibria (NE), one of which satisfies the refinement concept of Pareto dominance (PDNE). The experiments employ explicit instructions, salient payoffs via the "risk-neutralization" procedure described in Section 4.2, and a computerized matching protocol that rotates each player's opponents from one period to the next and that eliminates direct and indirect communication between subjects. The data on players' choices are informally analyzed in bar graphs, and formally analyzed using Fisher's exact test statistic (mentioned in Section 7.3.3). The authors conclude that outcomes generally are consistent with NE but not with PDNE, suggesting that other NE refinements such as risk dominance may be more important in practice.

Van Huyck, Battalio, and Beil (1990) exemplifies the work at Texas A&M. In this and later work, they found that none of the standard static NE refinements could explain the regularities they document in various coordination games. Game theorists such as Crawford (1991) have begun to create new dynamic branches of game theory in response. These evolutionary or learning models have recently attracted a lot of recent theoretical attention, which in turn has inspired new experiments and new data analysis. For example, Van Huyck et al. (1992) and Friedman (1992) emphasize convergence paths, rather than average behavior. Figures 9.1 and 9.2 show some typical results. Figure 9.1 shows the percentages of group 1 (row) players and group 2 (column) players choosing their first pure strategy in Run 2 (periods 11–20) of evolutionary game experimental session Exp5, and Figure 9.2 shows the percentages choosing their first pure strategy in Run 13 (periods 1–10) of evolutionary game experimental session Exp19. "No information" means that players did not view the history of other players' actions. "Mean Matching" means that each player was matched against all players in the other group and received his mean payoff. "Random Matching" means that each period each player was matched against a randomly selected player in the other group. The displayed payoff matrices are for group 1 players and the transpose for group 2 players. Nash equilibria are indicated by asterisks. In Figure 9.1 there is a unique Nash equilibrium, at (.75, .50). Figure 9.2 has three Nash equilibria, at (0,0), (1.00, 1.00), and (.33, .60).

The underlying game in Figure 9.1 has a single NE in mixed strategies. The figure shows clearly that the 12 players in the 10 periods examined

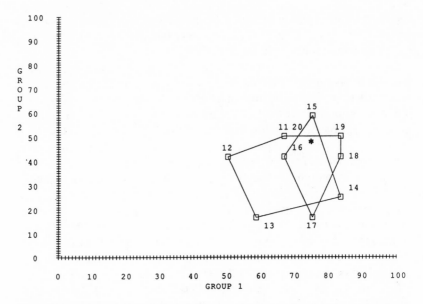

Fig. 9.1 Evolutionary game Exp5, Run2. The percentages of group 1 (row) players and group 2 (column) players chosing their first pure strategy in Run 2 (periods 11–20) of evolutionary game experimental session Exp5. "No information" means that players did not view the history of other players' actions. "Mean Matching" means that each player was matched against all players in the other group and received his mean payoff. The displayed payoff matrices are for group 1 players and the transpose of group 2 players. The unique Nash equilibrium is at (.75, .50), and is indicated by an asterisk (*).

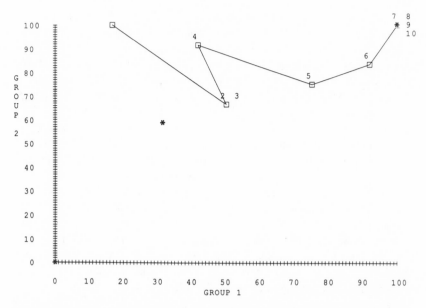

Fig. 9.2 Evolutionary game Exp19, Run13. The percentages of group 1 (row) players and group 2 (column) players chosing their first pure strategy in Run 13 (periods 1–10) of evolutionary game experimental session Exp19. "No information" means that players did not view the history of other players' actions. "Random Matching" means that each period each player was matched against a randomly selected player in the other group. The displayed payoff matrices are for group 1 players and the transpose for group 2 players. The three Nash equilibria, indicated by an asterisks (*) are at (0, 0), (1.00, 1.00), and (.33, .60).

chose strategies that on average were close to the NE, but the sequences of aggregate strategies circled around the NE with no clear tendency to actually converge or diverge. The underlying game in Figure 9.2 has three NE, two of which are in pure strategies and theoretically stable (in now standard evolutionary game theory) and one of which is in mixed strategies and theoretically unstable. The theoretical properties are generally consistent with the data shown in the figures.

Other recent laboratory studies look at various refinements, especially refinements of Bayesian Nash equilibrium. The studies use a variety of protocols for matching players, for implementing extensive forms and information, and use a variety of techniques for analyzing data.

At the present time, game-theory experiments are a microcosm of experimental economics as a whole. Dozens of different studies are underway around the world, pursuing several different issues of concern to contemporary game theorists. Many game theorists, both pure and applied, monitor the work closely and sometimes participate in (or even lead) the experimental research. As a result, the evolution of experimental technique and game theory both have accelerated.

Appendixes:
Supplemental materials

APPENDIX I.
READINGS IN EXPERIMENTAL ECONOMICS

We hope this primer has whetted your appetite to learn more about experimental economics. What should you read next? Here are our suggestions.

Davis and Holt (1992) is a graduate-level textbook on experimental economics. It integrates economic theory with interpretive surveys of experimental work in many fields of economics. The coverage is especially strong for posted offer and other market experiments and for individual choice experiments.

Kagel and Roth (1993) is a collection of research surveys by leading experimentalists, covering most major fields. We have already cited Camerer's chapter on individual decision making, Roth's chapter on bargaining experiments, Kagel's chapter on auctions, and Sunder's chapter on asset market experiments. You probably will want to read the other chapters dealing with your own research interests.

Hey (1991) is the first published textbook on experimental economics. Not surprisingly, the coverage is not as deep as in later books, but Hey is very readable and conveys the enthusiasm most experimentalists feel for the new horizons opened by experimental methods. He gives special attention to econometric perspectives and to individual choice experiments.

There are several general survey articles on experimental economics. The classics, Smith (1982b) and Plott (1982), are both still well worth reading. Roth (1988) gives special attention to early bargaining experiments and individual choice experiments. *The New Palgrave* dictionary article by Smith (1987) is a good short introduction to experimental economics.

Several books collect articles reporting research results. Smith (1990) collects fifteen classic articles from his experimental economics seminar reading list. Roth (1987c) contains six interpretive essays by leading experimentalists. Moriarty (1986) is a conference volume with nine original papers, and discussants' comments. Palfrey (1991) gathers ten original research articles on laboratory elections, committee decisions, and problems of cooperation and coordination in games. Friedman and Rust (1993) collects fourteen original papers dealing with the double-auction market institution. Six of the papers primarily analyze laboratory market data. The other papers are computer simulations, reports on field markets, theoretical analyses, surveys or combinations, but most of them interact closely with the laboratory evidence. In the future we hope to see more such interdisciplinary studies grounded in experimental economics.

Experimental research articles now appear regularly in most mainstream economics

143

journals. Among the first to consistently publish such articles are the *Economic Journal,* edited by John Hey, and the *Journal of Economic Behavior and Organization,* edited by Richard Day. Both journals have occasional special issues devoted to experimental economics and continue to carry many experimental articles in their regular issues. *Advances in Experimental Economics* (JAI Press, Greenwich, Connecticut) is a research annual going back to 1980. It often publishes research articles that are too long or too methodological for general-interest economics journals.

The Economic Science Association, founded in 1986, is the main professional organization for experimental economists. The ESA sponsors annual meetings (usually in October in Tucson, Arizona) and jointly sponsors spring conferences with the Public Choice Society as well as sponsoring sessions at major economics meetings such as the American Economic Association/ASSA annual winter meetings. The ESA maintains address lists of its members (numbering about 500 in 1992). Elizabeth Hoffman, a past president of ESA, began to compile a bibliography of papers on experimental economics. You can contact the ESA at Mark Isaac, Secretary/Treasurer, Economic Science Association, Economic Science Laboratory, College of Business and Public Administration, University of Arizona, Tucson, Arizona, 85721.

The rest of this appendix consists of three reading lists for courses in experimental economics. The first, compiled by Charles Plott in 1990 and partially updated in 1993, is the most extensive. It covers most substantive applications of experimental techniques in economics with the exceptions of individual choice and bargaining. James Cox compiled the second list in 1992 for a graduate-level semester course in experimental economics; the syllabus is included. Mark Isaac compiled the third list in 1992 for an undergraduate course.

Charles R. Plott

Experimental political economy reading list

I. Methodology and miscellaneous

Aspiration Levels in Bargaining and Economic Decision Making. Reinhard Tietz, ed. Lecture Notes in Economics and Mathematical Systems, no. 213. New York: Springer, 1983.

Berg, Joyce E., Lane A. Daley, John W. Dickhaut, and John R. O'Brien. "Controlling Preferences for Lotteries on Units of Experimental Exchange." *Quarterly Journal of Economics* (May 1986): 281–306.

Contributions to Experimental Economics. Vol. 3. Heinz Sauermann, ed. Tübingen, Germany: J. C. B. Mohr (Paul Siebeck), 1972.

Contributions to Experimental Economics. Vol. 8. *Coalition Forming Behavior.* Heinz Sauermann, ed. Tübingen, Germany: J. C. B. Mohr (Paul Siebeck), 1978.

Holt, Charles A., and Anne P. Villamil. "The Use of Laboratory Experiments in Economics: An Introductory Survey." In Shane Moriarity, ed., *Laboratory Market Research,* pp. 1–14. Norman: Center for Economic and Management Research, University of Oklahoma, 1986.

Plott, Charles R. "The Application of Laboratory Experimental Methods to Public Choice." In C. S. Russell, ed., *Collective Decision Making: Applications from Public Choice Theory,* pp. 137–60. Baltimore: Johns Hopkins Press for Resources for the Future, 1979.

"Dimensions of Parallelism: Some Policy Applications of Experimental Methods." Social Science Working Paper no. 569. Pasadena: California Institute of Technology. In A. E. Roth, ed., *Laboratory Experimentation in Economics: Six Points of View,* Cambridge: Cambridge University Press, 1987.

"Experimental Methods in Political Economy: A Tool for Regulatory Research." In Allen R. Ferguson ed., *Attacking Regulatory Problems: An Agenda for Research in the 1980s,* Cambridge, Mass.: Ballinger 1981.

"Experiments in Non-Classical Environments: A Survey." Paper presented at NSF Conference on Experimental Economics, University of Arizona, Tucson, 1979.

"Industrial Organization Theory and Experimental Economics." *Journal of Economic Literature* 20 (December 1982): 1485–1527.

"Laboratory Experiments in Economics: The Implications of Posted-Price Institutions." *Science* 232 (May 9, 1986): 732–8.

145

"Rational Choice in Experimental Markets." *Journal of Business* 59 (October 1986): S301–27.

"An Updated Review of Industrial Organization: Applications of Experimental Methods." In R. Schmalensee and R. D. Willig, eds., *Handbook of Industrial Organization*, Vol. 2, pp. 1009–176. Amsterdam: Elsevier Science Publishers B.V., 1989.

Vernon L. Smith, ed., *Research in Experimental Economics*. Vol. 1. Greenwich, Conn.: JAI Press, 1979.

Vernon L. Smith, ed., *Research in Experimental Economics*. Vol. 2. Greenwich, Conn.: JAI Press, 1982.

Review of Economic Studies 36 (October 1979) (special issue of Experimental Economics).

Roth, Alvin E. "Laboratory Experimentation in Economics." Working Paper no 198. University of Pittsburgh, February 1986. (forthcoming in *Advances in Economic Theory*).

Laboratory Experimentation in Economics: Six Points of View. Cambridge: Cambridge University Press, 1987.

Roth, Alvin E., Michael W. K. Malouf, and J. K. Murnighan. "Sociological versus Strategic Factors in Bargaining." *Journal of Economic Behavior and Organization* 2 (June 1981): 153–78.

Smith, Vernon L. "Experimental Economics: Induced Value Theory." *American Economic Review* 66 (May 1976): 274–9.

"Experimental Methods in Economics." In *The New Palgrave: A Dictionary of Economic Theory and Doctrine*, edited by John Eatwell, Murray Milgate, and Peter Newman. New York: Stockton Press, 1987.

"Experimental Methods in the Political Economy of Exchange." *Science* 234 (October 10, 1986): 167–73.

"Microeconomic Systems as an Experimental Science." *American Economic Review* 72 (December 1982): 923–55.

"Reflections on Some Experimental Mechanisms for Classical Environments." In Leigh McAlister, ed., *Choice Models for Buyer Behavior. Research in Marketing, Supplement 1*. Greenwich, Conn.: JAI Press, 1982.

"Relevance of Laboratory Experiments to Testing Resource Allocation Theory." In J. Kmenta and J. Ramsey, eds., *Evaluation of Econometric Models*. New York: Academic Press, 1980.

"A Survey of Experimental Market Mechanisms for Classical Environments." NSF Conference on Experimental Economics, University of Arizona, Tuscon, 1979.

Wilde, Louis L. "On the Use of Laboratory Experiments in Economics." In J. C. Pitt, ed., *Philosophy in Economics*, pp. 137–48. Amsterdam: D. Reidel, 1981.

II. **Market organization and behavior**

A. *Open outcry auctions*

Buccola, Steven T., and Vernon L. Smith. "Uncertainty and Partial Adjustment in Double-Auction Markets." Unpublished paper (mimeo), March 10, 1986.

Burns, Penny. "Market Structure and Behavior: Price Adjustment in a Multi-Object Progressive Oral Auction." *Journal of Economic Behavior and Organization* 6 (September 1985): 275–300.

Carlson, J. A. "The Stability of an Experimental Market with a Supply-Response Lag." *Southern Economic Journal* 33 (January 1967): 305–21.

Coppinger, Vicki M., Vernon L. Smith, and Jon A. Titus. "Incentives and Behavior in

English, Dutch and Sealed-Bid Auctions." *Economic Inquiry* 18 (January 1980): 1–22.

Daniels, Brian P., and Charles R. Plott. "Inflation and Expectations in Experimental Markets." In R. Tietz, W. Albers, and R. Selten, eds., *Proceedings of the Fourth Conference on Experimental Economics, Bielefeld, West Germany, September 1986.* Lecture Notes in Economics and Mathematical Systems, no. 314, pp. 198–218. Berlin-Heidelberg: Springer, 1988.

Frahm, D., and L. F. Schrader. "An Experimental Comparison of Pricing in Two Auction Systems." *American Journal of Agricultural Economics* 52 (November 1969): 528–34.

Gray, Peter, and Charles R. Plott. "The Multiple Unit Double Auction." *Journal of Economic Behavior and Organization* 13 (1990): 245–58.

Grether, David M, R. Mark Isaac, and Charles R. Plott. "Alternative Methods of Allocating Slots: Performance and Evaluation." Prepared for the CAB and FAA. Polinomics Research Laboratories, Pasadena, Calif., August 1979.

Harrison, Glenn W., Vernon L. Smith, and Arlington W. Williams. "Learning Behavior in Experimental Auction Markets." Unpublished paper (mimeo), Department of Economics, University of California at Los Angeles, 1983.

Hess, Alan C. "Experimental Evidence on Price Formation in Competitive Markets." *Journal of Political Economy* 80 (March-April 1972): 375–85.

Holt, Charles A., Loren W. Langan and Anne P. Villamil. "Market Power in Oral Double Auctions." *Economic Inquiry* 24 (January 1986): 107–23.

Johnson, Michael D., and Charles R. Plott. "The Effect of Two Trading Institutions on Price Expectations and the Stability of Supply-Response Lag Markets." *Journal of Economic Psychology* 10 (1989): 189–216.

Mestelman, Stuart, and Douglas Welland. "Advance Production in Oral Double Auction Markets." *Economic Letters* 23 (1987): 43–8.

Plott, Charles R., and Vernon L. Smith. "An Experimental Examination of Two Exchange Institutions." *Review of Economic Studies* 45 (February 1978): 133–53.

Smith, Vernon L. "Bidding and Auctioning Institutions: Experimental Results." In Yakov Amihud, ed., *Bidding and Auctioning for Procurement and Allocation*, pp. 43–63. New York: New York University Press, 1976.

"Effect of Market Organization on Competitive Equilibrium." *Quarterly Journal of Economics* 78 (May 1964): 181–201.

"Experimental Auction Markets and the Walrasian Hypothesis." *Journal of Political Economy* 73 (August 1965): 387–393.

"An Experimental Study of Competitive Market Behavior." *Journal of Political Economy* 70 (April 1962): 111–37.

Smith, Vernon L. and Arlington W. Williams. "The Boundaries of Competitive Price Theory: Convergence, Expectations and Transaction Cost." In L. Green and J. Kagel, eds., *Advances in Behavioral Economics,* Vol. 2, Norwood, N.J. Ablex, 1989.

"The Effects of Rent Asymmetries in Experimental Auction Markets." *Journal of Economic Behavior and Organization* 3 (1982): 99–116.

"An Experimental Comparison of Alternative Rules for Competitive Market Exchange." In M. Shubik, ed., *Auctions, Bidding and Contracting: Uses and Theory.* New York: New York University Press, 1982.

"Price Adjustment Processes, 1: PLATO Double Auction Experiments." Unpublished paper (mimeo), Department of Economics, University of Arizona, 1977.

Walker, James M., and Arlington W. Williams. "Market Behavior in Bid, Offer and

Double Auctions: A Reexamination." *Journal of Economic Behavior and Organization* 9 (1988): 301–14.

Williams, Arlington W. "Computerized Double-Auction Markets: Some Initial Experimental Results." *Journal of Business* 53 (3 Part 1) (July 1980): 235–58.

"The Formation of Price Forecasts in Experimental Markets." *Journal of Money, Credit, and Banking* (February 1987): 1–18.

B. Theory of Double Auctions

Easley, David, and John Ledyard. "A Theory of Price Formation and Exchange in Oral Auctions." Northwestern University Discussion Paper no. 461, revised, January 1983.

Friedman, Daniel. "On the Efficiency of Experimental Double Auction Markets." *American Economic Review* 74 (March 1984): 60–72.

"Price Formation in Double Auction Markets." UCLA Discussion Paper no. 278, November 1982.

Wilson, Robert. "Double Auctions." Unpublished paper (mimeo), Stanford University, 1982.

C. Posted price

Alger, Daniel R. "Laboratory Tests of Equilibrium Predictions with Disequilibrium Data." *Review of Economic Studies* 54 (January 1987): 105–46.

Cook, William D., and E. C. H. Veendorp. "Six Markets in Search of an Auctioneer." *Canadian Journal of Economics* 8 (May 1975): 238–57.

Coursey, Don, and Vernon L. Smith. "Price Controls in a Posted-Offer Market." *American Economic Review* 73 (March 1983).

Davis, Douglas D., and Williams, Arlington W. "The Effects of Rent Asymmetries in Posted-Offer Markets." *Journal of Economic Behavior and Organization* 7 (September 1986): 303–16.

Hong, James T., and Charles R. Plott. "Rate Filing Policies for Inland Water Transportation: An Experimental Approach." *Bell Journal of Economics* 13 (Spring 1982): 1–19.

Ketcham, Jon, Vernon L. Smith, and Arlington W. Williams. "A Comparison of Posted-Offer and Double-Auction Pricing Institutions." *Review of Economic Studies* 51 (October 1984): 595–614.

Kruse, Jamie, Stephen Rassenti, Stanley S. Reynolds and Vernon L. Smith. "Bertrand-Edgeworth Competition in Experimental Markets." Department of Economics Discussion Paper no. 87-12. University of Arizona, Tucson. revised, November 1987.

Mestelman, Stuart, Deborah Welland, and Douglas Welland. "Advance Production in Posted Offer Markets," *Journal of Economic Behavior and Organization* 8 (1987): 249–64.

Mestelman, Stuart, and Douglas Welland. "Advance Production in Experimental Markets." Quantitative Studies in Economics and Population Research Report no. 172, McMaster University, Hamilton, Ontario, June 1986.

"Advance Production in Oral Double Auction Markets." *Economic Letters* (1987): 43–8.

Plott, Charles R., and Vernon L. Smith. "An Experimental Examination of Two Exchange Institutions." *Review of Economic Studies* 45 (February 1978): 133–53.

Williams, Fred E. "The Effect of Market Organization on Competitive Equilibrium: The Multiunit Case." *Review of Economic Studies* 40 (January 1973): 97–113.

D. Other competitive organizations

Banks, Jeffrey S., John O. Ledyard, and David P. Porter. "Allocating Uncertain and Unresponsive Resources: An Experimental Approach." *RAND Journal of Economics* 20 (Spring 1989): 1–25.

Chamberlin, E. H. "An Experimental Imperfect Market." *Journal of Political Economy* 56 (April 1948): 95–108.

Bull, Clive, Andrew Schotter, and Keith Weigelt. "Asymmetric Tournaments, Equal Opportunity Laws and Affirmative Action: Some Experimental Results." Economic Research Report no. 87-33, New York University, New York, September 1987.

Grether, David M., and Charles R. Plott. "The Effects of Market Practices in Oligopolistic Markets: An Experimental Examination of the Ethyl Case." *Economic Inquiry* 22 (October 1984): 479–507.

Hong, James T., and Charles R. Plott. "Rate Filing Policies for Inland Water Transportation: An Experimental Approach." *Bell Journal of Economics* 13 (Spring 1982): 1–19.

Joyce, Patrick. "Information and Behavior in Experimental Markets." *Journal of Economic Behavior and Organization* 4 (1983): 411–24.

"The Walrasian Tâtonnement Mechanism and Information." *RAND Journal of Economics* 15 (1984): 416–425.

McCabe, Kevin A., Stephen J. Rassenti, and Vernon L. Smith. "Auction Institutional Design: Theory and Behavior of Simultaneous Multiple-Unit Generalizations of the Dutch and English Auctions." *American Economic Review* 80 (5) (December 1990): 1276–83.

"Designing 'Smart' Computer-Assisted Markets: An Experimental Auction for Gas Networks." University of Arizona, Tucson. (forthcoming in *European Journal of Political Economy*, Special Issue on Economic Design, n.d.)

"A Comparison of the Dutch and English Clocks in Simultaneous Multiple Unit Nondiscriminatory Auctions." Department of Economics Discussion Paper no. 88-12, University of Arizona, Tucson, April 1988.

"A New Market Institution for the Exchange of Composite Goods." Department of Economics Discussion Paper no. 88-13, University of Arizona, Tucson. April 1988.

Rassenti, S. J., Vernon L. Smith, and R. L. Bulfin. "A Combinatorial Auction Mechanism for Airport Time Slot Allocation." *Bell Journal of Economics* 13 (Autumn 1982): 402–17.

Selten, Reinhard. "Ein Marktexperiment." In Heinz Sauermann, ed., *Beiträge zur Experimentellen Wirtschaftsforschung* (Contributions to Experimental Economics), Vol. 2, pp. 33–98. Tübingen, Germany: J. C. B. Mohr (Paul Siebeck), 1970.

Smith, Vernon L., Arlington W. Williams, W. Kenneth Bratton, and M. G. Vannoni. "Competitive Market Institutions: Double Auctions vs. Sealed Bid-Offer Auctions." *American Economic Review* 72 (March 1982): 58–77.

E. Sealed bid

Belovicz, Meyer W. "Sealed-Bid Auctions: Experimental Results and Applications." In Vernon L. Smith, ed., *Research in Experimental Economics,* Vol. 1, pp. 279–338. Greenwich, Conn.: JAI Press, 1979.

Cech, Paula-Ann, David Conn, James C. Cox, and R. Mark Isaac. "An Experimental Study of Competitive Bidding and Incentive Contracts in Procurement." Department of Economics. Discussion Paper no. 87-8, University of Arizona, Tucson. September 1987.

Cox, James C., Bruce Roberson, and Vernon L. Smith. "Theory and Behavior of Single

Object Auctions." In Vernon L. Smith, ed., *Research in Experimental Economics,* Vol. 2, pp. 1–43. Greenwich, Conn.: JAI Press.

Cox, James C., Vernon L. Smith, and James M. Walker. "Experimental Development of Sealed-Bid Auction Theory; Calibrating Controls for Risk Aversion." *American Economic Review* 75 (May 1985): 160–5.

Cox, James C., Vernon L. Smith, and James M. Walker. "Nash Equilibrium Bidding Behavior in Sealed Bid Auctions." Unpublished paper (mimeo). University of Arizona, Tucson, 1981.

"A Test That Discriminates between Two Models of the Dutch-First Auction Nonisomorphism." *Journal of Economic Behavior and Organization,* 4 (1983): 205–19.

"Theory and Behavior of Heterogeneous Bidders in Multiple Unit Auction." *Economics Letters* 12 (1983): 207–212.

"The Theory and Behavior of Multiple Unit Discriminative Auction." *Journal of Finance* 39 (September 1984): 983–1010.

"Expected Revenue in Discriminative and Uniform Price Sealed-Bid Auctions." In Vernon L. Smith, ed. *Research in Experimental Economics,* Vol. 3, pp. 183–232. Greenwich, Conn.: JAI Press, 1985.

Cox, James C., Vernon L. Smith, and James M. Walker. "Theory and Individual Behavior of First-Price Auctions." *Journal of Risk and Uncertainty* 1 (1988): 61–99.

Guler, Kemal, Charles R. Plott, and Quang H. Vuong. "A Study of Zero-Out Auctions: Experimental Analysis of a Process of Allocating Private Rights to the Use of Public Property." Social Science Working Paper no. 650, California Institute of Technology, Pasadena, revised, November 1992.

Hoffman, Elizabeth, and James R. Marsden. "Empirical Evidence on Competitive Bidding: Some Surprising Results." *Economics Letters* 22 (1986): 15–21.

Hoffman, Elizabeth, James R. Marsden, and Reza Saidibaghgandomi. "Testing the Continuity of Individual Bid Density Functions." *Economics Letters* 24 (1987): 117–120.

Kagel, John H., and Dan Levin. "The Winner's Curse and Public Information in Common Value Auctions." *American Economic Review* (December 1986): 894–920.

Kagel, John H., Dan Levin, Raymond C. Battalio, and Donald J. Mayer. "Common Value Auctions: Some Initial Experimental Results." Unpublished paper (mimeo) November 1983.

Miller, Gary J., and Charles R. Plott. "Revenue Generating Properties of Sealed-Bid Auctions: An Experimental Analysis of One-Price and Discriminative Processes." In Vernon L. Smith, ed., *Research in Experimental Economics,* Vol. 3. Greenwich, Conn.: JAI Press, 1985.

Radner, Roy, and Andrew Schotter. "The Sealed-Bid Mechanism: An Experimental Study." *Journal of Economic Theory* 48 (1989): 179–220.

Smith, Vernon L. "Experimental Studies of Discrimination vs. Competition in Sealed-Bid Auction Markets." *Journal of Business* 40 (January 1967): 56–84.

III. Conspiracy and monopoly

Coursey, Don, R. Mark Isaac, M. Luke, and Vernon L. Smith. "Market Contestability in the Presence of Sunk (Entry) Cost." *RAND Journal of Economics* 15 (Spring 1984): 69–84.

Coursey, Don, R. Mark Isaac, and Vernon L. Smith. "Natural Monopoly and Contested Markets: Some Experimental Results." *Journal of Law and Economics* 8 (April 1984): 91–113.

Cox, James C., and Isaac, R. Mark. "Incentive Regulation: A Case Study in the Use of Experimental Analysis in Economics." In Shane Moriarity, ed., *Laboratory Market*

Research, Norman: University of Oklahoma, Center for Econometrics and Management Research, 1986.

"Incentive Regulation and Innovation." Department of Economics Discussion Paper no. 86-15, University of Arizona, Tucson, 1986.

"A New Mechanism For Incentive Regulation: Theory and Experiment." Department of Economics Discussion Paper no. 86-1, University of Arizona, Tucson, 1986.

Friedman, James W. "An Experimental Study of Cooperative Duopoly." *Econometrica* (October 1967): 379–97.

Harrison, Glenn W. "Experimental Evaluation of the Contestable Markets Hypothesis." In E. E. Bailey, ed., *Public Regulation: New Perspectives on Institutions and Policies,* Cambridge, Mass.: MIT Press, 1987.

"Predatory Pricing in a Multiple-Market Experiment," *Journal of Economic Behavior and Organization* 9 (1988): 405–17.

Harrison, Glenn W., and Michael McKee. "Monopoly Behavior, Decentralized Regulation, and Contestable Markets: An Experimental Evaluation." *RAND Journal of Economics* 16 (Spring 1985): 51–69.

Harrison, Glenn W., Michael McKee, and E. E. Rutstrom. "Experimental Evaluation of Institutions of Monopoly Restraint." In L. Green and J. Kagel, eds., *Advances in Behavioral Economics,* edited Norwood, N. J.: Ablex, 1981.

Isaac, R. Mark, and Charles R. Plott. "The Opportunity for Conspiracy in Restraint of Trade: An Experimental Study." *Journal of Economic Behavior and Organization* 2 (March 1981): 1–30.

Isaac, R. Mark, Valerie Ramey, and Arlington W. Williams. "The Effects of Market Organization on Conspiracies in Restraint of Trade." *Journal of Economic Behavior and Organization* 5 (June 1984): 191–222.

Isaac, R. Mark, and Vernon L. Smith. "In Search of Predatory Pricing." *Journal of Political Economy* 26 (April 1985): 320–45.

Isaac, R. Mark, and James M. Walker. "Information and Conspiracy in Sealed Bid Auctions." *Journal of Economic Behavior and Organization* 6 (June 1985): 139–59.

Smith, Vernon L. "An Empirical Study of Decentralized Institutions of Monopoly Restraint." In George Horwich and James P. Quirk, eds., *Essays in Contemporary Fields of Economics in Honor of Emanuel T. Weiler (1914–1979),* pp. 83–106. West Lafayette, Ind.: Purdue University Press, 1981.

IV. Tacit collusion and facilitating practices

A. Concentrated markets and repeated conflicts

Alger, Daniel R. "Laboratory Tests of Equilibrium Predictions with Disequilibrium Data." *Review of Economic Studies* 54 (January 1987): 105–46.

Cooper, Russell, Douglas V. DeJong, Robert Forsythe, and Thomas W. Ross, "Selection Criteria in Coordination Games: Some Experimental Results," *American Economic Review* 80 (1) (March 1990): 218–33.

Davis, Douglas D., and Arlington W. Williams. "Further Evidence on the Hayak Hypothesis in Experimental Auctions: Institutional Effects and Market Power." Unpublished paper (mimeo), Virginia Commonwealth University, Richmond, February 1988.

Dolbear, Jr., F. T., L. Lave, G. Bowman, et al. "Collusion in Oligopoly: An Experiment on the Effect of Numbers and Information." *Quarterly Journal of Economics* 82 (May 1968): 240–59

Fouraker, L., and S. Siegel. *Bargaining Behavior.* New York: McGraw-Hill, 1963.

Friedman, James W. "Equal Profits as Fair Division." In Heinz Sauermann, ed., *Beiträge zur Experimentellen Wirtschaftsforschung* (Contributions to Experimental Economics), Vol. 2, pp. 19–32. Tübingen, Germany: J. C. B. Mohr (Paul Siebeck), 1970.

"Individual Behavior in Oligopolistic Markets: An Experimental Study." *Yale Economic Essays* 3 (Fall 1963): 359–417.

"On Experimental Research in Oligopoly." *Review of Economic Studies* 36 (October 1969): 399–415.

Friedman, James W., and Austin C. Hoggatt. *An Experiment in Noncooperative Oligopoly. Research in Experimental Economics,* Vol. 1, Supplement 1. Greenwich, Conn.: JAI Press, 1980.

Harnett, D. L. "Bargaining and Negotiation in a Mixed-Motive Game: Price Leadership Bilateral Monopoly." *Southern Economic Journal* 33 (April 1967): 479–87.

Hoggatt, Austin C. "An Experimental Business Game." *Behavioral Science* 4 (July 1959): 192–203.

"Measuring the Cooperativeness of Behavior in Quantity Variation Duopoly Games." *Behavioral Science* 12 (March 1967): 109–21.

"Response of Paid Subjects to Differential Behavior of Robots in Duopoly Games." *Review of Economic Studies* 36 (October 1969): 417–32.

Holt, Charles A. "An Experimental Test of the Consistent-Conjectures Hypothesis." *American Economic Review* 75 (June 1985): 314–25.

Isaac, R. Mark, and Vernon L. Smith. "In Search of Predatory Pricing." *Journal of Political Economy* 26 (April 1985).

Sauermann, Heinz, and Reinhard Selten. "An Experiment in Oligopoly." In Ludwig von Bertalanffy and Anatol Rapoport, eds., *General Systems Yearbook of the Society for General Systems Research,* Vol. 5, pp. 85–114. (Translation of "Ein Oligopolexperiment," *Zeitschrift für die Gesamte Staatswissenschaft* 115 (1959): 427–71.) Ann Arbor, Mich.: Society for General Systems Research, 1960.

Selten, Reinhard. "Die Strategiemethode zur Erforschung des Eingeschränkt Rationalen Verhaltens im Rahmen eines Oligopolexperimentes." In Heinz Sauermann, ed., *Beiträge zur Experimentellen Wirtschaftsforschung,* Vol. 1, pp. 136–68. Tübingen, Germany: J. C. B. Mohr (Paul Siebeck), 1967.

"Ein Oligopolexperiment mit Preisvariation und Investition." In Heinz Sauermann, ed., *Beiträge zur Experimentellen Wirtschaftsforschung,* Vol. 1, pp. 103–35. Tübingen, Germany: J. C. B. Mohr (Paul Siebeck), 1967.

"Investitionsverhalten im Oligopolexperiment." In Heinz Sauermann, ed., *Beiträge zur Experimentellen Wirtschaftsforschung,* Vol. 1, pp. 60–102. Tübingen, Germany: J. C. B. Mohr (Paul Siebeck), 1967.

Selten, Reinhard, and Claus C. Berg. "Drei Experimentelle ligopolspielserien mit Kontinuierlichem Zeitablauf." In Heinz Sauermann, ed., *Beiträge zur Experimentellen Wirtschaftsforschung* (Contributions to Experimental Economics), Vol. 2, pp. 162–221. Tübingen, Germany: J. C. B. Mohr (Paul Siebeck), 1970.

Siegel, Sidney, and Lawrence E. Fouraker, *Bargaining and Group Decision Making: Experiments in Bilateral Monopoly.* Reprint of 1960 edition. Westport, Conn.: Greenwood Press, 1977.

Stoecker, Rolf. *Experimentelle Untersuchung des Entscheidungsverhaltens im Bertrand-Olipopol.* Vol. 4 of *Wirtschaftstheoretische Entscheidungsforschung.* Institut für Mathematische Wirtschaftsforschung, Universität Bielefeld. Bielefeld, West Germany: Pfeffersche Buchhandlung, 1980.

B. *Market practices*

Coursey, Donald L., and Vernon L. Smith. "Price Controls in a Posted-Offer Market." *American Economic Review* 73 (March 1983): 218–21.

Grether, David M., and Charles R. Plott. "The Effects of Market Practices in Oligopolistic Markets: An Experimental Examination of the Ethyl Case." *Economic Inquiry* 22 (October 1984): 479–507.

Hong, James T., and Charles R. Plott. "Rate Filing Policies for Inland Water Transportation: An Experimental Approach." *Bell Journal of Economics* 13 (Spring 1982): 1–19.

Isaac, R. Mark, and Charles Plott. "Price Controls and the Behavior of Auction Markets: An Experimental Examination." *American Economic Review* 71 (June 1981): 448–59.

Ochs, Jack. "The Coordination Problem in Decentralized Markets: An Experiment." *Quarterly Journal of Economics* 105 (2) (May 1990): 545–59.

Smith, Vernon L., and Arlington W. Williams. "On Nonbinding Price Controls in a Competitive Market." *American Economic Review* 71 (June 1981): 467–74.

V. **Assets and Time**

Camerer, Colin. "Bubbles and Fads in Asset Prices: A Review of Theory and Evidence." Draft 7, The Wharton School, Philadelphia, April 1987. Revision of a previous working paper, "Speculative Price Bubbles in Asset Markets: A Theoretical Survey and Experimental Design," 1984.

Camerer, Colin, and Keith Weigelt. "Experimental Tests of a Sequential Equilibrium Reputation Model," *Econometrica* 56 (1) (January 1988): 1–36.

Copeland, Thomas E., and Daniel Friedman. "The Effect of Sequential Information Arrival on Asset Prices: An Experimental Study." *Journal of Finance* 42 (3), (July 1987): 763–97.

Coursey, Don, and Edward A. Dyl. "Trading Suspensions, Daily Price Limits, and Information Efficiency: A Laboratory Examination." In Shane Moriarity, ed., *Laboratory Market Research*, pp. 153–68. Norman: University of Oklahoma, Center for Econometrics and Management Research, 1986.

Forsythe, R., T. R. Palfrey, and C. R. Plott. "Asset Valuation in an Experimental Market." *Econometrica* 50 (May 1982): 537–67.

"Futures Markets and Informational Efficiency: A Laboratory Examination." *Journal of Finance* (September 1984): 955–981.

Friedman, Daniel, Glenn W. Harrison, and Jon W. Salmon. "The Informational Efficiency of Experimental Asset Markets." *Journal of Political Economy* 92 (1984): 349–408.

Harrison, Glenn W. "Experimental Futures Markets." In B. A. Goss, ed., *Futures Markets: Their Establishment and Performance*, pp. 43–76. London: Croom Helm, 1986.

Knez, Marc, and Vernon L. Smith. "Hypothetical Valuations and Preference Reversals in the Context of Asset Trading." In A. E. Roth, ed., *Laboratory Experimentation in Economics: Six Points of View*, pp. 131–54. Cambridge: Cambridge University Press, 1987.

Miller, Ross M., Charles R. Plott, and Vernon L. Smith. "Intertemporal Competitive Equilibrium: An Empirical Study of Speculation." *Quarterly Journal of Economics* 91 (November 1977): 599–624.

Plott, Charles R., and Gul Agha. "Intertemporal Speculation with a Random Demand in an Experimental Market." In Reinhard Tietz ed., *Aspiration Levels in Bargaining and Economic Decision Making,* pp. 201–16. Lecture Notes in Economics and Mathematical Systems, no. 213. New York: Springer, 1983.

Plott, Charles R., and Jonathan T. Uhl. "Competitive Equilibrium with Middlemen: An Empirical Study." *Southern Economic Journal* 47 (April 1981): 1063–71.

Smith, Vernon L., Gerry L. Suchanek, and Arlington W. Williams. "Bubbles, Crashes and Endogenous Expectations in Experimental Asset Markets." Department of Economics Working Paper no. 86-2, University of Arizona, Tucson, revised, June 1986.

Smith, Vernon L., and Arlington W. Williams. "Bubbles, Crashes, and Endogenous Expectations in Experimental Spot Asset Markets." *Econometrica* 56 (5) (September 1988): 1119–151.

Williams, Arlington W. "Intertemporal Competitive Equilibrium: On Further Experimental Results." In Vernon L. Smith, ed., *Research in Experimental Economics,* Vol. 1, pp. 255–78. Greenwich, Conn.: JAI Press, 1979.

Williams, Arlington, W., and Vernon L. Smith. "Cyclical Double-Auction Markets with and without Speculators." *Journal of Business* 57 (January 1984): 1–33.

VI. Information: Finance

Banks, Jeffrey S. "Price-Conveyed Information vs. Observed Insider Behavior: A Note on Rational Expectations Convergence." *Journal of Political Economy* 93 (4), (1985): 807–15.

Copeland, Thomas E., and Daniel Friedman. "The Market Value of Information: Some Experimental Results." Unpublished paper (mimeo), University of California at Los Angeles, revised May 1988.

Copeland, Thomas E., and Daniel Friedman. "The Effect of Sequential Information Arrival on Asset Prices: An Experimental Study." *Journal of Finance* 42 (6) (July 1987): 763–97.

Coursey, Don L., and Edward A. Dyl. "Trading Suspensions, Daily Price Limits, and Information Efficiency: A Laboratory Examination." In Shane Moriarity, ed., *Laboratory Market Research,* pp. 153–68. Norman: University of Oklahoma, Center for Econometrics and Management Research, 1986.

Forsythe, Robert, and Russell J. Lundholm. "Information Aggregation in an Experimental Market." *Econometrica* 58 (2) (March 1990): 309–47.

Plott, Charles R., and Shyam Sunder. "Efficiency of Experimental Security Markets with Insider Information: An Application of Rational Expectations Models." *Journal of Political Economy* 90 (1982): 663–98.

"Rational Expectations and the Aggregation of Diverse Information in Laboratory Security Markets." *Econometrica* 56 (5) (September 1988): 1085–1118.

Sunder, Shyam. "Market for Information: Experimental Evidence." Graduate School of Management Working Paper no. 1984-3. University of Minnesota, Minneapolis, June 1984.

Sunder, Shyam. "Rational Expectations Equilibrium in Asset Markets with Costly Information: Experimental Evidence." Graduate School of Management Working Paper no. 1984-3, University of Minnesota, Minneapolis, February 1984.

VII. Information: Product quality

Berg, Joyce E., Lane A. Daley, John W. Dickhaut, and John R. O'Brien. "Tests of the Principal-Agent Theory in an Experimental Setting." Working Paper no. 1985-3, University of Minnesota, Minneapolis, 1985.

Berg, Joyce E., John W. Dickhaut, and David W. Senkow. "Signaling Equilibria in

Experimental Markets: Rothschild and Stiglitz vs. Wilson vs. Riley." Unpublished paper (mimeo), University of Minnesota, Minneapolis, 1987.

Bull, Clive, Andrew Schotter, and Keith Weigelt. "Tournaments and Piece Rates: An Experimental Study." *Journal of Political Economy* 95(1), (1987): 1–33.

Camerer, Colin, and Keith Weigelt. "Experimental Tests of a Sequential Equilibrium Reputation Model." *Econometrica* 56 (1) (January 1988): 1–36.

Daughety, Andrew F., and Robert Forsythe. "Regulation and the Formation of Reputations: A Laboratory Analysis." College of Business Administration Working Paper no. 85-32, University of Iowa, Iowa City, July 1985.

DeJong, Douglas V., Robert Forsythe, Russell J. Lundholm, and Wilfred Uecker. *Journal of Accounting Research* 23 (Supplement), 1985.

DeJong, Douglas V., Robert Forsythe, and Wilfred Uecker. *Journal of Accounting Research* 23 (Supplement) Autumn 1985.

DeJong, Douglas V., Robert Forsythe, and Russell J. Lundholm. "Ripoffs, Lemons, and Reputation Formation in Agency Relationships: A Laboratory Market Study." *Journal of Finance* 40 (July 1985): 809–23.

- Holt, Charles A. "Advertising and Product Quality in Posted-Offer Experiments." *Economic Inquiry* 28 (January 1990): 39–56.

Holt, Charles A., and Roger Sherman. "Quality Uncertainty and Bundling." In P. M. Ippolito and D. T. Scheffman, eds., *Empirical Approaches to Consumer Protection Economics*, pp. 221–50. Washington, D.C.: Federal Trade Commission, March 1986.

Lynch, Michael, Ross Miller, Charles R. Plott, and Russell Porter. "Experimental Studies of Markets with Buyers Ignorant of Quality before Purchase: When Do 'Lemons' Drive Out High Quality Products?" A Report to the Federal Trade Commission, May 1986.

"Product Quality, Consumer Information and 'Lemons' in Experimental Markets." In P. M. Ippolito and D. T. Scheffman, eds., *Empirical Approaches to Consumer Protection Economics*, pp. 251–306. Washington, D.C.: Federal Trade Commission, March 1986.

Miller, Ross M., and Charles R. Plott. "Product Quality Signaling in Experimental Markets." *Econometrica* 53 (July 1985): 837–72.

Palfrey, Thomas R. "Bundling Decision by a Multiproduct Monopolist with Incomplete Information." *Econometrica* 51 (March 1983): 463–83.

"Buyer Behavior and Welfare Effects of Bundling by a Multiproduct Monopolist: A Laboratory Test." In Vernon L. Smith, ed., *Research in Experimental Economics*, Vol. 3. Greenwich, Conn.: JAI Press, 1985.

Palfrey, Thomas R., and Thomas Romer. "An Experimental Study of Warranty Coverage and Dispute Resolution in Competitive Markets." In P. M. Ippolito and D. T. Scheffman, eds., *Empirical Approaches to Consumer Protection Economics*, pp. 307–72. Washington, D.C.: Federal Trade Commission, March 1986.

Pitchik, Carolyn, and Andrew Schotter. "The 'Big Lie' Hypothesis in Markets with Asymmetric Information: An Experimental Study." New York: New York University, November 1983.

"Regulating Markets with Asymmetric Information: An Experimental Study." Unpublished paper (mimeo). New York University, New York, July 1984 (revised).

Plott, Charles R., and Louis L. Wilde. "Professional Diagnosis versus Self Diagnosis: An Experimental Examination of Some Special Features of Markets with Uncertainty." In Vernon L. Smith, ed. *Research in Experimental Economics*, Vol. 2. Greenwich, Conn.: JAI Press, 1982.

VIII. Information: Search

Braunstein, Yale, and A. Schotter. "Optimal Economic Search and Labor Market Policy: An Experimental Study." C. V. Starr Center for Applied Economics no. 79-22, New York University, New York, August 1979.

Grether, David M., Alan Schwartz, and Louis L. Wilde. "Uncertainty and Shopping Behavior, An Experimental Analysis." *Review of Economic Studies* 55 (1988): 323–42.

Grether, David M., and Louis L. Wilde. "Consumer Choice and Information: New Experimental Evidence." *Information Economics and Policy* 1 (1983): 1–29.

"Experimental Economics and Consumer Research." In Thomas Kinnear, ed., *Advances in Consumer Research,* pp. 724–8. Provo, Utah: Association for Consumer Research, 1984.

McKelvey, Richard D., and Talbot Page. "Public and Private Information: An Experimental Study of Information Pooling." *Econometrica* 58 (6) (November 1990): 1321–39.

Wilde, Louis L. "Consumer Behavior under Imperfect Information: A Review of Psychological and Marketing Research as It Relates to Economic Theory." In Len Green and John Kagel, eds., *Advances in Behavioral Economics,* Vol. 2. Norwood, N.J.: Ablex, 1984.

IX. Externalities, public goods, and commons dilemma

A. Externalities

Coursey, Don L., Elizabeth Hoffman, and Matthew L. Spitzer. "Fear and Loathing in the Coase Theorem: Experimental Tests Involving Physical Discomfort." *Journal of Legal Studies* 16 (1) (January 1987): 217–48.

Harrison, Glenn W., E. Hoffman, E. E. Rutstrom, and M. L. Spitzer. "Coasian Solutions to the Externality Problem in Experimental Markets." *Economic Journal* 97 (June 1987): 388–402.

Harrison, Glenn W., and Michael McKee. "Experimental Evaluation of the Coase Theorem." *Journal of Law and Economics* 28 (October 1985): 653–70.

Hoffman, Elizabeth, and Matthew L. Spitzer. "The Coase Theorem: Some Experimental Tests." *Journal of Law and Economics* 25 (1982): 73–98.

"Entitlements, Rights, and Fairness: An Experimental Examination of Subjects' Concepts of Distributive Justice." *Journal of Legal Studies* 14 (June 1985): 259–97.

"Experimental Law and Economics: An Introduction." *Columbia Law Review* 85 (June 1985): 991–1036.

"Experimental Tests of the Coase Theorem with Large Bargaining Groups." *Journal of Legal Studies* 15 (1) (January 1986): 149–71.

Plott, Charles R. "Externalities and Corrective Policies in Experimental Markets." *Economic Journal* 93 (March 1983): 106–27.

B. Public goods and free riding

Alfano, Geraldine, and Gerald Marwell. "Experiments on the Provision of Public Goods by Groups III: Nondivisibility and Free Riding in 'Real' Groups." *Social Psychology Quarterly* 43 (1980): 300–09.

Banks, Jeffrey S., Charles R. Plott, and David Porter. "An Experimental Analysis of Public Goods Provision Mechanisms with and without Unanimity." *Review of Economic Studies* 55 (1988): 301–22.

Bohm, P. "Estimating Demand for Public Goods: An Experiment." *European Economic Review* 3 (1973): 111–30.

Brewer, Marilynn B., and Roderick M. Kramer. "Choice Behavior in Social Dilemmas: Effects of Social Identity, Group Size, and Decision Framing." Unpublished paper (mimeo), University of California at Los Angeles, 1985.

Brookshire, David S., and Don L. Coursey. "Measuring the Value of a Public Good: An Empirical Comparison of Elicitation Procedures." *American Economic Review* 77 (4) (September 1987): 554–66.

Brookshire, David S., Don L. Coursey, Mark Dickie, Ann Fisher, Shelby Gerking, and William D. Schulze. "Tests of Parallelism between the Laboratory and the Field." Unpublished paper (mimeo), February 1985.

Caldwell, M. "Communication and Sex Differences in a Five-Person and Prisoner's Dilemma Game." *Journal of Personality and Social Psychology* 33 (1976): 273–80.

Chamberlin, John R. "The Logic of Collective Action: Some Experimental Results." *Behavioral Science* 23 (1978): 441–5.

Dawes, Robyn M. "Social Dilemmas." *Annual Review of Psychology* 31 (1980): 169–93.

Dawes, Robyn M., Jeanne McTavish, and Harriet Shaklee. "Behavior Communication and Assumptions about Other People's Behavior in a Commons Dilemma Situation." *Journal of Personality and Social Psychology* 1 (1977): 1–11.

Dawes, Robyn M., and John M. Orbell. "Cooperation in Social Dilemma Situations: Thinking about It Doesn't Help." In Vernon L. Smith, ed., *Research in Experimental Economics*, Vol. 2, pp. 167–73. Greenwich, Conn.: JAI Press, 1982.

Dawes, Robyn M., John M. Orbell, and Alphons J. C. van de Kragt. "A 'Great Society' or a 'Small Society'?: The Threshold-of-the-Room Effect in Social Dilemmas." Paper prepared for the Public Choice Society Meetings, New Orleans, February 1985, University of Oregon, Eugene.

Harrison, Glenn W., and Jack Hirshleifer. "An Experimental Evaluation of Weakest-Link/Best-Shot Models of Public Goods." *Journal of Political Economy* 97 (1) (1989): 201–25.

"Experiments Testing Weakest-Link/Best-Shot Models For Provision of Public Goods." *Journal of Political Economy* 95, 1987, forthcoming.

Harrison, Glenn W., Elizabeth Hoffman, E. E. Rutstrom, and M. L. Spitzer. "Coasian Solutions to the Externality Problem in Experimental Markets." *Economic Journal* 97 (June 1987): 388–402.

Isaac, R. Mark, Kenneth F. McCue, and Charles R. Plott. "Public Goods Provision in an Experimental Environment." *Journal of Public Economics* 26 (1985): 51–74.

Isaac, R. Mark, David Schmidtz, and James M. Walker. "The Assurance Problem in a Laboratory Market." *Public Choice* 62 (1989): 217–36.

Isaac, R. Mark, and James M. Walker. "Communication and Free Riding Behavior: The Voluntary Contribution Mechanism." *Economic Inquiry* 26 (1988): 585–608.

"The Effects of Communication on Free Riding Behavior." Unpublished paper (mimeo), University of Arizona, Tucson, October 1984.

"Group Size Hypotheses of Public Goods Provision: An Experimental Examination." Unpublished paper (mimeo), University of Arizona, Tucson, April 1984.

"Marginal Private Returns and Public Goods Provision." Unpublished paper (mimeo), University of Arizona, Tucson, revised, December 1983.

Isaac, R. Mark, David Schmidtz, and James M. Walker. "The Assurance Problem in a Laboratory Market." *Public Choice* 62 (1989): 217–36.

Kim, Oliver, and Mark Walker. "The Free Rider Problem: Experimental Evidence." *Public Choice* 43 (1984): 3–24.

Marwell, Gerald. "Altruism and the Problem of Collective Action." In Valerian J. Derlega and Januse Grzelak, eds., *Cooperation and Helping Behavior: Theories and Research,* New York: Academic Press, 1982.

Marwell, Gerald and Ruth E. Ames. "Economists Free Ride, Does Anyone Else? Experiments on the Provision of Public Goods, IV. *Journal of Public Economics* 15 (1981): 295–310.

"Experiments on the Provision of Public Goods: Resources, Interest, Group Size, and the Free-Rider Problem." *American Journal of Sociology* 84 (May 1979): 1335–60.

"Experiments on the Provision of Public Goods II: Provision Points, Stakes, Experience and the Free-Rider Problem." *American Journal of Sociology* 85 (1980): 926–37.

Orbell, John M., and Robyn M. Dawes. "Social Dilemmas." In J. M. Stephenson and J. H. Davis, eds., *Progress in Applied Social Psychology,* Vol. 1, pp. 117–33. New York: Wiley, 1981.

Palfrey, Thomas R., and Howard Rosenthal. "Altruism and Participation in Social Dilemmas." Working paper no. 35-84-85, Carnegie-Mellon University, Pittsburgh.

"Private Incentives in Social Dilemmas: The Effects of Incomplete Information and Altruism." *Journal of Public Economics* 35 (1988): 309–32.

Palfrey, Thomas R., and Howard Rosenthal. "Testing for Effects of Cheap Talk in a Public Goods Game with Private Information." *Games and Economic Behavior* 3 (1991): 183–220.

Rapoport, Amnon. "Provision of Public Goods and the MCS Experimental Paradigm." Laboratory for Informational Processing and Decision Making Report no. 13. Haifa, Israel: University of Haifa, July 1984.

"Research Paradigms and Expected Utility Models for the Provision of Step Level Public Goods." *Psychological Review* 94 (1) (1987): 74–83.

Schneider, Friedrich, and Werner W. Pommerehne. "On the Rationality of Free Riding: An Experiment." *Quarterly Journal of Economics* 96 (November 1981): 689–704.

Schwartz-Shea, Peregrine, and Randy T. Simmons. "Cooperation and Framing." Unpublished paper (mimeo), n.d.

Simmons, Randy T., Robyn M. Dawes, and John M. Orbell. "An Experimental Comparison of the Two Motives for Not Contributing to a Public Good: Desire to Free Ride and Fear of Being Gypped." Unpublished paper (mimeo).

Smith, Vernon L. "The Principle of Unanimity and Voluntary Consent in Social Choice." *Journal of Political Economy* 85 (December 1977): 1125–40.

Van de Kragt, A., J. M. Orbell, and R. M. Dawes. "The Minimal Contributing Set as a Solution to Public Goods Problems." *American Political Science Review* 77 (1983): 112–22.

C. Incentive compatible processes

Banks, Jeffrey S., Charles R. Plott, and David P. Porter. "An Experimental Analysis of Unanimity in Public Goods Provision Mechanisms." *Review of Economic Studies* 55 (1988): 301–22.

Binger, Brian R., Elizabeth Hoffman, and Arlington W. Williams. "Implementing a Lindahl Equilibrium with a Modified Tâtonnement Mechanism: Some Preliminary Experimental Results." Preliminary Draft. February 1985.

Coursey, Don L, and Vernon L. Smith. "Experimental Tests of an Allocation Mechanism for Private, Public, or Externality Goods." *Scandinavian Journal of Economics* 86(4) (1984): 468–84.

Ferejohn, John A., Robert Forsythe, and Roger Noll. "An Experimental Analysis of Decision Making Procedures for Discrete Public Goods: A Case Study of a Problem in Institutional Design." In Vernon L. Smith, ed., *Research in Experimental Economics,* Vol. 1, pp. 1–58. Greenwich, Conn.: JAI Press, 1982.

"Practical Aspects of the Construction of Decentralized Decisionmaking Systems for Public Goods." In C. S. Russell, ed., *Collective Decision Making: Applications from Public Choice Theory,* pp. 173–88; Comments, E. H. Clark, pp. 189–95, Charles Clotfelter, pp. 196–8; Reply, pp. 199–203. Baltimore: Johns Hopkins University Press for Resources for the Future, 1979.

Ferejohn, John A., Robert Forsythe, Roger Noll, and Thomas R. Palfrey. "An Experimental Examination of Auction Mechanisms for Discrete Public Goods." In Vernon L. Smith, ed., *Research in Experimental Economics,* Vol. 2, Greenwich, Conn.: JAI Press, 1982.

Ferejohn, John A., and Roger Noll. "An Experimental Market for Public Goods: The PBS Station Program Cooperative." *American Economic Review* 66 (May 1976): 267–73.

Harstad, Ronald M., and Michael Marrese. "Behavioral Explanations of Efficient Public Good Allocations." *Journal of Public Economics* 19 (1982): 367–83.

"Implementation of Mechanisms by Processes: Public Good Allocation Experiments." *Journal of Economic Behavior and Organization* 2 (1981): 129–51.

McKelvey, Richard D., and Talbot Page. "Public and Private Information: An Experimental Study of Information Pooling." *Econometrica* 58 (6) (November 1990): 1321–39.

Scherr, B., and E. Babb. "Pricing Public Goods: An Experiment with Two Proposed Pricing Systems." *Public Choice* (Fall 1975): 35–48.

Smith, Vernon L. "An Experimental Comparison of Three Public Good Decision Mechanisms." *Scandinavian Journal of Economics* 81 (1979): 198–215.

"Experimental Mechanisms for Public Choice." In P. C. Ordeshook, ed., *Game Theory and Political Science,* pp. 323–55. New York: New York University Press, 1978.

"Experimental Tests of an Allocation Mechanism for Private, Public, or Externality Goods." *Scandinavian Journal of Economics* 86(4) (1984): 468–84.

"Experiments with a Decentralized Mechanism for Public Good Decisions." *American Economic Review* 70 (September 1980): 584–99.

"Incentive Compatible Experimental Processes for the Provision of Public Goods." In Vernon L. Smith, ed., *Research in Experimental Economics,* Vol. 1, pp. 59–168. Greenwich, Conn.: JAI Press, 1979.

"The Principle of Unanimity and Voluntary Consent in Social Choice." *Journal of Political Economy* 85 (December 1977): 1125–40.

X. Committees: Majority rule

A. Agenda

Altfeld, Michael, and Gary J. Miller. "Sources of Bureaucratic Influence: Expertise and Agenda Control." *Journal of Conflict Resolution* 28 (December 1984): 701–30.

Cohen, Linda, Michael E. Levine, and Charles R. Plott. "Communication and Agenda Influence: The Chocolate Pizza Design." In Heinz Sauermann, ed., *Coalition Forming Behavior: Contributions to Experimental Economics,* Vol. 8. Tübingen, Germany: J. C. B. Mohr (Paul Siebeck), 1978.

Eavey, Cheryl. L., and Gary J. Miller. "Bureaucratic Agenda Control: Imposition or Bargaining?" *American Political Science Review* 78 (September 1984): 719–33.

"Fairness in Majority Rule Games with a Core." *American Journal of Political Science* 28 (August 1984): 570–86.

Eckel, Catherine, and Charles A. Holt. "Strategic Voting Behavior in Agenda-Controlled Committees." *American Economic Review* 79 (4) (1989): 763–73.

Levine, Michael E., and Charles R. Plott. "Agenda Influence and Its Implications." *Virginia Law Review* 63 (May 1977): 561–604.

Miller, Gary J. "Experimental Results in Two-Party Agenda Setting: What's It Worth to Be a Party?" Unpublished paper (mimeo), Michigan State University, East Lansing, 1980.

"The Politics of Collective Consumption and Bureaucratic Supply." National Science Foundation Proposal, 1983.

Miller, Gary J., and Daniel Stengel. "Sophistication in Committee Agenda Control." Unpublished paper (mimeo), Michigan State University, East Lansing, 1984.

Plott, Charles R. "Transcript of a Five-Member Committee Experiment." Social Science Working Paper no. 110, California Institute of Technology, 1976.

Plott, Charles R. and Michael E. Levine. "A Model of Agenda Influence on Committee Decisions." *American Economic Review* 68 (March 1978): 146–60.

B. Simple majority rule

Berl, Janet E., Richard D. McKelvey, Peter C. Ordeshook, and Mark Winer. "An Experimental Test of the Core in a Simple *N*-Person Cooperative Nonsidepayment Game." *Journal of Conflict Resolution* 20 (September 1976): 453–79.

Fiorina, Morris P., and Charles R. Plott. "Committee Decisions under Majority Rule." *American Political Science Review* 72 (June 1978): 575–98.

Herzberg, Roberta, and Rick K. Wilson. "Decision Making Costs and Simple Voting Games: Theory and Experiments on Real-Valued Time Costs." Unpublished paper (mimeo), n.d. Paper presented at the Annual Meeting of the Midwest Political Science Association, April 18–20, 1985, Chicago.

McKelvey, Richard D., and Peter C. Ordeshook. "Competitive Coalition Theory. In P. C. Ordeshook, *Competitive Coalition Theory*, pp. 1–37. New York: New York University Press, 1978.

"Elections with Limited Information: A Fulfilled Expectations Model Using Contemporaneous Poll and Endorsement Data as Information Sources." *Journal of Economic Theory* 36 (1985): 55–85.

"An Experimental Study of the Effects of Procedural Rules on Committee Behavior." *Journal of Politics* 46 (1984): 182–205.

"An Experimental Study of Two-Candidate Elections without Majority Rule Equilibria." *Simulation and Games* 13 (September 1982): 311–35.

"An Experimental Test of Cooperative Solution Theory for Normal Form Games." In P. C. Ordeshook and K. A. Shepsle, eds., *Political Equilibrium*, pp. 118–30. Boston: Kluwer-Nijhoff, 1982.

"An Experimental Test of Several Theories of Committee Decision-Making under Majority Rule." In S. J. Brams, A. Schotter, and G. Schwodiauer. eds., *Applied Game Theory*, Wurzburg: Physica Verlag, 1979.

"Experiments on the Core: Some Disconcerting Results for Majority Rule Voting Games." *Journal of Conflict Resolution* 25 (December 1981): 709–24.

"Rational Expectations in Elections: Some Experimental Results Based on a Multi-dimensional Model." *Public Choice* 44 (1984): 61–102.

"Some Experimental Results That Fail to Support the Competitive Solution." *Public Choice* 40 (1983): 281–91.

"Vote Trading: An Experimental Study." *Public Choice* 35 (1980): 151–84.

McKelvey, Richard D., Peter C. Ordeshook, and Mark D. Winer. "The Competitive

Solution for *N*-Person Games without Transferable Utility, with an Application to Committee Games." *American Political Science Review* 72 (June 1978): 599–615.

Miller, Gary J. and Joe A. Oppenheimer. "Universalism in Experimental Committees." *American Political Science Review* 76 (September 1982): 561–74.

Plott, Charles R. and William P. Rogerson. "Committee Decisions under Majority Rule: Dynamic Theories and Experimental Results." Social Science Working Paper no.280, California Institute of Technology, 1979.

Riker, William H. "An Experimental Examination of Formal and Informal Rules of a Three-Person Game." In B. Lieberman, ed. *Social Choice,* New York: Gordon and Breach, 1971.

Riker, William H., and W. J. Zavoina. "Rational Behavior in Politics: Evidence from a Three-Person Game." *American Political Science Review* 64 (1970).

Selten, Reinhard. "Equity and Coalition Bargaining in Experimental 3-Person Games." In A. E. Roth, ed., *Laboratory Experimentation in Economics: Six Points of View,* pp. 42–98. Cambridge: Cambridge University Press, 1987.

C. Voting over time

Hoffman, Elizabeth, and Charles R. Plott. "Pre-Meeting Discussions and the Possibility of Coalition-Breaking Procedures in Majority Rule Committees." *Public Choice* 40 (1983): 21–39.

Laing, James D., and Scott Olmsted. "An Experimental and Game-Theoretic Study of Committees." In P. C. Ordeshook, ed., *Game Theory and Political Science.* New York: New York University Press, 1978.

McKelvey, Richard D., and Peter C. Ordeshook. "Vote Trading: An Experimental Study." *Public Choice* 35(2) (1980): 151–84.

Plott, Charles R. "The Application of Laboratory Experimental Methods to Public Choice." In C. S. Russell, ed., *Collective Decision Making: Applications from Public Choice Theory,* pp. 137–60. Baltimore: Johns Hopkins Press for Resources for the Future, 1979.

XI. Committees: Nonmajority rules

Grether, David M., R. Mark Isaac, and Charles R. Plott. "The Allocation of Landing Rights by Unanimity among Competitors." *American Economic Review* 71 (May 1981): 166–71.

Grether, David M., R. Mark Isaac, and Charles R. Plott. "Alternative Methods of Allocating Slots: Performance and Evaluation." Prepared for the CAB and FAA. Polinomics Research Laboratories, Pasadena, Calif., August 1979.

Isaac, R. Mark and Charles R. Plott. "Cooperative Game Models of the Influence of the Closed Rule in Three Person, Majority Rule Committees: Theory and Experiments." In P. C. Ordeshook, eds., *Game Theory and Political Science.* New York: New York University Press, 1978.

Kormendi, Roger C. and Charles R. Plott. "Committee Decisions under Alternative Procedural Rules: An Experimental Study Applying a New Nonmonetary Method of Preference Inducement." *Journal of Economic Behavior and Organization* 3 (1982): 21–39.

Krehbiel, Keith. "Sophistication, Myopia, and the Theory of Legislatures: An Experimental Study." Social Science Working Paper no. 551, California Institute of Technology, Pasadena, 1984.

Laing, James D., and Benjamin Slotznick, eds. *When Anyone Can Veto: A Laboratory*

Study of Committees Governed by Unanimous Rule, Philadelphia: Wharton School, University of Pennsylvania, 1983.

Miller, Gary J., and Joe A. Oppenheimer. "Universalism in Experimental Committees." *American Political Science Review* 76 (September 1982): 561–74.

Roth, Alvin E., Michael W. K. Malouf, and J. Keith Murnighan. "Sociological versus Strategic Factors in Bargaining." *Journal of Economic Behavior and Organization* 2 (1981): 153–77.

Roth, Alvin E., and J. Keith Murnighan, "The Role of Information in Bargaining: An Experimental Study." *Econometrica* 50 (September 1982): 1123–42.

Roth, Alvin E., J. Keith Murnighan, and Francoise Schoumaker, "The Deadline Effect in Bargaining: Some Experimental Evidence." *American Economic Review* 78 (4) (September 1988): 806–23.

XII. Elections

McKelvey, Richard D., and Peter C. Ordeshook. "An Experimental Study of the Effects of Parliamentary Rules on Committee Behavior." *Journal of Politics* 46 (1984): 182–205.

"An Experimental Study of Two-Candidate Elections without Majority Rule Equilibria." *Simulation and Games* 13 (September 1982): 311–35.

"Rational Expectations in Elections: Some Experimental Results Based on a Multidimensional Model." *Public Choice* 44 (1984): 61–102.

Plott, Charles R. "A Comparative Analysis of Direct Democracy, Two Candidate Elections and Three Candidate Elections in an Experimental Environment." In T. R. Palfrey, ed., *Laboratory Research in Political Economy,* 11–32. Ann Arbor: University of Michigan Press, 1991.

XIII. The individual (a few studies)

Becker, Joao L., and Rakesh K. Sarin. "Lottery Dependent Utility." *Management Science* 33 (November 1987): 1367–82.

Berg, Joyce E., Lane A. Daley, John W. Dickhaut, and John R. O'Brien. "Controlling Preferences for Lotteries on Units of Experimental Exchange." *Quarterly Journal of Economics* (May 1986): 281–306.

Bolle, Friedel. "Testing for Rational Expectations in Experimental Predictions." Unpublished paper (mimeo), Universitat Hamburg, Germany, n.d.

Coursey, Don L., Elizabeth Hoffman, and Matthew L. Spitzer. "Fear and Loathing in the Coase Theorem: Experimental Tests Involving Physical Discomfort." *Journal of Legal Studies* 16 (1) (January 1987): 217–48.

Cox, James C., and Epstein, Seth. "Preference Reversals without the Independence Axiom." *American Economic Review* 79 (3) (June 1989): 408–26.

Einhorn, Hillel J., and Robin M. Hogarth. "Ambiguity and Uncertainty in Probabilistic Inference." *Psychological Review* 92 (October 1985): 433–61.

Goldstein, William M. "Judgement versus Choice: The Preference Reversal Phenomenon." Unpublished paper University of Michigan, Ann Arbor, n.d.

Goldstein, William M., and Hillel J. Einhorn. "Expression Theory and the Preference Reversal Phenomena." *Psychological Review* 94 (1987): 236–54.

Grether, David M. "Bayes Rule as a Descriptive Model: The Representativeness Heuristic." *Quarterly Journal of Economics* 95 (November 1980): 537–57.

"Financial Incentive Effects and Individual Decisionmaking." Social Science Working Paper no. 401, California Institute of Technology, Pasadena, September 1981.

"Recent Psychological Studies of Behavior under Uncertainty." *American Economic Review: Papers and Proceedings* 68 (May 1978): 70–4.

Grether, David M., and Charles R. Plott. "Economic Theory of Choice and the Preference Reversal Phenomenon." *American Economic Review* 69 (September 1979): 623–38.

Grether, David M., and Louis L. Wilde. "An Analysis of Conjunctive Choice: Theory and Experiments." *Journal of Consumer Research* 10 (March 1984): 373–85.

"Consumer Choice and Information: New Experimental Evidence on Information Overload Hypothesis." *Information Economics and Policy* 1 (1983): 1–29.

"Consumer Choice and Information: New Experimental Evidence." *Information Economics and Policy* 1 (1983): 1–29.

"Experimental Economics and Consumer Research." In Thomas Kinnear, ed., *Advances in Consumer Research*, pp. 724–8. Provo, Utah: Association for Consumer Research, 1984.

Harrison, Glenn W. "An Experimental Test for Risk Aversion." *Economics Letters* 21 (1986): 7–11.

"Risk Aversion and Preference Distortion in Deterministic Bargaining Experiments." *Economics Letters* 22 (1986): 191–96.

Kagel, John H. "Economics According to the Rats (and Pigeons too): What Have We Learned and What Can We Hope to Learn?" In A. E. Roth, ed., *Laboratory Experimentation in Economics: Six Points of View*, pp. 55–192. Cambridge: Cambridge University Press.

Slovic, Paul, and Sarah Lichtenstein. "Preference Reversals: A Broader Perspective." *American Economic Review* 73 (1983): 596–605.

Thaler, Richard. "The Psychology of Choice and the Assumptions of Economics." In Alvin Roth, ed., *Laboratory Experiments in Economics: Six Points of View*. Cambridge: Cambridge University Press, 1987.

Tversky, Amos, and Daniel Kahneman. "The Framing of Decisions and the Psychology of Choice." *Science* 211 (January 1981): 453–8.

Tversky, Amos, and Paul Slovic. "Compatibility Effects and Preference Reversals." Unpublished paper (mimeo), n.p., n.d.

XIV. Bargaining (A Few Studies)

Siegel, Sidney, and Lawrence E. Fouraker. *Bargaining and Group Decision Making: Experiments in Bilateral Monopoly.* Reprint of 1960 edition. Westport, Conn.: Greenwood Press, 1977.

James C. Cox

Syllabus and reading lists for Economics 506 (Fall 1992) and Economics 696
(Spring 1992)

Course Objectives
This course is an introduction to experimental economics that is intended to:

a. expose you to a varied set of experimental research papers;
b. guide you to think about economic theory from the perspective of an empirical science; and
c. provide you with a working knowledge of techniques for conducting laboratory experiments in economics.

Course Requirements
There are four graded course requirements, each of which counts for 25 percent of your course grade:

1. a midterm exam;
2. a survey paper on experimental research, due on the last day the class meets;
3. an experimental research proposal, due during the scheduled final exam period for this course; and
4. a class presentation based on your survey paper, your experimental research proposal, or both.

Nongraded course requirements include participation in class discussions and in laboratory experiments during the scheduled class period. During participation in experiments, each of you will accumulate a subject payoff amount. These are the amounts that are paid to the subjects in U.S. currency ("cold cash") when the subjects' responses are to be used in research papers. Your subject payoff amounts from class-period experiments will *not* be paid to you in cash; instead, they will be paid in "priority rights" in the following way. The student with the highest cumulative (over all experiments) payoff amount will have first choice from the scheduled days for student class presentations. The student with the second-highest cumulative payoff will have second choice, and so on.

Class assignments for the first part of the semester are listed on "Course Outline I" and on the "Core Reading List." Class assignments for the second part of the semester will consist of student presentations and discussion of topics that we all will select.

The instructor's office is room 401-NN in McClelland Hall. His office hours are Tuesdays and Thursdays, 5:00–6:30 P.M. and Wednesdays, 10:00 A.M.–12:00 P.M., and by appointment.

Econ 506: Course outline I

August 20:	Discussion of course content and some elementary economic models.
August 25:	Laboratory experiment.
August 27:	Discussion of papers 1 and 2 on the core reading list.
September 1:	Discussion of papers 3 and 4 on the core reading list.
September 3:	Laboratory experiment.
September 8:	Discussion of papers 5, 6, and 7 on the core reading list.
September 10:	Continuation of discussion of pages 5, 6, and 7.
September 15:	Laboratory experiment.
September 17:	Discussion of papers 8 and 9 on the core reading list.
September 22:	Continuation of discussion of pages 8 and 9.
September 24:	Laboratory experiment.
September 29:	Discussion of papers 10 and 11 on the core reading list.
October 1:	Laboratory experiment.
October 6:	Discussion of papers 12 and 13 on the core reading list.
October 8:	Continuation of discussion of papers 12 and 13.
October 13:	Laboratory experiment.
October 15:	Discussion of papers 14 and 15 on the core reading list.
October 20:	Discussion: integration and wrap-up.
October 22:	Midterm exam.

Econ 506: Core reading list

1. V. Smith, "Markets as Economizers of Information: Experimental Examination of the Hayek Hypothesis," *Economic Inquiry,* vol. 20, April 1982, pp. 165–179.
2. V. Smith, "An Empirical Study of Decentralized Institutions of Monopoly Restraint," pp. 83–106 in G. Horwich and J. Quirk (eds.), *Essays in Contemporary Fields of Economics* (West Lafayette, Ind.: Purdue University Press, 1981).
3. V. Smith, "Experimental Methods in Economics," pp. 241–249 in J. Eatwell, *et al.* (eds.), *The New Palgrave: A Dictionary of Economics* (New York: The Stockton Press, 1987).
4. V. Smith, "Theory, Experiment, and Economics," *Journal of Economic Perspectives,* vol. 3, Winter 1989, pp. 151–169.
5. D. Grether and C. Plott, "Economic Theory of Choice and the Preference Reversal Phenomenon," *American Economic Review,* vol. 69, September 1979, pp. 623–638.
6. J. Cox and M. Isaac, "Experimental Economics and Experimental Psychology: Ever the Twain Shall Meet?" pp. 647–669 in A. J. MacFadyen and H. W. MacFadyen (eds.), *Economic Psychology: Intersections in Theory and Application* (New York: North-Holland, 1986).
7. J. Cox and D. Grether, "The Preference Reversal Phenomenon: Response Mode, Markets and Incentives," discussion paper, University of Arizona, August 1992.
8. J. Cox, B. Roberson, and V. Smith, "Theory and Behavior of Single Object Auctions," pp. 1–43 in V. Smith (ed), *Research in Experimental Economics,* vol. 2 (Greenwich, Conn.: JAI Press, 1982).

9. J. Cox, V. Smith, and J. Walker, "Theory and Behavior of First-Price Auctions," *Journal of Risk and Uncertainty,* vol. 1, March 1988, pp. 61–100.

10. R. Forsythe, T. Palfrey, and C. Plott, "Asset Valuation in an Experimental Market," *Econometrica,* vol. 50, May 1982, pp. 537–567.

11. V. Smith, G. Suchanek, and A. Williams, "Bubbles, Crashes and Endogenous Expectations in Experimental Spot Asset Markets," *Econometrica,* vol. 56, September 1988, pp. 1119–1151.

12. V. Smith, "Experiments with a Decentralized Mechanism for Public Goods Decisions," *American Economic Review,* vol. 70, September 11980, pp. 584–599.

13. M. Isaac and J. Walker, "Group Size Effects in Public Goods Provision: The Voluntary Contributions Mechanism," *Quarterly Journal of Economics,* February 1988, vol. 103, pp. 179–199.

14. A. Roth and F. Schoumaker, "Expectations and Reputations in Bargaining: An Experimental Study," *American Economic Review,* vol. 73, June 1983, pp. 362–372.

15. E. Hoffman, K. McCabe, K. Shachat, and V. Smith, "Preferences, Property Rights, and Anonymity in Bargaining Games," discussion paper, University of Arizona, 1992.

Econ 506: Main reading list

A. Methodology

1. V. Smith, "Microeconomic Systems as an Experimental Science," *American Economic Review,* December 1982, pp. 923–955.

2. V. Smith, "Experimental Methods in Economics," in J. Eatwell, *et al.* (eds.), *The New Palgrave: A Dictionary of Economics* (New York: The Stockton Press, 1987).

3. V. Smith, "Theory, Experiment, and Economics," *Journal of Economic Perspectives,* Winter 1989, pp. 151–169.

4. J. Cox and M. Isaac, "Experimental Economics and Experimental Psychology: Ever the Twain Shall Meet?," in A. J. MacFadyen and H. W. MacFadyen (eds.), *Economic Psychology: Intersections in Theory and Application* (New York: North-Holland, 1986).

B. Markets

1. V. Smith, "Bidding and Auctioning Institutions: Experimental Results," in Y. Amihud (ed.) *Bidding and Auctioning for Procurement and Allocation* (New York University Press, 1976).

2. V. Smith, "Markets as Economizers of Information: Experimental Examination of the Hayek Hypothesis," *Economic Inquiry,* April 1982, pp. 165–179.

3. A. Williams, "Intertemporal Competitive Equilibrium," in V. Smith (ed.), *Research in Experimental Economics,* vol. 1 (Greenwich, Conn.: JAI Press, 1979).

4. V. Smith and A. Williams, "Cyclical Double-Auction Markets with and without Speculators," *Journal of Business,* Jan. 1984, pp. 1–33.

C. Market structure and price discrimination

1. M. Isaac and C. Plott, "Price Controls and the Behavior of Auction Markets," *American Economic Review*, June 1981, pp. 448–459.
2. V. Smith and A. Williams, "On Nonbinding Price Controls in a Competitive Market," *American Economic Review*, June 1981, pp. 467–474.
3. D. Coursey and V. Smith, "Price Controls in a Posted Offer Market," *American Economic Review*, March 1983, pp. 218–221.
4. V. Smith, "An Empirical Study of Decentralized Institutions of Monopoly Restraint," in G. Horwich and J. Quirk (eds.), *Essays in Contemporary Fields of Economics* (West Lafayette, Ind.: Purdue University Press, 1981).
5. C. Holt, L. Langan, and A. Villamil, "Market Power in Oral Double Auctions," *Economic Inquiry*, Jan. 1986, pp. 107–123.
6. V. Smith and A. Williams, "The Boundaries of Competitive Price Theory: Convergence, Expectation, and Transaction Costs," in L. Green and J. Kagel (eds.), *Advances in Behavioral Economics*, vol. 2 (Norwood, N.J.: Ablex Publishing, 1990).

D. Incentive mechanisms for control of monopolies

1. M. Loeb and W. Magat, "A Decentralized Method for Utility Regulation," *Journal of Law and Economics*, Oct. 1979, pp. 399–404.
2. J. Cox and M. Isaac, "Incentive Regulation: A Case Study in the Use of Laboratory Experimental Analysis in Economics," in S. Moriarity (ed.), *Laboratory Market Research* (Norman: The University of Oklahoma, Center for Economic and Management Research, 1986).
3. J. Cox and M. Isaac, "Mechanisms for Incentive Regulation: Theory and Experiment," *RAND Journal of Economics*, Autumn 1987, pp. 348–359.

E. Experimental evaluation of econometric estimators

1. J. Cox and R. Oaxaca, "Using Laboratory Market Experiments to Evaluate Econometric Estimators of Structural Models," discussion paper, University of Arizona, revised 1991.

F. Individual choice under certainty

1. R. Battalio, J. Kagel, et al., "A Test of Consumer Demand Theory Using Observations of Individual Consumer Purchases," *Western Economic Journal*, Dec. 1973, pp. 411–428.
2. J. Cox, "On Testing the Utility Hypothesis," unpublished paper, Department of Economics, University of Arizona, revised 1992.
3. D. Brookshire, D. Coursey, and W. Schulze, "The External Validity of Experimental Economics Techniques: Analysis of Demand Behavior," *Economic Inquiry*, 25, April 1987, pp. 239–250.
4. J. Kagel, R. Battalio, et al., "Experimental Studies of Consumer Demand Behavior Using Laboratory Animals," *Economic Inquiry*, 13, March 1975, pp. 22–38.

5. R. Battalio, L. Green, and J. Kagel, "Income-Leisure Tradeoffs of Animal Workers," *American Economic Review*, Sept. 1981, pp. 621–632.
6. R. Battalio, J. Kagel, *et al.*, "Commodity Choice Behavior with Pigeons as Subjects," *Journal of Political Economy*, 89, Feb. 1981, pp. 67–91.
7. R. Battalio, G. Dwyer, and J. Kagel, "Tests of Competing Theories of Consumer Choice and the Representative Consumer Hypothesis," *Economic Journal*, 97, Dec. 1988, pp. 842–856.
8. R. Battalio, J. Kagel, and C. Kogut, "Experimental Confirmation of the Existence of a Giffen Good," *American Economic Review*, 81, Sept. 1991, pp. 961–970.

G. Theories of choices under uncertainty

1. P. Schoemaker, "The Expected Utility Model: Its Variants, Purposes, Evidence and Limitations," *Journal of Economic Literature*, June 1982, pp. 529–563.
2. M. Machina, "Choice under Uncertainty: Problems Solved and Unsolved," *Journal of Economic Perspectives*, 1, Summer 1987, pp. 121–154.
3. D. Kahneman and A. Tversky, "Prospect Theory: An Analysis of Decision under Risk," *Econometrica*, 47, March 1979, pp. 263–291.

H. Individual choice under uncertainty

1. D. Grether, "Bayes Rule as a Descriptive Model: The Representativeness Heuristic," *Quarterly Journal of Economics*, Nov. 1980, pp. 537–557.
2. D. Grether and C. Plott, "Economic Theory of Choice and the Preference Reversal Phenomenon," *American Economic Review*, Sept. 1979, pp. 623–638.
3. C. Holt, "Preference Reversals and the Independence Axiom," *American Economic Review*, June 1986, pp. 508–515.
4. J. Cox and S. Epstein, "Preference Reversals without the Independence Axiom," *American Economic Review*, June 1989, pp. 408–426.
5. J. Knetsch and J. Sinden, "Willingness to Pay and Compensation Demanded," *Quarterly Journal of Economics*, Aug. 1984, pp. 507–521.
6. R. Battalio, J. Kagel, and D. MacDonald, "Animals' Choices over Uncertain Outcomes: Some Initial Experimental Results," *American Economic Review*, 75, Sept. 1985, pp. 597–613.
7. C. Camerer, "An Experimental Test of Several Generalized Utility Theories," *Journal of Risk and Uncertainty*, 2, April 1989, pp. 61–104.
8. R. Battalio, J. Kagel, and K. Jiranyakul, "Testing Between Alternative Models of Choice Under Uncertainty: Some Initial Results," *Journal of Risk and Uncertainty*, 3, March 1990, pp. 25–50.
9. J. Kagel, D. MacDonald, and R. Battalio, "Tests of 'Fanning Out' of Indifference Curves: Results from Animal and Human Experiments," *American Economic Review*, 80, Sept. 1990, pp. 912–921.

I. Market feedback and choice under uncertainty

1. D. Coursey, J. Hovis, and W. Schulze, "The Disparity between Willingness to Accept and Willingness to Pay Measures of Value," *Quarterly Journal of Economics*, Aug. 1987, pp. 679–690.
2. C. Camerer, "Do Biases in Probability Judgment Matter in Markets? Experimental Evidence," *American Economic Review*, Dec. 1987, pp. 981–997.

3. C. Camerer, G. Loewenstein, and M. Weber, "The Curse of Knowledge in Economic Settings: An Experimental Analysis," *Journal of Political Economy*, 97, Oct. 1989, pp. 1232–1254.
4. J. Cox and D. Grether, "The Preference Reversal Phenomenon: Response Mode, Markets and Incentives," discussion paper, Oct. 1991, revised 1992.

J. Search Decisions

1. Y. Braunstein and A. Schotter, "Economic Search: An Experimental Study," *Economic Inquiry*, 19, Jan. 1981, pp. 1–25.
2. Y. Braunstein and A. Schotter, "Labor Market Search: An Experimental Study," *Economic Inquiry*, 20, Jan. 1982, pp. 133–144.
3. J. Cox and R. Oaxaca, "Laboratory Experiments with a Finite Horizon Job Search Model," *Journal of Risk and Uncertainty*, 2, Sept. 1989, pp. 301–329.
4. J. Cox and R. Oaxaca, "Tests for a Reservation Wage Effect," in John Geweke (ed.), *Decision Making under Risk and Uncertainty: New Models and Empirical Findings*, Dordrecht: Kluwer Academic Publishers (in press).
5. J. Cox and R. Oaxaca, "Direct Tests of the Reservation Wage Property," *Economic Journal*, forthcoming.
6. J. Cox and R. Oaxaca, "Finite Horizon Search Behavior with and without Recall," discussion paper, University of Arizona, 1991.
7. J. Cox and R. Oaxaca, "Search Behavior with an Unknown Distribution of Offers," discussion paper, University of Arizona, 1992 (if available).
8. D. Grether, A. Schwartz, and L. Wilde, "Uncertainty and Shopping Behavior: An Experimental Analysis," *Review of Economic Studies*, April 1988, pp. 239–250.
9. G. Harrison and P. Morgan, "Search Intensity in Experiments," *Economic Journal*, 100, June 1990, pp. 478–486.

K. Auction markets

1. V. Smith, "Auctions," forthcoming in J. Eatwell, et al. (eds.), *The New Palgrave: A Dictionary of Economics* (New York: The Stockton Press, 1987).
2. J. Cox, B. Roberson, and V. Smith, "Theory and Behavior of Single Object Auctions," in V. Smith (ed.), *Research in Experimental Economics*, vol. 2 (Greenwich, Conn.: JAI Press, 1982).
3. J. Cox, V. Smith, and J. Walker, "Theory and Individual Behavior of First Price Auctions," *Journal of Risk and Uncertainty*, March 1988, pp. 61–99.
4. V. Harlow and K. Brown, "Understanding and Assessing Financial Risk Tolerance: A Biological Perspective," *Financial Analysts Journal*, Nov.–Dec. 1990, pp. 50–62, 80.
5. J. Cox, V. Smith, and J. Walker, "Theory and Behavior of Multiple Unit Discriminative Auctions," *Journal of Finance*, Sept. 1984, pp. 983–1010.
6. G. Miller and C. Plott, "Revenue Generating Properties of Sealed-Bid Auctions: An Experimental Analysis of One-Price and Discriminative Processes," in V. Smith (ed.), *Research in Experimental Economics*, vol. 3 (Greenwich, Conn.: JAI Press, 1985).
7. J. Cox, V. Smith, and J. Walker, "Expected Revenue in Discriminative and Uniform Price Sealed Bid Auctions," in V. Smith (ed.), *Research in Experimental Economics*, vol. 3 (Greenwich, Conn.: JAI Press, 1985).

8. M. Isaac and J. Walker, "Information and Conspiracy in Sealed Bid Auctions," *Journal of Economic Behavior and Organization*, 6, 1985, pp. 139–159.

9. J. Kagel, R. Harstad, and D. Levin, "Information Impact and Allocation Rules in Auctions with Affiliated Private Values: A Laboratory Study," *Econometrica*, Nov. 1987, pp. 1275–1304.

10. J. Kagel and D. Levin, "The Winner's Curse and Public Information in Common Value Auctions," *American Economic Review*, Dec. 1986, pp. 894–920.

11. J. Cox and V. Smith, "Common Value Auctions with Entry and Exit," discussion paper, University of Arizona, 1992 (if available.).

12. P. Cech, D. Conn, J. Cox, and M. Isaac, "An Experimental Study of Incentive Contracts in Procurement: Market Performance Results," unpublished paper, Department of Economics, University of Arizona, 1988.

L. Methodology: Lottery payoffs and the random decision selection procedure

1. J. Berg et al., "Controlling Preferences for Lotteries on Units of Experimental Exchange," *Quarterly Journal of Economics*, 101, pp. 281–306.

2. J. Walker, V. Smith, and J. Cox, "Inducing Risk-Neutral Preferences: An Examination in a Controlled Market Environment," *Journal of Risk and Uncertainty*, 3, March 1990, pp. 5–24.

3. T. Rietz, "Controlling Risk Preferences in Sealed Bid Auctions: Some Experimental Results," discussion paper, Northwestern University, 1991.

4. C. Starmer and R. Sugden, "Does the Random-Lottery Incentive System Elicit True Preferences? An Experimental Investigation," *American Economic Review*, 81, Sept. 1991, pp. 971–978.

M. Methodology: The metric war

1. G. Harrison, "Theory and Misbehavior in First-Price Auctions," *American Economic Review*, 79, Sept. 1989, pp. 749–762.

2. D. Friedman, " 'Theory and Misbehavior': A Comment," *American Economic Review*, forthcoming.

3. J. Kagel and A. Roth, "Comment on Harrison versus Cox, Smith, and Walker: 'Theory and Misbehavior in First-Price Auctions'," *American Economic Review*, forthcoming.

4. J. Cox, V. Smith, and J. Walker, "Theory and Misbehavior in First-Price Auctions: Comment and Reply to Harrison, Kagel and Roth," *American Economic Review*, forthcoming.

N. Expectations and asset valuation

1. R. Forsythe, T. Palfrey, and C. Plott, "Asset Valuation in an Experimental Market," *Econometrica*, May 1982, pp. 537–567.

2. C. Plott and S. Sunder, "Efficiency of Experimental Security Markets with Insider Information: An Application of Rational Expectations Models," *Journal of Political Economy*, Aug. 1982, pp. 663–698.

3. D. Friedman, G. Harrison, and J. Salmon, "The Informational Efficiency of Experimental Asset Markets," *Journal of Political Economy*, June 1984, pp. 349–408.

4. V. Smith, G. Suchanek, and A. Williams, "Bubbles, Crashes and Endogenous Expectations in Experimental Spot Asset Markets," *Econometrica*, Sept. 1988, pp. 1119–11151.
5. C. Plott and S. Sunder, "Rational Expectations and the Aggregation of Diverse Information in Laboratory Security Markets," *Econometrica*, 56, Sept. 1988, pp. 1085–1118.
6. S. Sunder, "Market for Information: Experimental Evidence," *Econometrica*, May 1992.
7. C. Camerer and H. Kunreuther, "Experimental Markets for Insurance," *Journal of Risk and Uncertainty*, 2, Sept. 1989, pp. 265–300.

Mark Isaac

Syllabus and reading list for Economics 406 (undergraduate, Spring 1992)

This course is an introduction to the use of laboratory experimental economics, a relatively new method of economics research in which the University of Arizona is one of a handful of world leaders. The course is designed to familiarize undergraduate students with a broad range of research which has been conducted using experimental methods, and, in the process, guide the student to rethink the methodological connections between theory and data.

Books

Beveridge, *The Art of Scientific Investigation*

In addition, there will be other readings from journals and books.

Course Requirements

Two midterm exams, one final exam, and one final project, each worth one-fourth of the total course grade.

Final exam date: Thursday, May 14, 11 A.M.–1 P.M.

Policy on missing exams: I do not give make-up exams. Students who miss an exam receive a grade of "zero" for that exam unless they provide me, in a timely fashion, a written, signed explanation of their absence. Health, family emergencies, out-of-town job interviews, etc. are standard, acceptable excuses for a midterm. Students who miss an exam with an acceptable excuse simply have their course work reweighted on the remaining components. You may not be excused from both midterms. Final exams are rescheduled only on the most extreme of circumstances: death, hospitalization, or jail sentence (your own or that of a close family member). Supersaver airline tickets are *not* an acceptable reason to reschedule a final exam.

Office hours: My office hours are Tuesday and Thursday from 2:00 to 3:00 p.m., and by appointment (621-4831). My office is 205 Econ.

Reading List:

1. V. L. Smith, "Experimental Methods in Economics," from *The New Palgrave.*
2. C. R. Plott, "Experimental Methods in Political Economy: A Tool for Regulatory Research," in *Attacking Regulatory Problems: An Agenda for the 1980s,* A. R. Ferguson, ed. (Cambridge, Mass: Ballinger, 1982).
3. V. L. Smith, "An Experimental Study of Competitive Market Behavior," *Journal of Political Economy* (April 1962).
4. V. L. Smith and A. W. Williams, "The Boundaries of Competitive Price Theory," mimeo.
5. C. R. Plott and V. L. Smith, "An Experimental Examination of Two Exchange Institutions," *Review of Economic Studies"* (February 1978).
6. J. Hong and C. R. Plott, "Rate Filing Policies for Inland Water Transportation: An Experimental Approach," *Bell Journal.*
7. R. M. Isaac and J. M. Walker, "Group Size Effects in Public Goods Provision: The Voluntary Contribution Mechanism," *Quarterly Journal of Economics.*
8. C. R. Plott and S. Sunder, "Efficiency of Experimental Security Markets with Insider Information: An Application of Rational Expectations Models," *Journal of Political Economy.*
9. D. M. Grether, R. M. Isaac, and C. R. Plott, Chapters 5, 6, and 7 of *The Allocation of Scarce Resources: Experimental Economics and the Problem of Allocating Airport Slots* (Boulder, Colo.: Westview Press, 1989).
10. Elizabeth Hoffman, Dale J. Menkhaus, Ray A. Field, and Glen D. Whipple et al. "Using Laboratory Experimental Auctions in Marketing Research: A Case Study of New Packaging for Fresh Beef." University of Arizona Working Paper.

APPENDIX II: INSTRUCTIONS
AND PROCEDURES

This appendix collects instructions and procedures for several different kinds of experiments, including oral double auction and posted offer markets, committee decisions, bargaining, computerized asset markets, overlapping generations economies, and normal form games. You may want to use simplified versions for classroom demonstrations or may want to elaborate the procedures in some respects for your own research experiments. If you can't find instructions or procedures here for the kind of experiment you wish to conduct, do not hesitate to request them from the author of a relevant article. Most experimentalists will be happy to comply.

Charles R. Plott and Vernon L. Smith

Instructions for experiments

Instructions

General

This is an experiment in the economics of market decision making. Various research foundations have provided funds for the conduct of this research. The instructions are simple, and if you follow them carefully and make good decisions you might earn a considerable amount of money which will be paid to you in cash after the experiment.

In this experiment we are going to stimulate a market in which some of you will be buyers and some of you will be sellers in a sequence of market days or trading periods. Two kinds of sheets will now be distributed—information for buyers and information for sellers. The sheets are identified and numbered. The number is only for data-collecting purposes. If you have received sellers' information, you will function only as a seller in this market. Similarly, if you have received buyers' information, you will function only as a buyer in this market. The information you have received is for your own private use. **Do not reveal it to anyone.**

This is a one commodity market in which there is no product differentiation. That is, each seller produces a product which is similar in all respects to the products offered by the other sellers. A seller is free to sell to any buyer or buyers. Likewise, a buyer may purchase from any seller or sellers.

Specific Instructions for Sellers

During each market period you are free to produce and sell any of the amounts listed on your information sheet. Assume that you produce only for immediate sale—there are no inventories. The dollar amounts listed in column 2 on your information sheet are your costs of producing that quantity.

Your payoffs are computed as follows: At the beginning of the experiment you will receive starting capital of $0.30. If you are able to make any sales, you will receive the difference between your sales revenue and your cost. For example, if you were to sell two units at $100 each, total revenue would be $200. Suppose your information sheet

Reprinted from Charles R. Plott and Vernon L. Smith, 1978, "An Experimental Examination of Two Exchange Institutions," *Review of Economic Studies* 45:1 (February): 133–152.

indicated that the cost of producing two units was $190. Your total profit would then be $200 − $190 = $10 for the trading period. If you sold two units for less than $190 you would incur a loss. Column 3 will be useful to a seller in deciding at any time during a given trading period whether to sell an additional unit. Suppose a seller has already sold one unit at a profit, and wants to know if he should sell a second unit. If the additional cost of producing the second unit is $10, then he will lose money on that unit if he sells it at any price below $10. Obviously, these figures are illustrative only and should not be assumed to apply to the actual sellers in this experiment.

All of your profits will be added to your starting capital, and any losses you might incur will be subtracted. Your total payoffs will be accumulated over several trading periods and the total amount will be paid to you after the experiment.

Specific Instructions for Buyers

During each market period you are free to purchase any of the quantities listed on your information sheet. Assume that you are buying this commodity for the purpose of reselling it in an entirely different market. The dollar amounts listed beside each quantity are the total value of that quantity. That is, they are the amounts you can sell that quantity for in the other market.

Your payoffs are computed as follows: You will receive starting capital of $0.30. If you are able to make any purchases, you will receive the difference between the total value as shown on your information sheet and the total amount you paid for the purchases. For example, if you were to purchase one unit for $105 and another for $95, you would obviously have paid a total of $200 for the two units. Suppose your information sheet indicated that the revenue from two units was $210. Your profit for the market period would then be $210 − $200 = $10. If you had paid more than $210 for the two units, you would have incurred a loss. Column 3 will be useful to a buyer in deciding at any time during a given period whether to buy an additional unit. Suppose a buyer has already bought two units at a profit, and wants to know if he should buy a third unit. If the additional revenue he gets from the third unit is $7, then he will lose money on that unit if he buys it at any price above $7. Obviously, these figures are illustrative only and should not be assumed to apply to the actual buyers in this experiment. All of your profits will be added to your starting capital, and any losses you might incur will be subtracted.

Your total payoffs will be accumulated over several trading periods and the total amount will be paid to you after the experiment.

Market Organization (included in Exp. 1 instructions but not Exp. 2)

The market for this commodity is organized as follows: we open the market for each trading day. Each buyer decides on a purchase price which he will write on one of the cards provided. The buyers will be given two minutes to submit their prices. The cards will be collected and the prices written on the blackboard. Sellers will then be free to make offers to sell whatever quantities they desire and to specify the buyer to whom they wish to sell. Offers will be made as follows: a seller will raise his hand and, when called upon, will state the quantity he wishes to sell and the buyer to whom he wishes to sell. The buyer will then accept any part of the seller's offer by stating the quantity he wishes to buy. However, when a buyer posts a price, he must be prepared *to buy at least one unit* if any seller wishes to sell to him. If a number of sellers desire to make simultaneous offers, one of them will be selected at random and he will then make his desired sales. If the first buyer will not purchase all units the seller wants to sell, the seller is free to make contracts with another buyer or buyers.

When the first seller has made all his contracts, another seller will be selected at random

TABLE IV

Incentive schedules: Experiments 1 and 2

Seller Number......
SELLER'S COST SCHEDULE

Quantity of commodity Q in each trading period	Total cost of producing Q units of commodity	Additional cost of producing the last or Qth unit of commodity
0	$0·00	
		$0·26
1	0·26	
		0·38
2	0·64	
		0·50
3	1·14	
		0·60
4	1·74	
		0·70
5	2·44	
		0·78
6	3·22	
		0·86
7	4·08	
		0·94
8	5·02	

Seller Number......
SELLER'S COST SCHEDULE

Quantity of commodity Q in each trading period	Total cost of producing Q units of commodity	Additional cost of producing the last or Qth unit of commodity
0	$0·00	
		$0·28
1	0·28	
		0·32
2	0·60	
		0·36
3	0·96	
		0·42
4	1·38	
		0·50
5	1·88	
		0·60
6	2·48	
		0·70
7	3·18	
		0·82
8	4·00	
		0·94
9	4·94	
		1·06
10	6·00	

Buyer Number......
BUYER'S REVENUE SCHEDULE

Quantity of commodity Q in each trading period	Total revenue from Q units of commodity	Additional revenue from the last or Qth unit of the commodity
0	$0·00	
		$0·92
1	0·92	
		0·88
2	1·80	
		0·84
3	2·64	
		0·78
4	3·42	
		0·70
5	4·12	
		0·60
6	4·72	
		0·50
6	5·22	
		0·38
8	5·60	
		0·26
9	5·86	
		0·14
10	6·00	

Buyer Number......
BUYER'S REVENUE SCHEDULE

Quantity of commodity Q in each trading period	Total revenue from Q units of commodity	Additional revenue from the last or Qth unit of the commodity
0	$0·00	
		$0·94
1	0·94	
		0·82
2	1·76	
		0·70
3	2·46	
		0·60
4	3·06	
		0·50
5	3·56	
		0·42
6	3·98	
		0·34
7	4·32	
		0·26
8	4·58	

and he will make his desired purchases. The process will be continued until there are no offers to sell. This completes the trading day. We will reopen the market for a new trading day by having buyers submit new prices and the process will be repeated.

Are there any questions?

Market Organization (included in Exp. 2 instructions but not Exp. 1)

The market for this commodity is organized as follows: we open the market for a trading day. Any buyer is free at any time to raise his hand and make a verbal bid to buy one unit of the commodity at a specified price. Any seller is free to accept or not accept the bid of any buyer but sellers cannot make counter offers. If a bid is accepted a binding contract has been closed for a single unit between that buyer and seller.

This process continues for a period of time. You will be warned in advance before the market closes and more bids will be called for before actually closing. This completes a market "day". We will then reopen the market for a new trading period. The cost and revenue tables apply to each new trading period, and represent cost or revenue per period.

Are there any questions?

C. Instructions: Experiments 3 and 4

Instructions used in Experimental Sessions 3 and 4 are identical with the exception of the section entitled "Market Organization." The Market Organization sections outline the change in the treatment variable. Both forms are included below.

Instructions

General

This is an experiment in the economics of market decision making. Various research foundations have provided funds for this research. The instructions are simple and if you follow them carefully and make good decisions you might earn a considerable amount of money which will be paid to you in cash.

In this experiment we are going to simulate a market in which some of you will be buyers and some of you will be sellers in a sequence of market days or trading periods. Attached to the instructions you will find a sheet, labelled Buyer or Seller, which describes the value to you of any decisions you might make. **You are not to reveal this information to anyone.** It is your own private information.

Specific Instructions to Buyers

During each market period you are free to purchase from any seller or sellers as many units as you might want. For the first unit that you buy *during a trading period* you will receive the amount listed in row (1) marked *1st unit redemption value;* if you buy a second unit you will receive the additional amount listed in row (5) marked *2nd unit redemption value; etc.* The profits from each purchase (which are yours to keep) are computed by taking the difference between the redemption value and purchase price of the unit bought. *Under no conditions may you buy a unit for a price which exceeds the redemption value.* In addition to this profit you will receive a 5-cent commission for each purchase. That is

[your earnings = (redemption value) − (purchase price) + 0·05 commission].

Suppose for example that you buy two units and that your redemption value for the first unit is $200 and for the second unit is $180. If you pay $150 for your first unit and $160 for the second unit, your earnings are:

$ earnings from 1st = 200 − 150 + 0·05 = 50·05
$ earnings from 2nd = 180 − 160 + 0·05 = 20·05
total $ earnings = 50·05 + 20·05 = 70·10

The blanks on the table will help you record your profits. The purchase price of the first unit you buy during the first period should be recorded on row (2) *at the time of purchase.* You should then record the profits on this purchase as directed on rows (3) and (4). At the end of the period record the total of profits and commissions on the last row (41) on the page. Subsequent periods should be recorded similarly.

Specific Instructions to Sellers

During each market period you are free to sell to any buyer or buyers as many units as you might want. The first unit that you sell *during a trading period* you obtain at a cost of the amount listed on the attached sheet in the row (2) marked *cost of 1st unit;* if you sell a second unit you incur the cost listed in the row (6) marked *cost of the 2nd unit; etc.* The profits from each sale (which are yours to keep) are computed by taking the difference between the price at which you sold the unit and the cost of the unit. *Under no conditions may you sell a unit at a price below the cost of the unit.* In addition to this profit you will receive a 5 cent commission for each sale. That is

[your earnings = (sale price of unit) − (cost of unit) + (0.05 commission).]

Your total profits and commissions for a trading period, which are yours to keep, are computed by adding up the profit and commissions on sales made during the trading period.

Suppose, for example, your cost of the 1st unit is $140 and your cost of the second unit is $160. For illustrative purposes we will consider only a two-unit case. If you sell the first unit at $200 and the second unit at $190, your earnings are:

$ earnings from 1st $= 200 - 140 + 0.05 = 60.05$
$ earnings from 2nd $= 190 - 160 + 0.05 = 30.05$
total $ earnings $= 60.05 + 30.05 = 90.10$

The blanks on the table will help you record your profits. The sale price of the first unit you sell during the 1st period should be recorded on row (1) *at the time of sale.* You should then record the profits on this sale as directed on rows (3) and (4). At the end of the period record the total of profits and commissions on the last row (41) on the page. Subsequent periods should be recorded similarly.

Market Organization (included in instructions for Exp. 3 but not Exp. 4)

The market for this commodity is organized as follows: we open the market for each trading day. Each buyer decides on a purchase price which he will write on one of the cards provided. The buyers will be given two minutes to submit their prices. The cards will be collected and the prices written on the blackboard. Sellers will then be free to make offers to sell whatever quantities they desire and to specify the buyer to whom they wish to sell. Offers will be made as follows: a seller will be chosen using random numbers, and will state the quantity he wishes to sell and the buyer to whom he wishes to sell. The buyer will then accept any part of the seller's offer by stating the quantity he wishes to buy. However, when a buyer posts a price, he must be prepared *to buy at least one unit.* If the first buyer will not purchase all units the seller wants to sell, the seller is free to choose a second buyer, and so on.

When the first seller has made all his contracts, another seller will be selected at random and he will make his desired purchases. The process will be continued until there are no offers to sell. This completes the trading day. We will reopen the market for a new trading day by having buyers submit new prices and the process will be repeated. Except for the

Unit Sold		Trading Period Number	1	2	3	4	5	6	7	8	9	10	11	12	13	14	15
1	1	1st unit redemption value	.92	.92	.92	.92	.92	.92	.92	.92	.92	.92	.92	.92	.92	.92	.92
	2	Purchase price															
	3	Profit (row 1 − row 2)															
	4	Profit + 5 cents commission															
2	5	2nd unit redemption value	.88	.88	.88	.88	.88	.88	.88	.88	.88	.88	.88	.88	.88	.88	.88
	6	Purchase price															
	7	Profit (row 5 − row 6)															
	8	Profit + 5 cents commission															
3	9	3rd unit redemption value	.84	.84	.84	.84	.84	.84	.84	.84	.84	.84	.84	.84	.84	.84	.84
	10	Purchase price															
	11	Profit (row 9 − row 10)															
	12	Profit + 5 cents commission															
4	13	4th unit redemption value	.78	.78	.78	.78	.78	.78	.78	.78	.78	.78	.78	.78	.78	.78	.78
	14	Purchase price															
	15	Profit (row 13 − row 14)															
	16	Profit + 5 cents commission															
5	17	5th unit redemption value	.70	.70	.70	.70	.70	.70	.70	.70	.70	.70	.70	.70	.70	.70	.70
	18	Purchase price															
	19	Profit (row 17 − row 18)															
	20	Profit + 5 cents commission															
6	21	6th unit redemption value	.60	.60	.60	.60	.60	.60	.60	.60	.60	.60	.60	.60	.60	.60	.60
	22	Purchase price															
	23	Profit (row 21 − row 22)															
	24	Profit + 5 cents commission															
7	25	7th unit redemption value	.50	.50	.50	.50	.50	.50	.50	.50	.50	.50	.50	.50	.50	.50	.50
	26	Purchase price															
	27	Profit (row 25 − row 26)															
	28	Profit + 5 cents commission															
8	29	8th unit redemption value	.38	.38	.38	.38	.38	.38	.38	.38	.38	.38	.38	.38	.38	.38	.38
	30	Purchase price															
	31	Profit (row 29 − row 30)															
	32	Profit + 5 cents commission															
9	33	9th unit redemption value	.26	.26	.26	.26	.26	.26	.26	.26	.26	.26	.26	.26	.26	.26	.26
	34	Purchase price															
	35	Profit (row 33 − row 34)															
	36	Profit + 5 cents commission															
10	37	10th unit redemption value	.14	.14	.14	.14	.14	.14	.14	.14	.14	.14	.14	.14	.14	.14	.14
	38	Purchase price															
	39	Profit (row 37 − row 38)															
	40	Profit + 5 cents commission															
	41	Total per period earnings															
	42	Damages															
	43	Net income															
	44	Capital payment															

Name_____ Soc. Sec. No._____ Total Payment_____

Address_____

Fig. 10   Record of Purcases and Earnings, Buyers No. 1 & 2

offers and their acceptance you are not to speak to any other subject. You are free to make as much profit as you can.

Are there any questions?

Market Organization (included in instructions for Exp. 4 but not Exp. 3)

The market for this commodity is organized as follows: we open the market for a trading period (a trading "day"). The period lasts for minutes. Any buyer is free at any time during the period, to raise his hand and make a verbal bid to buy one unit of the commodity at a specified price. Any seller is free to accept or not accept the bid of any buyer but *sellers cannot make counter offers.* If a bid is accepted a binding contract has been closed for a single unit and the buyer and seller will record the contract price to be included in their earnings. Any ties in bids or acceptances will be resolved by a random choice of buyer or seller. Except for the bids and their acceptance you are not to speak to any other subject. There are likely to be many bids that are not accepted, but you are free to keep trying, and as a buyer or a seller you are free to make as much profit as you can.

Are there any questions?

Morris P. Fiorina and Charles R. Plott

Instructions for full communication experiments

General.

You are about to participate in a committee process experiment in which one of numerous competing alternatives will be chosen by majority rule. The purpose of the experiment is to gain insight into certain features of complex political processes. The instructions are simple. If you follow them carefully and make good decisions, you might earn a considerable amount of money. You will be paid in cash.

Instructions to Committee Members.

The alternatives are represented by points on the blackboard. The committee will adopt as the committee decision one and only one point. *Your* compensation depends on the particular point chosen by the committee (see attached payoff chart). For example, suppose your payoff chart is that given in Figure 1 and that the committee's final choice of alternative is the point $(x,y) = (170,50)$. Your compensation in this event would be $7,000. If the policy of the committee is $(140,125)$ your compensation would be computed as follows:

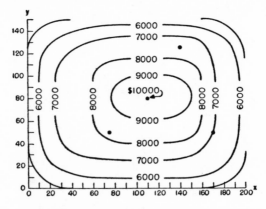

Reprinted from the appendix to Morris P. Fiorina and Charles R. Plott, 1978, "Committee Decisions under Majority Rule: An Experimental Study," *American Political Science Review* 72 (June): 575–98.

182

The point (140,125) is halfway between the curve marked $7,000 and the curve marked $8,000. So, your compensation is halfway between $7,000 and $8,000, i.e., $7,500. If the policy is one-quarter of the distance between two curves, then your payoff is determined by the same proportion (i.e., at (75,50) which is one-quarter of the way between $8,000 and $9,000, you get $8,250).

The compensation charts may differ among individuals. *This means that the patterns of preferences differ and the monetary amounts may not be comparable. The point which would result in the highest payoff to you may not result in the highest payoff to someone else.* You should decide what decision you want the committee to make and do whatever you wish within the confines of the rules to get things to go your way. *The experimenters, however, are not primarily concerned with whether or how you participate so long as you stay within the confines of the rules.* [Under no circumstances may you mention anything *quantitative* about your compensation. You are free, if you wish, to indicate which ones you like best, etc., but you cannot mention anything about the actual monetary amounts. Under no circumstances may you mention anything about activities which might involve you and other committee members after the experiment, i.e., no deals to split up afterward or no physical threats.]*

Parliamentary Rules.

The process begins with an existing motion (200,150) on the floor. You are free to propose *amendments* to this motion. Suppose, for example, (170,50) is the motion on the floor and you want the group to consider the point (140,125). Simply raise your hand and when you are recognized by the chair, say "I move to amend the motion to (140,125)." The group will then proceed to vote on the amendment. If the amendment passes by a majority vote, the point (140,125) is the new motion on the floor and is subject, itself, to amendments. If the amendment fails the motion (170,50) remains on the floor and is subject to further amendment. Thus, amendments simply change the motion on the floor. You may pass as many amendments as you wish.

At any time during the consideration of an amendment or the motion on the floor a *motion to end debate* is in order. If there are no objections, an immediate vote will take place. If there are objections, the motion to end debate will itself be put to a majority vote. If the motion to end debate fails, the amendment process continues. If it passes, a vote on the amendment or motion will take place.

To sum up, the existing motion on the floor is (200,150). You are free to amend this motion as you wish. The meeting will not end until a majority consents to end debate and accept some motion. Your compensation will be determined by the motion on the floor finally adopted by the majority.

Are there any questions?

We would like you to answer the questions on the attached page. These should help you understand the instructions.

Test

1. At _____I would make the most possible money. The amount I would receive is _____.
2. At _____I would make the least possible money. The amount I would receive is _____.
3. Suppose (200,150) is the motion on the floor and an amendment to move to

---

* This section omitted in no-communication condition.

point (199,149) passes (fails), then the new motion on the floor is _____,
_____(_____,_____)?

4. Suppose an amendment to move to (100,100) passes and no further amendments
   pass. If the motion on the floor is then adopted by a majority, my compensation
   is _____.

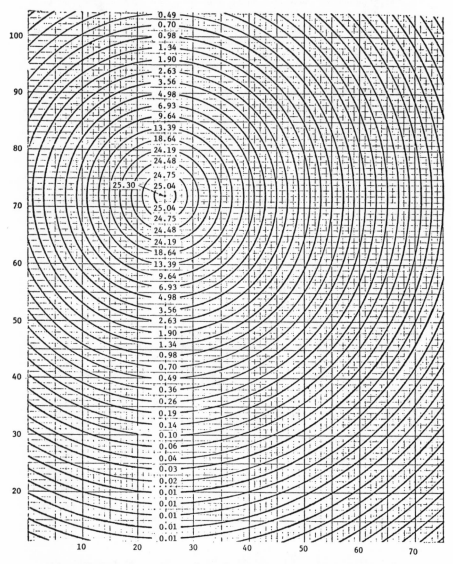

Appendix B. Sample Indifference Map—Player 3, Series 1, High Payoff

Alvin E. Roth and Michael W. K. Malouf

Instructions

Method

Subjects

The subject pool consisted mainly of college sophomores from an introductory business administration course. No special skill or experience was required for participation. Pretests were run with the same subject pool to ensure that the instructions to participants were clear and easily understandable.

Procedure

Each participant was seated at a visually isolated terminal of a computer-assisted instruction system (called PLATO) developed at the University of Illinois, whose features include advanced graphic displays and interactive capability. The experiment was conducted in a room containing over 70 terminals, most of which were occupied at any given time by students uninvolved in this experiment. No more than 9 of the terminals were used for the experiment at any time (8 terminals occupied by participants, and 1 terminal used by the experimenter to monitor the proceedings). Participants were seated by the experimenter in order of their arrival at scattered terminals throughout the room, and for the remainder of the experiment they received all of their instructions and conducted all communication through the terminal.

Background information such as a brief review of probability theory was first presented. The main tools of the bargaining were then introduced. These consisted of sending messages or sending proposals. A proposal was a pair of numbers, the first of which was the sender's probability of receiving his/her prize and the second was the receiver's probability. The use of the computer enabled any asymmetry in the presentation to be avoided. PLATO also computed the expected value of each proposal and displayed the proposal on a graph of the feasible region. After being made aware of these computations, the bargainer was given the option of canceling the proposal before its transmittal. Proposals were said to be binding on the sender, and an agreement was reached whenever one of the bargainers returned a proposal identical to the one he or she had just received.

Reprinted from Alvin E. Roth and Michael W. K. Malouf, 1979, "Game-Theoretic Models and the Role of Information in Bargaining," *Psychological Review* 86: 574–94.

Messages were not binding. Instead, they were used to transmit any thoughts that the bargainers wanted to convey to each other. To ensure anonymity, the monitor intercepted any messages that revealed the identity of the players. In the partial information condition, the monitor also intercepted messages containing information about the available prizes. The intercepted message was returned to the sender with a heading indicating the reason for such action.

To verify their understanding of the basic notions, the subjects were given some drills followed by a simulated bargaining session with the computer. As soon as all the participants finished this portion of the experiments, they were paired at random and the bargaining started.

At the end of 12 minutes or when agreement was reached (whichever came first), the subjects were informed of the results of that game and were asked to wait until all the other bargainers were finished. For the subsequent game there were new random pairings, and the bargaining resumed. The cycle continued until all four games were completed. At no point in the experiment were the players aware of what the other participants were doing, or of the identity of their opponents.

The bargaining process consisted of the exchange of messages and proposals, and participants were instructed that "your objective should be to maximize your own earnings by taking advantage of the special features of each session." Only if the bargainers reached agreement on what percentage of the "lottery tickets" each would receive were they allowed the opportunity to participate in the lottery for the particular game being played. All transactions were automatically recorded.

The lotteries were held after all four games were completed, and each player was informed of the outcomes and the amount of his winnings. A brief explanation of the purpose of the experiment was then given, and the subjects were offered the opportunity to type any comments, questions, and so on, and were directed to the monitor who paid them.

Shyam Sunder

Instructions

Markets were conducted in three steps: (1) training with the mechanism used to draw the states of nature, (2) explanations of procedures and rules of the market, and (3) conduct of markets for several periods.

Step 1: Training with the mechanism used to draw the states of nature
Instruction Set 1 (see summary below) was distributed and read out. Subjects had the opportunity to observe the operation of a bingo cage with 40 balls kept on a table between them and the experimenter. The subjects were asked to predict the outcome of 10 draws, one at a time, with replacement and received announced rewards ($0.25 for correct and $-$0.10 for incorrect predictions). No mention was made of probabilities.

Step 2: Explanation of procedures and rules of the market
Instruction Set 2 (see summary below) was distributed and read out. The experimenter illustrated a sequence of hypothetical transactions on the blackboard so each subject would understand how transactions were to be recorded on the record sheet and how his/her profit would be reckoned. The example was designed to minimize its normative effect on subsequent bidding behavior. The importance of accurate records of all transactions was emphasized. Instruction Set 2 was modified in Markets 1 and 3A to allow for the sale of information to a fixed number of traders through a sealed bid auction. In PLATO computer auctions (Markets 6 and 7), a part of Instruction Set 2 was substituted by PLATO online instructions for double auctions.

Step 3: Conduct of markets
Five minutes were permitted for each period with warning at four minutes. The experimenter drew a ball from the bingo cage. In Markets 1 and 3A, sealed bids for information were gathered from all traders; after tallying the bids, information was recorded on the bidding forms of four winning bidders, bidding forms were returned to all traders, and the price at which information was sold (i.e., fifth highest bid) publicly announced. In Markets 2, 3B, 4, 5, 6, and 7, the experimenter announced the price of information, collected information purchase order forms from all traders, recorded in-

Reprinted from Shyam Sunder, 1992, "Market for Information: Experimental Evidence," *Econometrica* 60 (3): 667–695.

formation on appropriate forms, and returned all forms to traders. The bingo cage was operated in full view of the subjects. A running log of bids, offers and transactions of the current and previous few periods was maintained on the blackboard. A cumulative table of trading activity of each period showing the following data was also maintained on the blackboard: period, opening price, closing price, high price, low price, average price, number of transactions, realized state, price of information and the number of traders who had bought information.

Summary of Instruction Set 1

The bingo cage has forty balls numbered 1 through 40. If the ball drawn is numbered 1 through 16, outcome of the draw is called X; if a ball numbered 17 through 40 is drawn, the outcome is called Y.

You have to predict the outcome of each draw before it is announced. If your prediction is correct you win **$0.25**, if wrong you lose **$0.10**.

| | | | | | Circle One | |
Number	Circle One Decision		Outcome X or Y	Win ($)	Lose ($)
1.	X	Y	_____	0.25	−0.10
2.	X	Y	_____	0.25	−0.10
3.	.	.	.	.	.
4.	.	.	.	.	.
5.	.	.	.	.	.

Total winnings $ _____
Total losses $ _____
Net winnings/losses $ _____

Summary of Instruction Set 2

General

This is an experiment in decision making. The instructions are simple, and if you follow them carefully and make good decisions, you might earn a considerable amount of money which will be paid to you in cash.

In this experiment a market for buying and selling certificates will be operated over a sequence of market years. The attached Information and Record Sheet will help you determine how much money you make from your decisions. The information contained in it is your private information.

All trading and earnings will be in terms of francs. Each franc is worth ____ dollars to you. At the end of the experiment your francs will be converted to dollars at this rate.

Specific instructions

At the beginning of each year you are provided with an initial holding of certificates. This is recorded on row 0 of the year's information and record sheet. Within the following rules, you are free to buy and sell certificates. Your profits come from two sources – from collecting earnings on the certificates you hold at the end of the year *and* from buying and selling certificates.

The certificate earning each period will be one of the two numbers of francs listed on row 26 of your information and record sheet. The method by which one of the two numbers is selected each year is explained later. Note that earnings may be different for different investors. At the end of each year all your holdings are automatically sold to the experimenter at a price of 0.

In addition, at the beginning of each year you are provided with an initial amount of francs on hand. This is also recorded on row 0 of each year's information and record sheet. You may use it to purchase certificates. At the end of the year, you must return this amount to the experimenter and the rest is your profit for the year.

Information about dividends

Whether the dividend you receive from the certificate you hold is the X dividend or the Y dividend shown on row 26 is determined by the experimenter at the beginning of the year by drawing a ball from a bingo cage containing forty balls numbered 1 through 40. If the ball drawn is numbered 1–16, X dividend is paid; if the ball drawn is numbered 17–40, Y dividend is paid.

Before the market opens for trading each year you have the opportunity to buy information about whether X or Y dividend would be paid in that year. The experimenter will declare the price of information and invite you to submit your purchase order. Information will be distributed to all who wish to purchase information. The number of traders who purchase information, but not their identity, will be announced by the experimenter.

Trading and recording rules

(1) All transactions are for one certificate at a time.
(2) After each transaction you must calculate and record your new holdings of certificates and your new francs on hand. Your holdings of certificates must not be below zero at the end of the period. For every certificate "short," a fine must be paid equal to the highest price at which any unit is sold during the period plus 500 francs.
(3) At the end of the experiment add up your total profit on your profit sheet and enter this sum on row 21 of your profit sheet. To convert this number into dollars, multiply by the number on row 22 and record the product on row 23. The experimenter will pay you this amount of money.

Market organization

The market will be conducted in a series of years. Each period lasts for five minutes. Anyone wishing to purchase a certificate is free to raise his or her hand and make a verbal bid to buy one certificate at a specified price, and anyone with certificates to sell is free to accept or not accept the bid. Likewise, anyone wishing to sell a certificate is free to raise his or her hand and make a verbal offer to sell one certificate at a specified price. If a bid or offer is accepted, a binding contract has been closed for a single certificate, and the contracting parties will record the transaction on their information and record sheets. Any ties in bids or acceptance will be resolved by random choice. Except for the bids and their acceptance, you are not to speak to any other subject. There are likely to be many bids that are not accepted, but you are free to keep trying. You are free to make as much profit as you can.

Information and Record Sheet

Trader Number _____

Trading Period _____

	Transaction Number	Transaction Price		Certificates on Hand	Francs on Hand
		Purchase	Sale		
Beginning Period Holdings	0	////////// ////////// //////////	////////// ////////// //////////	2	Beg. 10,000 Cost ( ) Bal. _____
	1				
	2				
	3				
	4				
	5				
	6				
	7				
	8				
	9				
	10				
	11				
	12				
	13	Total Certificate Earnings = Cert. on hand x Earnings per certificate =			
X-Div.____ Y-Div.____	14	Total Francs on Hand at the end of the period =			
	15	Less: Fixed cost			10,000
	16	Net Profit for the period			

Stephen Spear, Ramon Marimon, and Shyam Sunder

Design of Experimental Economies

Overlapping generations were created in the laboratory by recruiting $N \geq (3n + 1)$ subjects. Each subject was seated on a computer workstation and shielded from viewing the computer screens of others. In every period of the economy, n subjects entered the game to constitute the young generation, the n subjects who entered the game in the preceding period constituted the old generation, and the remaining ($\geq n + 1$) subjects, called outsiders, were inactive. In the following period, n outsiders were randomly picked to constitute the young generation of that period, before the subjects who had just finished serving as the old were added to the pool of outsiders. This procedure made sure that every subject sat out of the economy for at least one period before reentering the game, and that the number of periods for which the subject had to sit out was random.

Extrinsic uncertainty was generated by cyclically changing the color of a blinking square on the computer screen between red and yellow. The lower half of the computer screen displayed data (the realized price, inflation, etc.) for each period in the color of the blinking square for the respective period. For a certain number of consecutive periods in each economy . . . , the economy was imparted a real shock by cyclically varying the number of subjects in each generation between a high and a low number *in phase* with the color of the blinking square on computer screens. The advantage of this method of introducing extrinsic uncertainty into the economy was that subjects remained entirely unaware of the existence or absence of generation size shocks.[1] In-phase alteration of the color of

Reprinted from Stephen Spear, Ramon Marimon, and Shyam Sunder, 1993, "Expectationally-Driven Volatility: Experimental Evidence," *Journal of Economic Theory* (forthcoming).

[1] We conducted eight pilot economies to explore the feasibility of several other modes of introducing extrinsic uncertainty into laboratory environment. An extra payment of cash contingent on the color of the blinking square could not be used without the individual subjects being aware of its presence or absence. Changing the endowment of the young to impart a real shock to the economy had the same problem. Alteration of generation size, on the other hand, was quite opaque to individual subjects. Its real impact could be seen by subjects in the price behavior of the economy, but they had no information to attribute this impact to variation in generation size. Further, once subjects form second-order adaptive expectations on the basis of their observations in the presence

blinking squares and data display, and the unobserved generation size were the key features of the "sunspot" implementation in the laboratory.

In order to minimize the effect of the terminal conditions on the economy, the subjects played a price-prediction game. In addition to P^{et+1}, subjects were also solicited for their prediction of P^{et} at the beginning of every period t with the promise of a \$2.00 reward for the best that came closest to the actual market-clearing price in the period. The results of this prediction game were announced at the end of each period. As part of the initial instructions, the subjects were informed that the economy may be terminated in any period after solicitation of these predictions; the units of fiat money in the hands of the subjects who play "young" in the last period of the economy will be converted into "chips" at the average predicted price for the unplayed period. To the extent the subjects were able to make accurate predictions after some experience, their concerns about the impact of abrupt termination of the economy on their welfare were minimized.

A full set of instructions for one of the economies is given below. The time sequence of operating the economies can be described as follows:

1. n subjects are randomly chosen from the pool of outsiders to enter the economy in period t before the subjects who served as old in period $t - 1$ were added to the pool of outsiders.
2. The Markovian transition matrix pi is used to generate the color (orange or yellow) of a blinking square which is displayed in the middle of the computer screen of all subjects. The color of the square is a potential candidate for extrinsic uncertainty. Transition probabilities in the economies reported here were always 1.
3. Subjects are asked to submit their forecast of the market clearing price of chips in period t as their entry to the forecasting competition. In addition, they are asked to enter their forecasts for period $t + 1$.
5. Computer uses the forecasts of each member of the "young" generation to construct a money demand function. Individual demands are aggregated to form money demand for the generation.
6. The central computer computes the point of intersection of money demand with the (constant) supply of money ($25n$ for all economies reported here). Market clearing price is announced and individual subjects are informed of their allocations.
7. The old are informed of the number of dollars they earned on the basis of the chips they consumed in their young and the old period. Members of the old generation then join the pool of outsiders.
8. The young are informed of the units they consume in period t, and the number of units of fiat money they carry into period $t + 1$.
9. The results of the price-prediction competition are announced and the winner receives the prediction prize.
10. Cycle resumes at step 1.

Instructions for Economy 1

This is an experiment in decision making. Various research foundations have provided funds for this research. The instructions are simple; if you follow them carefully and make good decisions, you might earn a considerable number of points.

of the shock, the cyclic price behavior is supported by such expectations in an economy when the generation shock is absent.

We shall operate a market in which you may buy and sell chips in a sequence of periods. Your computer will prompt you for your decisions and keep track of the amount of money you earn. You may also keep your own account of the points you make as a result of your decisions.

The type of currency used in this market is francs. The only use of this currency is to buy and sell chips. It has no other use. The points you take home with you are called dollars. The procedures for determining the number of dollars you take home with you is explained in these instructions.

You will participate in the market for two consecutive periods at a time. Let us call the first of these periods your entry period (because you begin your participation then) and the second of these periods your exit period (because that is when you end your participation in the market). Different individuals may have different entry and exit periods and your computer will inform you about when you will enter and exit the market. You may be asked to enter and exit more than once depending on the number of periods for which the market is operated.

When you enter the market, you will see a flashing square in the middle of your screen in either orange or yellow color. The color of the square alternates between orange and yellow.

The first part of your dollar earnings from the game are determined on the basis of the color of these squares will always be zero.

The second part of your dollar earnings from the game are determined on the basis of your sale and purchase of chips. At the beginning of your entry period, you will be given a prespecified number (w_1) of chips. You may keep these chips or sell some of the chips to others in exchange for francs. You cannot buy chips in this period. The number of chips you sell in your entry period depends on the number of chips you offer to sell at various prices, and on the prevailing market price of chips during that period (we come back to this point below). The number of chips you "consume" at the end of the entry (c_1) period will be w_1 minus the number you sell. The francs you receive from selling any of your chips will be carried over into the following period which is your exit period.

In your exit period, you will be given no chips. You can use the francs carried over from your entry period to buy chips from others. The number of chips you buy in your exit period is determined by the prevailing market price of chips in that period and the number of francs that you obtained by selling chips in the preceding entry period. Francs have no use for you after you exit; they cannot be traded outside the market or saved for some future use. Your computer has been programmed to automatically use up all your francs to purchase as many chips as possible at the market price. You cannot sell chips in your exit period. Thus the number of chips you "consume" in your exit period (c_2) is the number of chips your francs will buy.

The number of points you earn at the end of your exit period is determined by the following formula:

$$\text{Earnings} = \text{maximum} \{0, 4 + ((8c_1/w_1)^{0.5} - 0.5 \times (w_1/2c_2)^2)\}$$

where

w_1 = the number of chips you are given in entry period, i.e., 10,
c_1 = the number of chips you "consume" (w_1—what you sell) in your entry period, and
c_2 = the number of chips you "consume" (what you buy) in your exit period.

Your computer will calculate this dollar amount and inform you about it at the end of each period. Thus, suppose you are given 7 chips in the entry period and 1 in the exit period. If you end up selling 3 units at the prevailing market price of 10 francs per chip, then you will finish the entry period with a balance of 30 francs (because you had no francs when you entered the market) and "consume" the remaining $7 - 3 = 4$ chips. Suppose the market price in the following period (which is your exit period) is 8.75 francs per chip, then by (automatically) using all your francs you will purchase and "consume" $30/8.75 = 3.43$ chips during this period. Your dollar earnings for these two periods will be given by the above formula as:

$$\text{Maximum } \{0,\ 4 + ((8 \times 4/10)^{0.5} - 0.5 \times (10/2/3.43)^2)\} = 4.7$$

Note that the earnings formula makes sure that your earnings will not be negative. All chips are forfeited at the end of each period. Exhibit 1 shows various combinations of chip consumptions needed to earn a given dollar amount.

The first period of the market will be an entry period for some of you (as described above). For some of you, however, this first period itself will be an exit period and you will receive the exit period endowment of 0 chip at the beginning of this period. In addition, each of you for whom the first period is an exit period will be given 25 francs at the beginning of this period. In this case you will not be asked to do anything (since your computer will automatically use all your francs to purchase chips). If, for example, the price of a chip in this first period is 15 francs per chip, then you will purchase and consume (25/15) chips. Your dollar earnings for this period will be determined by the following formula:

$$\text{Maximum } \{0,\ (8c_2/w_1)^{0.5}\}.$$

In every period, the market price is determined by the "willingness" of entry participants to sell, the number of francs in the hands of the exit participants (their ability to buy). The central computer calculates this price and displays it on your screen.

The third source of your dollar earnings is a prediction game. If a given period is not your entry or your exit period, then you are "outside" the market in that period. At the beginning of each period, each of these outside participants is asked to predict the market price for that period and the following period. Each period a $1.00 prize is given to the participant whose prediction of the current period price is the closest to the actual market price. If there is a tie, the prize is split equally among the winners.

All players are required to enter two price predictions at the beginning of every period on the price-prediction sheet provided to you. The first prediction is for the current period and the next prediction is for the immediately following period. Note that you will therefore record separate price predictions for, say, period 14 at the beginning of period 13 as well as at the beginning of period 14.

At any point through the session, after the outside participants have entered their price forecasts, the experimenter may announce that the period just concluded was the last period of the current experiment. In this case, the francs being held by the exit participants are transformed into chips using the "average predicted price" provided by the outside participants. Note, however, that more than one experiment might be conducted within a single session and that an experiment might be continued into another session, possibly with a different group of subjects.

Let us now review the specific rules:

(1) All entry-period players are sellers and all exit-period players are buyers.
(2) Computers are programmed so all franc holdings of every exit-period player will be used up to buy chips from the entry-period players at the market price of chips for the period.

(3) On the basis of the price prediction you have provided for the next period ($t + 1$), the computer figures out what is the the the number of chips you should sell at various prices in order to maximize your points. It does the same for all entry players, and figures out the number of chips all entry players would like to sell at various prices.

(4) After considering the amount of francs in the hands of the exit-period players and the number of chips entry-period players would like to sell, the computer calculates and informs you about the market clearing price. Exit-period players and the experimenter pay this price for each chip they buy. Each entry-period player will be informed of the number of chips he/she has been able to sell at the market price, and each exit-period player will be told of the number of chips that he/she has been able to buy with his/her francs on hand.

The actual number of chips you sell will almost always be in fractions, depending on the market-clearing price. The way the market-clearing mechanism works, if you are willing to sell, say two units at unit price x and 3 units at unit price y, you may end up selling, say 2.4 units at a price between x and y.

(5) After the transaction information is determined, the computer determines the chips remaining on hand and the francs received from sale of chips for each entry-player. These numbers can be viewed on F1 screen (see screen design sheets). The francs received by the entry-period players in the entry period will be used to buy chips in the exit period which follows immediately.

(6) The computer determines the number of chips purchased by each exit-player and the number of dollars earned by each of these players after considering the chips held at the end of entry and exit periods according to the formula given earlier. This amount, and your cumulative profit for the experiment is shown in the left middle window on your screen. If you wish to keep a profit record of your own, you may write it down on your Profit Record Sheet.

(7) At the beginning of each period, all players are prompted by the computer for a market price prediction for the current as well as the following period. At the end of each period, the computer informs you about the average predicted market price for the current period and the winner(s) – the outside players whose prediction of the current period price was the closest to the actual market price. This player receives a $1.00 prize that shows on his computer screen. When there is more than one winner, the prize is split equally among them. In addition, *all* players will be asked to record their price prediction for the current and the following period at the beginning of each period on a prediction sheet.

(8) At the end of the experiment, francs held by all entry-period players are converted into chips using the average of predicted current period market prices by outside-market players.

(9) At the end of the experiment, the computer screen shows your cumulative profit. This should match with your own profit record if you have kept one. This is the number of points you have earned from the game.

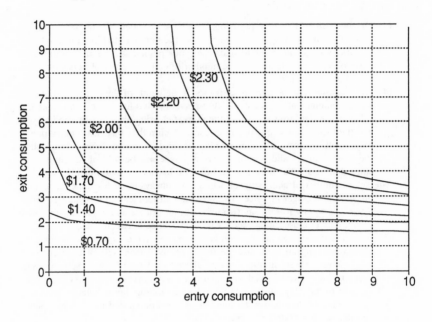

Daniel Friedman

Instructions for evolutionary games experiments

I. General

You are about to participate in an experiment in the economics of group decision making. The funding for this project has been provided by the National Science Foundation. If you follow these instructions carefully and make good decisions, you can earn a considerable amount of money which will be paid to you in cash at the end of the experiment.

The experiment will consist of between 30 and 200 periods of strategic interaction among a group of 6–24 players. As one of the players, you will choose an action each period and enter your choice at your computer terminal. As explained below, your payoff (or earnings) in each period will be determined by your choice and by the choices of the other players. Your goal in this experiment is to earn as much money as you can.

Remember that the information on your screen is private. To ensure the best results for yourself and complete data for the experimenters, please do not talk with your fellow players while the experiment is in progress and please do not discuss your information with others at any point during the experiment.

II. Specific instructions

After you log onto your terminal, the right-hand side of your computer screen will display a "payoff matrix" which defines how your earnings in each period depend on your choices and the choices of other players. In each period you will view the current payoff function and your payoffs from previous periods. You will choose an action from a menu of two or more possible actions. The payoff matrix will often remain the same from one period to the next, but sometimes it will change, so remember to look carefully at the payoff matrix each period before you choose an action.

Other players may have the same payoff matrix as you, or they may have different payoff matrices. The conductor may make a public announcement about how many different payoff matrices are being used in the same period.

The effect of other players' choices on your payoff is determined either by mean matching or by random matching. In each period your computer screen will tell you which matching method applies.

Unpublished normal-form game instructions.
UCSC Economics Department, December 1992.

round	Total (A,B,C)	Your Choice	Payoff
1	(5,7,#)	A	3.8
2	(4,8,#)	A	4.7
3	(3,9,#)	A	5.5
4	(7,5,#)	B	1.7
5	(6,6,#)	A	3.0

Overall % of (A,B,C): (41,58, #)

Your total earnings: − 2.00

Please choose "a" or "b":

# of As	A payoff	B payoff
0	N/A	4.0
1	7.2	3.7
2	6.3	3.3
3	5.5	3.0
4	4.7	2.7
5	3.8	2.3
6	3.0	2.0
7	2.2	1.7
8	1.3	1.3
9	0.5	1.0
10	− 0.3	0.7
11	− 1.2	0.3
12	− 2.0	N/A

Figure 1: Mean Matching Screen

A. Mean matching

Figure 1 is an example of what your computer screen will look like under mean matching. At the bottom left-hand side of the screen, you will see a request for you to choose either action "A" or "B." There is no time limit for you to make your decision. Now look at the payoff box on the right-hand side of the screen. The first column, # of A's, refers to the number of players (including yourself) that choose A in the current period. The middle column, A payoff, gives the amount that you will receive if you have chosen "A," given the number of players who have chosen "A." The last column, B payoff, gives the amount that you will receive if you have chosen "B," again given the number of players who have chosen "A." In the payoff matrix in Figure 1, for example, if 3 players have chosen "A" and you are among them, then you would receive a payoff of 5.5 cents. If, however, you had chosen "B" when other players had chosen "A," then you would receive a payoff of 3.0 cents.

In each period the column you choose (A or B) is highlighted. The central computer will count the number of players choosing A. When all players have chosen, the appropriate row is also highlighted and your payoff (at the highlight intersection) is then displayed in the "history" box in the upper left of your screen.

B. Random matching

Figure 2 is an example of what your computer screen will look like during a random matching period. As in a mean matching period, you will be asked to choose either "A" or "B" and there will be no time limit. Please look at the payoff matrix at the right side of the sample screen. Notice that the rows are labeled "You" and the columns are labeled "Other Player." You will choose either row "A" or "B" and then you will be randomly matched against another player to determine your payoff. For example, if you choose "A" and the other player chooses "B" you will receive a payoff of 8.0 cents (and the other player will receive a payoff of 0.0 if he or she has the same payoff matrix).

In each period, the row you choose (A or B) is highlighted in the payoff box. When all players have chosen, the central computer will randomly match you with another player,

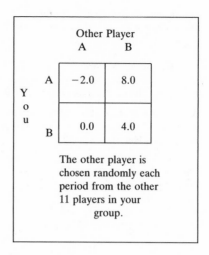

Overall % of (A,B,C): (41,58, #)		
	Total	Your	
round	(A,B,C)	Choice	Payoff
1	(5,7,#)	A	8.0
2	(4,8,#)	A	8.0
3	(3,9,#)	A	−2.0
4	(7,5,#)	B	0.0
5	(6,6,#)	A	8.0

Your total earnings: 22.00

Please choose "a" or "b":

The other player is chosen randomly each period from the other 11 players in your group.

Figure 2: Random Matching Screen

compute the payoffs, and highlight the appropriate column on your screen. The payoff you receive that period (at the highlight intersection) is then displayed in the history box in the upper left of your screen.

Each period a new matching is chosen randomly, so you can expect to interact with a different player every period.

C. Split groups and opposing groups

Your conductor may announce at the beginning of the experiment that the groups will be split or opposing. During split groups, the players will be divided into two or more groups and you will be matched (mean or random) only with the members of your group. During opposing groups, the players will be divided into two or more groups and you will be matched only with the members of a group that you are not a part of.

D. History

At the upper left-hand side of your screen is the "history" area. Data from previous periods are displayed here in order to assist you in your decision making. The first column lists the period number. The second column lists the number of players who choose "A" in that period. The third column reminds you of what you chose that period. The fourth column lists the payoff that you received. Whenever your payoff matrix or group assignment is changed, the history box is started over again.

Some experiments involve some periods in which no history is given. The number of players choosing "A", etc, then is listed as "#".

E. Earnings

The computer determines your gross earnings by adding up your payoffs over all periods in the experiment. At the beginning of each experiment, the conductor will announce the percentage of gross earnings that you will actually receive in cash, for example, 20% of gross earnings. After all of the periods have been completed, the conductor will call you up individually to calculate your net earnings. You will sign a receipt and receive your net earnings in cash. Net earnings usually average $15.00 or more, but if your net earnings are below $5.00 then you will receive the minimum cash payment of $5.00.

III. **Before We Begin**

Before we begin, you should check your understanding of how payoffs will be calculated. Please take a moment to complete the following quiz:

A. Mean matching: In the example screen in the instructions, if you choose "B" and 6 other people choose "A," what will your payoff be? _____
What if you had chosen "A"? _____

B. Random matching: If you choose "B" and are randomly matched against someone who has chosen "A," what will your payoff be? _____
What if you had chosen "A"? _____

APPENDIX III: FORMS

We have used the forms reproduced below in our own recent experiments. You may find it useful to adapt them for your own purposes.

1. Checklist for experimental session

Experiment number: _____

Experimenter: _____

Date: _____

    Announcements
    Sign-up sheets
    Consent forms
    Instructions
    Trial example
    List of file contents
    Trial profit record sheet
    Profit record sheet
    Comment sheet
    IOU forms
    Receipt forms
    File folders
    List of subjects
    Cash/checkbook
    Backup diskettes
    Pencils
    Calculators
    Research assistant
    Lab reservation
    Overhead projector and transparency blanks
    Still or video camera

2. Recruitment announcement

To: CMU Students

From: Steve Spear and Shyam Sunder (Room 215 GSIA, x2103, ss8a)

We shall conduct a series of economics research experiments in February and March, 1990. Some experiments will last for one 3-hour session while the others will last for two 3-hour sessions. During the experiment, you will be asked to play a game in which you will buy and sell things. I shall give you the money and things and provide you the instructions on how to play the game. The amount of money you earn will be determined by the rules of the game and your and other players' actions. Last time we played the game, each of the participants earned amounts varying from $10 to $41 for the single 3-hour sessions, and $48 to $75 for the two-session experiments. You can expect to earn similar amounts. However, since the money you earn depends on your and others' actions, we cannot guarantee you an amount. The money you earn will be paid to you in cash at the end of your participation in the experiment. (If you have signed up for a two-session experiment, the money will be paid to you at the end of your participation in the second session.)

All experiments will take place in Trailer D behind the CFA and GSIA building. If you sign up for an experiment, you must come *on time*. If you are late, you may not be able to participate in the experiment.

Experiment 2 (two 3-hour sessions)

Tuesday and Thursday (February 27 and March 1)   *6:00–9:00 PM*

1._____ Phone: Day_____ Eve._____

2._____ Phone: Day_____ Eve._____

3._____ Phone: Day_____ Eve._____

4._____ Phone: Day_____ Eve._____

5._____ Phone: Day_____ Eve._____

Call Mary Vaccaro at x3344 or Carla Smith at x2138 for signing up or questions.

3. Slips for recruited participants

Experiment 2 (two, three hour sessions)

Tuesday and Thursday (February 27 and March 1)   *6:00–9:00 PM*
Room 146, GSIA

It is important that you come on time to receive the $3 on-time bonus. If you are late, you may not be able to participate in the experiment.

Call Shyam Sunder (x2103, or 422-3135) or Rishore Kao (x8854), or Mary Vaccaro (x3344) in case of emergency.

4. Subject consent form

I have volunteered to participate in this experiment.
I understand that the experiment requires my presence at the following time and date(s):

_____

I have the right to withdraw from the experiment at any time, and forfeit any payments
    I may have earned from my participation.
I understand that the reports of this experiment will not identify me.
I understand that my participation in the experiment will not affect my academic standing
    at the University.
I understand that I can ask for a copy of this consent form and keep it.

Signed_____ Date_____

Name_____ Phone_____

5. Comment sheet

Experiment _____ Date _____

Name (optional) _____ Subject No. (optional) _____
    Please write down on this sheet any comments you may have about this experiment
and your participation in it.

6. Cash payment receipt

Received from _____ $_____ in cash
as payment for participation in research experiment.

Signed_____ Date_____

Name _____ Subject No. from Screen_____

Address_____

_____

Phone_____ Social Security No._____

Name of the Experiment_____

_____ Please call me again to participate in other experiments.

_____ I do not wish to participate in future experiments.

7. I-owe-you form for deferred payment in multisession experiments

I, _____, have earned $_____ for my participation
in research experiment on _____. I shall attend the second session
of the experiment to be held at _____ on _____ in
Room _____ of _____. I shall receive the total amount I earn for both
sessions at the end of the second session. I shall return this IOU at that time.

Signed_____ Date_____

Name_____

Experimenter's signature_____

_____

Received $_____

Signed_____ Date_____

APPENDIX IV: *ECONOMETRICA* GUIDELINES FOR EXPERIMENTAL ARTICLES

Given the growth of interest and activity in experimental economics and the considerable increase in the number of submissions, some reflection on submission guidelines may be in order.

Unlike most other manuscripts received, detailed information about experimental procedures is relevant to the decision of whether or not to publish an experimental manuscript. Such information is also very valuable to scholars who subsequently work on related research. Therefore, the author(s) should include with their submitted manuscript an appendix which adequately explains the details of the experimental procedures. For example, a copy of the instructions that were handed out or read aloud to the subjects should be included. Other materials, such as sample subject record sheets, are also often helpful for the referee. If experiments are conducted through a computer network, this may be more difficult to do, since instructions are sometimes given by a sequence of computer screens and "tests." If instructions were presented by computer, then a summary of the computer-aided learning algorithm, and, if possible, hard copies of the computer screens, should be included. If there are too many screens, this may not be practical. In some cases, a reasonable substitute might be for the author(s) to submit a detailed written description of the instructional procedures for the computer-conducted experiments. (Authors are not required to provide software to other researchers, but this is encouraged.) Enough information should be provided to permit valid replication.

The main body of the manuscript should contain a section on experimental procedures. This section should explain important procedural aspects of the experiments, including:

1. The subject pool and any special recruiting procedures.
2. The experimental technology (e.g., manual or computer, or which computer network).
3. Any procedures to test for comprehension before running the experiment.
4. Matching procedures (particularly in game-theory experiments).
5. Subject payments {use of artificial currency, average earnings, lotteries, grades, etc.).

Reprinted from Thomas Palfrey and Robert Porter, "Guidelines for Submission of Manuscripts on Experimental Economics," *Econometrica* 59(4) (July): 1991 1197–8.

6. Number of subjects used in a session.
7. Any use of experienced subjects.
8. Any use of practice trials.
9. Timing (how long a typical experimental session lasted, and how much of that time was instructional).
10. Where and when the experiments were conducted.
11. Any use of intentional deception, or presence of instructional inaccuracies.

When a manuscript has been accepted for publication, the lengthy appendix should be replaced by an appendix of no more than three "small font" (i.e., as in *Econometrica* appendixes) pages. This is probably on the order of 6 to 8 double-spaced typed pages. If instructions are essentially the same as those published elsewhere, then it is only necessary to briefly note the differences and cite that other article.

A footnote should appear in the procedures section to the effect that a full set of the procedures is available from the author(s) upon request (unless a full set of the procedures is already in the appendix). A full set of the procedures is taken to mean the appendix that was included in the manuscript at the time it was accepted. The relevant criterion is that enough detail be provided to enable another researcher to replicate the results in a manner that the original author(s) would accept as being valid.

The paper should also contain a footnote to the effect that a complete set of the data will be made available to anyone upon request. An additional appendix containing the data should be made available to the referees, particularly if the data set is not large. Exceptions can be requested. The data appendix should be sufficiently detailed to permit computation of the statistics, figures, and tables reported in the paper. In some cases, there may be compelling reasons for actually publishing the data directly in the article as an appendix. This is currently, and will remain, an editorial decision to be made on a case-by-case basis.

APPENDIX V: LIST OF EXPERIMENTAL ECONOMICS LABORATORIES

In this appendix we have assembled a partial list of universities where faculty have conducted experimental research in economics in recent years. We have provided a few names of researchers for each institution. Shawn LaMaster, Graham Loomes, and Martin Weber assisted us in compiling this list, though we alone are responsible for errors and omissions.

Academic Sinica, Taipei
Sheila Lin

University of Alberta
Karim Jamal

University of Amsterdam
Mark Olson

University of Arizona
James Cox
Elizabeth Hoffman
Mark Isaac
Shawn LaMaster
Ron Oaxaca
Stephen J. Rassenti
Stanley Reynolds
Jeff Schatzberg
Vernon L. Smith

University of Bielefeld
Wulf Albers

Rheinische Friedrich-Wilhelms-
Universität Bonn
Reinhard Selten

California Institute of Technology
David Grether
John Ledyard
Richard McKelvey
Peter Ordeshook
Thomas Palfrey
Charles R. Plott
Louis Wilde

University of California, Santa Cruz
Daniel Friedman

Carnegie-Mellon University
George Loewenstein
John Miller
John O'Brien
Howard Rosenthal
Stephen Spear
Sanjay Srivastava
Shyam Sunder

University of Chicago
Colin Camerer

University of Cincinnati
Brian D. Kluger
Steven Wyatt

University of Cologne
Friedel Bolle

University of Colorado
Jamie Brown Kruse
Gary McClleland
William Schultze

Concordia University
Greg Lypny

Drexel University
David Harless

University of East Anglia
Judith Mehta
Chris Starmer
Robert Sugden

Eastern Illinois University
Timothy I. Mason

European University Institute
(Florence)
Alan Kirman
Aurora Garcia

Florida State University
James S. Ang
Thomas Schwartz

University of Frankfurt
Werner Güth
Reinhard Tietz
Ockenfels Wendels

University of Giessen
Jan Krahnen

Université des Sciences Sociales de
Grenoble
Michel Hollard
Bernard Ruffieux

University of Helsinki
Raimo P. Hämäläinen

University of Houston
Dan Levin

University of Ibadan, Nigeria
Mufutau I. Raheem

University of Idaho
Raymond Dacey

University of Illinois
J. Keith Murningham
Anne P. Villamil

Indian Statistical Institute, Delhi
Dilip Mookherjee

Indiana University at Bloomington
Mark Bagnoli
Sheryl Ball
Roy Gardener
James Walker
Arlington Williams

University of Iowa
Douglas DeJong
Robert Forsythe
Forrest Nelson

University of Kentucky
James Marsden

University of Kiel
Martin Weber

University of Maryland
Joe Oppenheimer

McMaster University
Stuart Mestleman

University of Madrid
Isabel Sanchez

University of Manitoba
David Senkow

Memphis State University
Douglas Dyer

University of Michigan
Kenneth Binmore
Russell Lundholm

Michigan State University
Matthew J. Anderson

University of Minnesota
John Dickhaut
Kevin McCabe
Antonio Merlo

University of Mississippi
Robert Dorsey
Mark Van Boening

Mississippi State University
Dorla Evans

National Chung-Cheng University
Yu-Jane Liu

National Taiwan University
Rong-Ruey Duh

University of New Castle
Daniel Siedman

University of New Mexico
Shaul Ben-David
Michael McKee

New York University
Roy Radner
Andrew Schotter

Northwestern University
Paula Ann Cech
Thomas A. Rietz

Universität Erlangen-Nürnberg
Wolfgang Gerke

Odense University
Forrest Nelson

Ohio State University
David E. Wallin

University of Oslo
Bern Stigum

Oxford University
Michael Bacharach

University of Paris
Jean-Yves Jaffray
Bertrand Munier

University of Pennsylvania
Howard Kunreuther
Keith Weigelt

University of Pittsburgh
John Kagel
Jack Ochs
Alvin Roth

Universität Pompeu Fabra
Antoni Bosch
Ramon Marimon
Jeffrey Prisbrey

Rice University
Rick K. Wilson

University of Rome
Maria Theresa Fiocca
Daniella DeCagno

Rutgers University
Barry Sopher

University of Saarland,
Axel Ostmann

Seoul City University
Suk Sig Lim

University of South Carolina
Glenn Harrison

University of South Florida
Carl A. Kogut

University of Southern California
Timothy Cason
Charles Swenson

Southern Methodist University
Barbara Reagen

Stanford University
Russ Lundholm

University of Stockholm
Peter Bohm
Hans Lind

University of Texas at Austin
Steven Kachelmeier

Texas A&M University
Raymond Battalio
John Van Huyck

University of Turin
Guido Ortono

University of Virginia
Charles Holt

Virginia Commonwealth University
Douglas Davis

Virginia Polytechnic University
John Brozovsky

Washington University
Richard Boylan
Don Coursey
Nicholas Dopuch
Ron King

University of Waterloo
Andrew Muller

University of Western Illinois
Paul Nelson

University of Wisconsin
James Andreoni
John Rust

University of Wyoming
Charles F. Mason

University of York
John Hey
Graham Loomes

GLOSSARY

ABA. See *Experiment, design.*

Alternating offers. See *Bargaining.*

Auction, basic. An economic institution in which a single seller offers a single indivisible object to two or more potential buyers, who send messages (bids) indicating willingness to pay for the object. (Some versions of the auction allow several objects or divisible objects, and some versions interchange the role of seller and buyers.)

Oral auctions require public and adjustable bids (for example, in an *English auction* buyers submit successively higher public bids until no one is willing to go higher; the good is sold to the highest bidder).

Sealed auctions require private, committed bids. The highest bidder acquires the object and pays the seller his own bid price in a *first price (1P)* auction, and pays the second highest bid price in a *second price (2P)* or *Vickrey* auction.

The *first-price* auction has two multiunit generalizations – *discriminatory auction* in which the bidders who bid the highest prices pay their bid, and *uniform-price auction* in which all successful bidders pay the lowest accepted bid. In the U.S. investment community, the *uniform-price* sealed-bid auction is often referred to as *Dutch* auction. Terminology is confusing because of a more frequent use of the term as follows:

In a *Dutch auction* the price at which an item is offered for sale starts from a high level, and declines steadily (as indicated by a price clock) until one of the buyers stops the clock and buys the good at that price. This auction is often used in Holland for sale of flowers.

Double Dutch auction, a laboratory generalization of Dutch auction in which two price clocks are used alternately until they converge to a single price. The buyer clock starts high and moves down until a buyer stops it, promising to buy one unit of the good at this price or better, and kicking off the seller clock that starts low. The seller clock moves up until a seller stops it, promising to sell one unit at this price or better, kicking off the buyer clock again. This sequence is repeated until the two clocks meet and the transactions are completed at that single uniform price.

A *single-sided auction* is an oral or computer auction in which only one side (either buyers or sellers) are allowed to announce proposals (bids for buyers and offers for sellers). Traders on the other side can only accept (or not accept) the proposals. In a *double auction* all participants (buyers as well as sellers) may announce a proposal (bid or offer), or accept a valid counterparty proposal at any time; usually combined with *improvement*

211

rule (every new bid must be higher than the current best bid and every new offer must be lower than the current best offer.)

Bargaining, basic. An economic institution that involves two people and a fixed sum of money (the "pie" or prize) to be divided between them. In *alternating offers* bargaining, one person suggests a division of the pie, the second person either accepts (in which case the suggestion is implemented and the game ends) or else rejects and makes a counteroffer to the first person, who then either accepts (ending the game) or makes a counteroffer to the second person, etc. In a *shrinking pie* environment, the size of the pie decreases after each rejected offer in some specified (possibly stochastic) manner.

Block. See *Experiment*.

Common information/common knowledge. Theorists, especially game theorists, say that something is common knowledge if each agent in the model knows it, knows that others know it, knows that everyone knows that others know it, etc. Experimentalists say that something is common information if it is publicly announced to all subjects. (If subjects reason the same way as theorists' agents, then common information is a sufficient condition for common knowledge.)

Crossover. See *Experiment, design*.

Demand effect. The tendency of human subjects in laboratory to behave in accord with the subjects' beliefs about the experimenter's expectations of them.

Dual trial. See *Experiment, design*.

Economic institution. Specifies the set of permissible actions (or messages) for each type of agent (or role), and the outcomes (including information flows) resulting from each combination of permissible actions by all agents. For important examples of economic institutions, see *auction, bargaining, environment, markets*.

Environment. All circumstances relevant to agents' decisions, including the economic institution, the resource and information endowments, the number and type of interacting agents, etc. Often the word is used to refer to circumstances other than the economic institution. For example, in a *private values* environment, some parameters of each agent's payoff function are known by the agent but are not known (except probabilistically) by other agents.

Efficiency. Total profits of all participants as a fraction of the maximum possible total profit of all participants in a market.

Experiment. A set of observations gathered in a controlled environment. Ideally, all variables that significantly affect the observations are controlled either directly (as constants or as treatments) or indirectly through appropriate *randomization* procedures that ensure independence from the focus variables. In a *quasiexperiment* some important variables are controlled but others are not.

An *experimental design* specifies how variables are controlled within and across a block of trials. In a *crossover* design, a treatment variable is controlled at two or more levels in a set of consecutive trials. The most common example is the ABA design, in which a variable is controlled at one level (A) in the first block, then at a second level (B) in the second block, and returned to the original level (A) in the third and last block. A *within-subjects* design exposes subjects to two or more values of a treatment variable, while a *between-subjects* design exposes each subject to a single value but exposes different subjects to different values.

A *trial* is an indivisible unit of observation in an experiment. A *session* is a group of trials conducted on the same day, usually with the same set of subjects. A *block* is a group of trials within which one or more treatment variables are held constant, but across which the controlled values are different. In economic experiments, a *period* is a self-contained unit of time for observation, e.g., a single auction or a single round of market trading.

Factorial. See *Experiment, design.*

Human subjects committee. University committee, usually consisting of faculty, in charge of approving conduct of research experiments that require participation of human subjects. Most universities and government funding agencies in the United States require approval of research proposals by human subjects committees.

Improvement rule. A requirement that every valid bid has to be higher than the best bid on the floor, and every offer must be lower than the offer on the floor.

Induced-value theory. Principles for establishing control of preferences and technology in a laboratory economy.

Dominance is the property that the reward is the only significant motivation for each subject and is determinant of his or her actions.

Monotonicity is the property of laboratory rewards given to subjects that makes more of the reward always preferable to the subject.

Parallelism is the extent of similarities between laboratory and field environments that permit generalizing laboratory findings to field environments.

Privacy is the practice of keeping each subject's endowments and rewards (and the experimenter's goals) as private information not available to other subjects.

Saliency is the property of laboratory rewards given to subjects that makes the rewards a known function of experimental actions and events.

Inducing risk attitudes. A laboratory technique of inducing a chosen risk attitude in subjects with respect to experimental points; the probability of the subject winning a binary money lottery is made a chosen function of the number of points earned by the subject during the experiment.

Markets. *Economic institutions* whose final allocations (of money and a single other traded good) differ from initial allocations by one or more bilateral trades. A *bilateral trade* is an allocation change for two agents such that money holdings increase and good holdings decrease for one agent (the buyer), have the opposite signs for the other agent (the seller), and the sums of the allocation changes (− *transactions costs*) are nonpositive for money and for the traded good.

In an *asset market,* agents who hold units of the traded good (the asset) receive one or more cash flows per unit (dividends). Dividends are uncertain (e.g., they depend on a state revealed at the end of the trading period) and/or intertemporal (e.g., specified dividends at the end of two or more subperiods in each trading period). Dividends usually are independent of the allocation, and traders usually are two-way, i.e., they can both buy and sell the asset.

By contrast, in a *perishables market,* the traded good provides only a single cash flow at the end of the trading period, traders are usually specialized as buyers or as sellers, and the cash flow (redemption value for buyers and cost for sellers) often depends on the allocation, e.g., increasing costs for sellers.

In a *call market* buyers submit bids (i.e., limit price buy orders) which are aggregated into a demand curve, sellers submit asks (i.e, sell orders) which are aggregated into a supply curve, and a market-clearing price p is found. All bids above p and all asks below p are filled at price p. A rationing rule sometimes is needed for bids or for asks submitted exactly at the clearing price p.

In a *posted-offer* market one side of the market (e.g., sellers) is active, the other passive (e.g., buyers). Traders on the active side simultaneously announce prices at which they are committed to transact during the trading period. Then traders on the passive side choose their transaction quantities with each active side trader, subject perhaps to some rationing rule. In the laboratory, the passive side often is automated, i.e., represented by a computer program rather than by human subjects.

Period. See *Experiment.*

Session. See *Experiment.*

Survey. Gathering data from a group of people regarding their opinions, preferences, and circumstances. No salient economic incentives are used in a survey.

Test-bedding. Subjecting a new economic institution to a battery of tests under controlled laboratory conditions before taking it to the field.

Trial. See *Experiment.*

Validity. A conclusion drawn from experimental data has *internal validity* when new data from similar experiments reliably supports it, i.e., when it holds up under *replication.* A conclusion has *external validity* when data drawn from another source or sources, (e.g., field observation or different laboratory environments), reliably supports it.

Variable. Any aspect of an economic environment that can vary within or across sessions. A variable is *controllable* if the experimenter can fix it at one or more chosen values A variable controlled at a single value throughout an experiment is a *constant,* and one controlled at two or more different values is a *treatment* variable. Variables whose values are not chosen by the experimenter are *uncontrolled* and they are *unobserved* if the experimenter does not know their values. A *focus variable* is a variable whose effects are of primary interest to the experimenter; other variables whose effects may be significant are called *nuisance variables.* Two or more variables are *confounded* if you are not able to attribute the observed effects to specific variables and to specific interactions among the variables. It can be harmless or even desirable to confound nuisances (see discussion of fractional factorial designs in Section 3.4). A major goal of experimental design is to avoid confounding focus variables and their interactions with other variables.

Vickrey auction. See *Sealed-bid auction.*

Within/between subjects. See *Experiment, design.*

Zero-intelligence (ZI) trader. A simple computer program that generates random numbers from a specified distribution as its bids or asks.

REFERENCES

Alger, Dan, 1988. "A Policy Context for FERC-Sponsored Laboratory Experiments Concerning Market-Based Regulation of Natural Gas Transportation." Federal Energy Regulatory Commission, Office of Economic Policy Technical Report 88-1. {1.4, 3.6.2}

Alger, Dan, R. O'Neill, and M. Toman. 1987a. "Gas Transportation Rate Design and the Use of Auctions to Allocate Capacity." Federal Energy Regulatory Commission Staff Discussion Paper, July. {1.4, 3.6.2}

1987b. "Making a Market: A New Approach to Gas Pipeline Regulation." Resources for the Future Discussion Paper, EM 87-02, September. {1.4, 3.6.2}

Allais, Maurice. 1953. "Le Comportement de L'homme Rationnel Devant le Risque: Critique des Postulats et Axiomes de L'ecole Americane." *Econometrica* 21 (October): 503–46. {4.2}

Alpert, Bernard. 1967. "Non-Businessmen as Surrogates for Businessmen in Behavioral Experiments." *Journal of Business* 40: 203–7. {4.1.2}

Anderson, Matthew J., and Shyam Sunder. 1989. "Professional Traders as Intuitive Bayesians." Carnegie-Mellon University Working Paper. {4.1.2}

Anderson, Scott, David Johnston, James M. Walker, and Arlington W. Williams. 1989. "The Efficiency of Experimental Asset Markets: Empirical Robustness and Subject Sophistication." Indiana University Working Paper. {8.6}

Ang, James S., and Thomas Schwartz. 1985. "Risk Aversion and Information Structure: An Experimental Study of Price Volatility in the Security Markets." *Journal of Finance* 40: 824–44. {4.2, 4.4.2}

Arrow, Kenneth J. 1971. *Essays in the Theory of Risk Bearing.* Chicago: Markham. {9.2}

Ball, Sheryl B., and Paula-Ann Cech. 1990. "The What, When and Why of Picking a Subject Pool." Boston University and Northwestern University Working Paper. {4.1, 4.1.4}

Becker, G. M., Morris H. DeGroot, and Jacob Marschak. 1964. "Measuring Utility by a Single Response Sequential Method." *Behavioral Science* 9 (July): 226–32. {7.1}

Bellman, Richard, C. E. Clark, D. G. Malcolm, C. J. Craft, and F. M. Ricciardi. 1957.

Note: The numbers in curly braces { } at the end of each citation refer to the sections of the text that use the citation.

215

"On the Construction of a Multistage, Multiperson Business Game." *Journal of the Operations Research Society of America* 5 (August). {9.4}

Belovicz, Meyer W. 1967. "The Sealed Bid Auction: Experimental Studies." Unpublished Ph.D. dissertation, Purdue University. {9.6}

Berg, Joyce E., Lane A. Daley, John W. Dickhaut, and John R. O'Brien. 1986. "Controlling Preferences for Lotteries on Units of Experimental Exchange." *Quarterly Journal of Economics* 101 (May): 281–306. {4.2}

Berg, Joyce, John Dickhaut, and Kevin McCabe. 1992. "Risk Preference Instability across Institutions: A Dilemma." University of Minnesota Working Paper, September. {4.2}

Binmore, Ken, Peter Morgan, Avner Shaked, and John Sutton. 1991. "Do People Exploit Their Bargaining Power? An Experimental Study." *Games and Economic Behavior* 3 (August) 295–322. {4.8}

Binmore, Ken, Avner Shaked, and John Sutton. 1985. "Testing Noncooperative Bargaining Theory: A Preliminary Study." *American Economic Review* 75: 1178–80. {4.8}

Bishop, Jerry E. 1986. " 'All for One ... One for All?' Don't Bet on It," *Wall Street Journal,* December 4. {2.3}

Bohm, Peter. 1984. "Revealing Demand for an Actual Public Good." *Journal of Public Economics* 24: 135–351. {2.4}

Box, George E. P., William G. Hunter, and J. Stuart Hunter. 1978. *Statistics for Experimenters*. New York: John Wiley and Sons. {1.3, 3.3, 3.4, 7, 7.3.1}

Boylan, Richard, and Mahmoud A. El-Gamal. 1992. "Fictitious Play: A Statistical Study of Multiple Economic Experiments." California Institute of Technology Working Paper. {7.3.3}

Brown-Kruse, Jamie, and David Hummels. 1990. "Gender Effects in Public Good Contribution: Some Laboratory Experiments." Unpublished manuscript University of Colorado Economics Department (June).

Burns, Penny. 1985. "Experience and Decision-Making: A Comparison of Students and Businessmen in a Simulated Progressive Auction." In Vernon L. Smith, ed., *Research in Experimental Economics*. Vol 3, pp. 139–57. Greenwich, Conn.: JAI Press. {4.1.2}

Camerer, Colin F. 1993. "Individual Decision Making." In John Kagel and Alvin E. Roth, eds., *Handbook of Experimental Economics*. Princeton, N.J.: Princeton University Press. {4.2, 9.9?}

Camerer, Colin F., and K. Weigelt. 1990. "Bubbles and Convergence in Experimental Markets for Stochastically-Lived Assets." University of Pennsylvania Working Paper. {6.13}

Campbell, D. T., and J. C. Stanley. 1966. *Experimental and Quasi-Experimental Designs for Research*. Chicago: Rand McNally. {3.4}

Chamberlin, Edward H. 1948. "An Experimental Imperfect Market." *Journal of Political Economy* 56 (April): 95–108. {1.4, 2.6}

Coase, Ronald. 1960. "The Problem of Social Cost." *Journal of Law and Economics* 3 (October): 1–44.

Cohen, Judy. 1992. "White Consumer Response to Asian Models in Advertising." *Journal of Consumer Marketing* 9:2 (Spring): 17–27. {1.4}

Cohen, Linda, Michael E. Levine, and Charles R. Plott. 1978. "Communication and Agenda Influence: The Chocolate Pizza Design." In Heinz Sauermann, ed., *Coalition Forming Behavior: Contributions to Experimental Economics*. Vol. 8. Tübingen, Germany: J. C. B. Mohr (Paul Siebeck). {4.5.4}

Committee on the Conduct of Science, 1989. *On Being a Scientist*. National Academy of Sciences. Washington, D.C.: National Academy Press. {8.1}

Conover, William J. 1980. *Practical Nonparametric Statistics.* 2nd ed. New York: John Wiley and Sons. {7, 7.3.3}

Cooper, Russell W., Douglas V. Dejong, Robert Forsythe, and Thomas W. Ross. 1990. "Selection Criteria in Coordination Games: Some Experimental Results." *American Economic Review* 80:1 (March): 218–33. {9.9}

Copeland, Thomas E., and Daniel Friedman. 1987. "The Effect of Sequential Information Arrival on Asset Prices: An Experimental Study." *Journal of Finance* 42 (July): 763–98. {3.4, 8.3, 8.6}

——— 1991. "Partial Revelation of Information in Experimental Asset Markets." *Journal of Finance* 46:1 (March): 265–95. {8.3}

——— 1992. "The Market Value of Information: Some Experimental Results." *Journal of Business* 65:2 (April) 241–66. {8.3}

Coppinger, Vicki, Vernon L. Smith, and John Titus. 1980. "Incentives and Behavior in English, Dutch, and Sealed-Bid Auctions." *Economic Inquiry* 18 (January): 1–22. {7.5}

Cox, James C., and Ronald L. Oaxaca, 1991. "Tests for a Reservation Wage Effect." In J. Geweke, ed., *Decision Making under Risk and Uncertainty: New Models and Empirical Findings.* Boston: Kluwer Academic Publishers. {1.3.1}

Cox, James C., Bruce Roberson, and Vernon L. Smith. 1982. "Theory and Behavior of Single Object Auctions." In Vernon L. Smith, ed., *Research in Experimental Economics.* Vol. 2. Greenwich, Conn. JAI Press. {7.5}

Cox, James C., Vernon L. Smith, and James M. Walker. 1988. "Theory and Individual Behavior of First-Price Auctions." *Journal of Risk and Uncertainty* 1 (March): 61–99. {7.5}

——— 1992. "Theory and Misbehavior of First-Price Auctions: Comment." *American Economic Review* 82:5 (December): 1392–412. {7.5}

Crawford, Vincent P. 1991. "An Evolutionary Interpretation of Van Huyck, Battalio and Beil's Experimental Results on Coordination." *Games and Economic Behavior* 3:25–59. {9.9}

Cummings, Ronald G., Glenn W. Harrison, and E. E. Rutström. 1992. "Homegrown Values and Hypothetical Surveys: Is the Dichotomous Choice Approach Incentive Compatible?" University of New Mexico Working Paper, October. {1.4}

Cunningham, William H., Thomas Anderson, and John H. Murphy, 1974. "Are Students Real People?" *Journal of Business* 47: 399–409. {4.1.1}

Davis, Douglas, and Charles Holt. 1992. *Experimental Economics.* Princeton, N.J. Princeton University Press. {Appendix}

Davis, Douglas D., and Arlington W. Williams. 1991. "The Hayek Hypothesis in Experimental Auctions: Institutional Effects and Market Power." *Economic Inquiry* 29 (April): 261–74. {2.6}

DeJong, Douglas V., Robert Forsythe, and Wilfred C. Uecker. 1988. "A Note on the Use of Businessmen as Subjects in Sealed Offer Markets." *Journal of Economic Behavior and Organizations* 9: 87–100. {4.1.2}

De Long, J. Bradford, and Kevin Lang. 1992. "Are All Economic Hypothesis False?" *Journal of Political Economy* 100:6 (December): 1257–72. {7.3.1}

Dyer, Douglas, John H. Kagel, and Dan Levin. 1987. "Common Value Offer Auctions: Bidding Behavior of Student Subjects and Construction Contractors." University of Pittsburgh Working Paper. {4.1.2}

Ellsberg, Daniel. 1961. "Risk, Ambiguity, and the Savage Axioms." *Quarterly Journal of Economics* 75 (November): 643–69. {4.2}

Enis, Ben E., Keith Cox, and James Stafford, 1972. "Students as Subjects in Consumer Behavior Experiments." *Journal of Marketing Research* 9: 72–4. {4.1.1}

Estes, William K. 1954. "Individual Behavior in Uncertain Situations: An Interpretation in Terms of Statistical Association Theory." In R. M. Thrall, C. H. Coombs, and R. L. Davis, eds., *Decision Processes*. New York: John Wiley and Sons, pp. 127–37. {9.3, 9.8}

Farwell, Loring C. 1963. *The Stock Market*. New York: Ronald Press.

Ferejohn, John, Robert Forsythe, and Roger Noll. 1979. "An Experimental Analysis of Decision Making Procedures for Discrete Public Goods: A Case Study of a Problem in Institutional Design." In Vernon L. Smith, ed., *Research in Experimental Economics*. Vol. 2, pp. 1–58. Greenwich, Conn.: JAI Press. {3.6.2}

Fiorina, Morris P., and Charles R. Plott. 1978. "Committee Decisions under Majority Rule: An Experimental Study." *American Political Science Review* 72 (June): 575–98. {1.4, 6.1.8, 9.6}

Flood, Merrill M. 1954. "Game-Learning Theory and Some Decision-Making Experiments." In R. M. Thrall, C. H. Coombs, and R. L. Davis, eds., *Decision Processes*. New York: John Wiley and Sons, pp. 139–58. {9.8}

Forsythe, Robert, and Russell Lundholm. 1990. "Information Aggregation in an Experimental Market." *Econometrica* 58: 309–47. {8.6}

Forsythe, Robert, Forrest Nelson, George R. Neumann, and Jack Wright. 1992. "Anatomy of an Experimental Political Stock Market." *American Economic Review* 82:5 (December): 1142–61. {1.4}

Forsythe, Robert, Thomas R. Palfrey, and Charles R. Plott. 1982. "Asset Valuations in an Experimental Market." *Econometrica* 50:1 (May): 537–68. {8.6}

Fouraker Lawrence E., Martin Shubik, and Sidney Siegel. 1961. "Oligopoly Bargaining: The Quantity Adjuster Models." Research Bulletin 20, Pennsylvania State University, Department of Psychology. {9.3}

Fouraker, Lawrence E., and Sidney Siegel. 1961. "Bargaining Behavior II." Unpublished paper, Pennsylvania State University, Department of Psychology. {9.3}

1963. *Bargaining Behavior*. New York: McGraw-Hill. {4.8, 9.3}

Fouraker, Lawrence, Sidney Sigel, and Donald Harnett. 1961. "Bargaining Behavior I." Unpublished paper, Pennsylvania State University, Department of Psychology. {9.3}

Friedman, Daniel. 1984. "On the Efficiency of Experimental Double Auction Markets." *American Economic Review* 74 (March): 60–72. {4.3}

1988. "Experimental Methods: Points of Consensus and Points of Contention." University of California at Santa Cruz Working Paper. {Preface}

1992. "Theory and Misbehavior of First-Price Auctions: Comment." *American Economic Review* 82:5, 1374–8. {9.9}

1993. "How Trading Institutions Affect Financial Market Performance: Some Laboratory Evidence." *Economic Inquiry* (forthcoming). {1.4, 3.6.2}

Friedman, Daniel, Glenn W. Harrison, and Jon W. Salmon. 1983. "The Informational Role of Futures Markets and Learning Behavior – Some Experimental Evidence." In M. E. Streit, ed., *Futures Markets – Modelling, Managing and Monitoring Futures Trading*. Oxford: Basil Blackwell. {4.2}

1984. "The Informational Efficiency of Experimental Asset Markets." *Journal of Political Economy* (June): 349–408. {4.2}

Friedman, Daniel, and Joseph Ostroy. 1993. "Competitivity in Auction Markets: An Experimental and Theoretical Investigation." UCLA/UCSC Working Paper, February. {fig. 7.3}

Friedman, James. 1967. "An Experimental Study of Cooperative Duopoly." *Econometrica* 35: 379–97. {9.3}

Friedman, James, and Austin C. Hoggatt. 1980. *An Experiment in Noncooperative Oligopoly.* Series in Research in Experimental Economics, Supplement 1. Greenwich, Conn. T: JAI Press. {9.3}

Friedman, Milton. 1953. "The Methodology of Positive Economics." In M. Friedman, ed., *Essays in Positive Economics.* Chicago: University of Chicago Press. {1.4}

Garman, Mark B. 1976. "Market Microstructure." *Journal of Financial Economics* 3 (June). {1.4}

Gode, Dhananjay K., and Shyam Sunder. 1992. "A Comparative Analysis of Efficiency of Economic Institutions with Zero Intelligence Traders." Carnegie-Mellon University Working Paper. {2.6}

1993a. "Lower Bounds for Efficiency of Surplus Extraction in Double Auctions." In D. Friedman and J. Rust, eds., *The Double Auction Market: Institutions, Theories, and Evidence.* Santa Fe Institute Series in the Science of the Complexity, Proceedings. Vol 15. Reading, Mass.: Addison-Wesley. {2.6}

1993b. "Allocative Efficiency of Markets with Zero Intelligence Traders: Markets as a Partial Substitute for Individual Rationality." *Journal of Political Economy* 101 (February): 119–37. {2.6}

Gresik, T., and M. Satterthwaite. 1986. "The Rate at Which a Simple Market Becomes Efficient as the Number of Traders Increases: An Asymptotic Result for Optimal Trading Mechanisms." Northwestern University CMSEMS DPNO.708, October. {4.3}

Grether, David M., R. Mark Isaac, and Charles R. Plott. 1981. "The Allocation of Lending Rights by Unanimity among Competitors." *American Economic Review* 71 (May): 166–71. {3.6, 3.6.2}

Grether, David M., and Charles R. Plott. 1984. "The Effects of Market Practices in Oligopolistic Markets: An Experimental Examination of the Ethyl Case." *Economic Inquiry* 22:4 (October): 479–507. {1.4, 3.6, 3.6.1}

Grossman, Sanford J., and Robert J. Shiller. 1981. The Determinants of the Variability of Stock Market Prices." *American Economic Review* 71 (May): 222–7. {4.2}

Hamermesh, Daniel S. 1992. "The Young Economist's Guide to Professional Etiquette." *Journal of Economic Perspectives* 6:1 (Winter): 169–79. {8.3, 8.5}

Harrison, Glenn W. 1986. "An Experimental Test for Risk Aversion." *Economic Letters* 21:1. 7–11.

1989. "Theory and Misbehavior of First-Price Auctions." *American Economic Review* 79 (September): 749–62. {7.5}

1992. "Theory and Misbehavior of First-Price Auctions: Reply." *American Economic Review* 82:5 (December): 1426–43. {7.5}

Harsanyi, John C. 1967. "Games with Incomplete Information Played by 'Bayesian' Players, Part I." *Management Science* 14 (November): 159–89. {9.9}

1968a. "Games with Incomplete Information Played by 'Bayesian' Players, Part II." *Management Science* 14 (January): 320–34. {9.9}

1968b. "Games with Incomplete Information Played by 'Bayesian' Players, Part III." *Management Science* 14 (March): 486–502. {9.9}

Harsanyi, John C., and Reinhard Selten. 1988. *A General Theory of Equilibrium Selection in Games.* Cambridge, Mass.: MIT Press. {9.9}

Hayek, Friedrich A. 1945. "The Use of Knowledge in Society." *American Economic Review* 35: 519–30. {2.6}

Hey, John D. 1991. *Experiments in Economics.* Cambridge: Blackwell. {Appendix}

Hicks, John R. 1939. *Value and Capital.* Oxford: Oxford University Press. {2.3}

Hoffman, Elizabeth, and Matthew L. Spitzer. 1982. "The Coase Theorem: Some Experimental Tests." *Journal of Law and Economics* 25: 73–98. {4.8}

——— 1985. "Entitlements, Rights, and Fairness: An Experimental Examination of Subjects' Concepts of Distributive Justice." *Journal of Legal Studies* 14:2 (June): 259–97. {4.8}

Hoggatt, Austin C. 1959. "An Experimental Business Game." *Behavioral Science* 4 (July): 192–203. {1.4}

Holt, Charles A., Loren W. Langan, and Anne P. Villamil. 1986. "Market Power in Oral Double Auctions." *Economic Inquiry* 24:1 (January): 107–23. {2.6}

Hong, James T., and Charles R. Plott. 1982. "Rate Filing Policies for Inland Water Transportation: An Experimental Approach." *Bell Journal of Economics* 13 (Spring): 1–19. {1.4, 3.6, 3.6.1}

Hurwicz, L. 1972. "On Informationally Decentralized Systems." In C. B. McGuire and R. Radner, eds., *Decision and Organization,* pp 297–336. Amsterdam: North-Holland. {2}

Isaac, R. Mark, and Vernon L. Smith. 1985. "In Search of Predatory Pricing." *Journal of Political Economy* 93:2 (April): 320–45. {1.4, 2.1}

Isaac, R. Mark, James M. Walker, and Arlington W. Williams. 1992. "Group Size and the Voluntary Provision of Public Goods: Experimental Evidence Utilizing Large Groups." Indiana University Working Paper. {4.3}

Jackson, Douglas. 1976. *Jackson Personality Inventory Manual.* Goshen, N.Y.: Research Psychologists Press. {4.2}

Jackson, Douglas, D. Houdnay, and N. Vidmar. 1972. "A Four-Dimensional Interpretation of Risk Taking." *Journal of Personality* 40: 433–501. {4.2}

Jamal, Karim, and Shyam Sunder, 1991, "Money vs. Gaming: Effects of Salient Monetary Payments in Double Oral Auctions." *Organizational Behavior and Human Decision Processes* 49: 151–66. {2.3, 4.4}

Kachelmeier, Steven J., and Mohamed Shehata. 1992. "Examining Risk Preferences under High Monetary Incentives: Experimental Evidence from People's Republic of China." *American Economic Review* 82 (5): 1120–41. {7.1}

Kagel, John H. 1993. "Auctions." In John Kagel and Alvin Roth, eds, *Handbook of Experimental Economics.* Princeton, N.J.: Princeton University Press. {7.5}

Kagel, John H., and Dan Levin. 1986. "The Winner's Curse and Public Information in Common Value Auctions." *American Economic Review* 76:5 (December): 894–920. {3.4}

Kagel, John H., and Alvin E. Roth. 1992. "Theory and Misbehavior in First-Price Auctions: Comment." *American Economic Review* 82:5 (December): 1379–91. {7.5}

——— 1993. *Handbook of Experimental Economics.* Princeton, N.J.: Princeton University Press. {Appendix}

Kalish, G. K., J. W. Milnor, J. F. Nash, and E. D. Nering. 1954. "Some Experimental *n*-Person Games." In R. M. Thrall, C. H. Coombs, and R. L. Davis, eds., *Decision Processes,* pp. 301–27. New York: John Wiley and Sons. {9.4, 9.9}

Kaufman, H., and G. M. Becker. 1961. "The Empirical Determination of Game-Theoretical Strategies." *Journal of Experimental Psychology* 61: 462–8. {9.9}

Kendall, M. G., and A. Stuart. 1969. *The Advanced Theory of Statistics.* New York: Hafner.

Killingsworth, Mark R. 1983. *Labor Supply,* Cambridge Surveys of Economic Literature, Cambridge: Cambridge University Press. {1.3}

King, Ronald R. 1987. "Noisy Rational Expectations Equilibrium in Experimental Markets." Washington University Working Paper, October. {8.3}

King, Ronald R. Vernon L. Smith, Arlington W. Williams, and M. Van Boening. 1992. "The Robustness of Bubbles and Crashes in Experimental Stock Market." In I. Prigogine, R. Day, and P. Chen, eds., *Nonlinear Dynamics and Evolutionary Economics*. Oxford: Oxford University Press. {4.1.2}

Kirk, R. E. 1982. *Experimental Design: Procedures for the Social Sciences*. 2nd ed. Monterey, Calif.: Brooks/Cole. {3.4, 7, 7.3.3}

Koopmans, T. C. 1957. *Three Essays on the State of Economic Science*. New York: McGraw-Hill. {1.4}

Kormendi, Roger C., and Charles R. Plott. 1982. "Committee Decisions under Alternative Procedural Rules: An Experimental Study Applying a New Nonmonetary Method of Preference Inducement." *Journal of Economic Behavior and Organization* 3: 175–95. {4.1.3}

Kotlikoff, Laurence J., William Samuelson, and Stephen Johnson. 1988. "Consumption, Computation Mistakes, and Fiscal Policy." *American Economic Review* 78:2 (May): 408–12. {2.3}

Kroll, Yoram, Haim Levy, and Amnon Rapoport. 1988. "Experimental Tests of the Separation Theorem and the Capital Asset Pricing Model." *American Economic Review* 78 (June): 500–19.

Kuhn, Thomas. S. 1970. *The Structure of Scientific Revolutions*. 2nd ed. Chicago: University of Chicago Press. {1.2, 9}

Kyle, Albert S. 1989. "Informed Speculation with Imperfect Competition." *Review of Economic Studies* 56:3 (July): 317–55. {4.3}

Lakatos, Imre. 1978. *The Methodology of Scientific Research Programmes*. Vol. 1, J. Worrall and G. Currie, eds.), Cambridge: Cambridge University Press. {1.2,9}

LaLonde, Robert J. 1986. "Evaluating the Econometric Evaluations of Training Programs with Experimental Data." *American Economic Review* 76:4 (September): 604–20. {1.3.1}

Leamer, Edward E. 1978. *Specification Searches: Ad Hoc Inference with Nonexperimental Data*, New York: Wiley. {7.3.3}

——— 1983. "Let's Take the Con out of Econometrics." *American Economic Review* 73 (March): 31–43. {1.3, 8.1}

LeRoy, Stephen, and C. LaCivita. 1981. "Risk Aversion and the Dispersion of Asset Prices." *Journal of Business* 54: 535–47. {4.2}

Lim, Suk Sig, Edward C. Prescott, and Shyam Sunder. 1994. "Stationary Solution to Overlapping Generations Model of Fiat Money: Experimental Evidence." in J.D. Hey, ed. *Empirical Economics* (forthcoming). {5.5.1, 6.1.3}

Lloyd, G. E. R. 1984. "Hellenistic Science." In F. W. Walbeck et al., eds. *The Cambridge Ancient History. Vol. VII, Part 1: The Hellenistic World*, 2nd ed. Cambridge: Cambridge University Press. {9.1}

Lucas, Robert E., Jr. 1986. "Adaptive Behavior and Economic Theory." *Journal of Business* 59:4.2 (October): s401–26. {5.5}

Maccoby, Eleanor E., and Carol N. Jacklin. 1974. *The Psychology of Sex Differences*, Stanford, Calif.: Stanford University Press. {4.1.4}

Marimon, Ramon, Stephen Spear, and Shyam Sunder. 1993. "Expectationally-Driven Market Volatility: Experimental Evidence." *Journal of Economic Theory* 23 (forthcoming). {4.1.3, 5.5.3, 5.5.3.1, 5.5.3.2}

Marimon, Ramon, and Shyam Sunder. 1993. "Expectations and Learning under Alternative Monetary Regimes: An Experimental Approach." *Economic Theory* (forthcoming). {5.5.2, 5.5.3.1}

1993. "Indeterminacy of Equilibria in a Hyperinflationary World: Experimental Evidence." *Econometrica* 61:5 (September): 1073–107. {5.1.1, 5.5.2., 5.5.3.1}.

McAfee, R. Preston, and John McMillan. 1987. "Auctions and Bidding." *Journal of Economic Literature* 25 (June): 699–738. {4.3; 7.5}

McCabe, Kevin A., Stephen J. Rassenti, and Vernon L. Smith. 1988. "An Experimental Examination of Competition and 'Smart' Markets in Natural Gas Pipeline Networks." Federal Energy Regulatory Commission, Office of Economic Policy Technical Report 88-3. {3.6, 3.6.2}

1991. "Smart Computer-Assisted Markets." *Science* 254 (October): 534–38. {1.4, 3.6.2}

1993. "Designing a Uniform Price Double Auction: An Experimental Evaluation." In D. Friedman, and J. Rust, eds., *The Double Auction Market: Theories and Evidence*. Santa Fe Institute Series in the Science of the Complexity, Proceedings Vol. 15. Reading, Mass.: Addison-Wesley. {1.4, 3.6, 3.6.2}

McCloskey, Donald N. 1985. *The Rhetoric of Economics,* Madison: University of Wisconsin Press. {8.3}

1987. *The Writing of Economics.* New York: Macmillan. {8.3}

Merlo, Antonio, and Andrew Schotter. 1992. "Theory and Misbehavior of First-Price Auctions: Comment." *American Economic Review* 82:5 (December): 1413–25. {7.5}

Milgram, Stanley. 1974. *Obedience to Authority: An Experimental View.* New York: Harper & Row. {2.5}

Moriarty, Shane. 1986. *Laboratory Market Research.* Norman: Center for Economic and Management Research, University of Oklahoma. {Appendix}

The New Palgrave: A Dictionary of Economics. 1987 John Eatwell, Murray Milgate, and Peter Newman, eds. New York: Stockton Press. {1.3, 8.4}

O'Brien, John. 1989. "Experimental Stock Markets with Controlled Preferences." Carnegie-Mellon University Working Paper. {4.2}

Palfrey, Thomas R. ed. 1991. *Laboratory Research in Political Economy.* Ann Arbor.: University of Michigan Press.

Palfrey, Thomas, and Robert Porter. 1991. "Guidelines on Submission of Manuscripts on Experimental Economics." *Econometrica* 59:4 (July): 1197–8. {8.6}

Payne, Doug. 1992. "Undecided Voters Unswayed by Debate." *Atlanta Constitution,* October 16, A,7:1. {1.4}

Pencavel, John. 1986. "Labor Supply of Men." In Orley Ashenfelter and Richard Layard, eds. *Handbook of Labor Economics.* Amsterdam: North Holland. {1.3}

Plott, Charles R. 1979. "The Application of Laboratory Experimental Methods to Public Choice." In Clifford S. Russell, ed., *Collective Decision Making: Applications from Public Choice Theory.* Baltimore.: Johns Hopkins Press for Resources for the Future, pp. 137–60. {9.6}

1982. "Industrial Organization Theory and Experimental Economics." *Journal of Economic Literature* 20 (December): 1485–527. {1.4, 2.4, 4.3, 9.7}

1986. "An Introduction to Some Experimental Procedures." Unpublished paper (mimeo), California Institute of Technology, December. {Preface}

1987. "Dimensions of Parallelism: Some Policy Applications of Experimental Methods." In A. E. Roth, ed., *Laboratory Experimentation in Economics: Six Points of View.* Cambridge: Cambridge University Press. {1.4}

1988. "Research on Pricing in a Gas Transportation Network." Federal Energy Regulatory Commission, Office of Economic Policy Technical Report 88-2. {1.4, 3.6.2}

1991. "Will Economics Become an Experimental Science?" *Southern Economic Journal* 57 (April): 901–19. {9.1}

Plott, Charles R., and Michael Levine. 1978. "A Model of Agenda Influence on Committee Decisions," *American Economic Review* 68 (March): 146–60. {9.6}

Plott, Charles R., and David P. Porter. 1989. "An Experiment with Space Station Pricing Policies." California Institute of Technology Working Paper. {3.6, 3.6.2}

Plott, Charles R., and Vernon L. Smith. 1978. "An Experimental Examination of Two Exchange Institutions." *Review of Economic Studies* 45:1 (February): 133–53. {2.6, 9.6}

Plott, Charles R., and Shyam Sunder. 1982. "Efficiency of Experimental Security Markets with Insider Information: An Application of Rational-Expectations Models." *Journal of Political Economy* 90 (August): 663–98. {8.6}

1988. "Rational Expectations and the Aggregation of Diverse Information in Laboratory Security Markets." *Econometrica* 56: 1085–118. {8.6}

Plott, Charles R., and Louis L. Wilde. 1982. "Professional Diagnosis vs. Self-Diagnosis: An Experimental Examination of Some Special Features of Markets with Uncertainty." In Vernon L. Smith, ed., *Research in Experimental Economics*. Vol. 2. Greenwich, Conn.: JAI Press. {8.6}

Porter, David, and Vernon L. Smith. 1990. "The Scope of Bubbles and Crashes in Experimental Asset Markets." University of Arizona Working Paper. {8.6}

Prasnikar, Vesna, and Alvin E. Roth. 1992. "Considerations of Fairness and Strategy: Experimental Data from Sequential Games." *Quarterly Journal of Economics* 107:3 (August) 865–88. {4.8}

Radner, Roy, and Andrew Schotter. 1989. "The Sealed Bid Mechanism: An Experimental Study." *Journal of Economic Theory* 48:1 (June): 179–220. {4.2}

Rappoport, Anatol, and Carol Orwandt. 1962. Experimental Games: A Review." *Behavioral Science* 7: 1–37. {9.9}

Rassenti, Stephen J., S. Reynolds, and Vernon L. Smith. 1988. "Cotenancy and Competition in an Experimental Double Auction Market for Natural Gas Pipeline Networks." *Economic Theory* (forthcoming). {1.4, 7.2.2}

Rhode, Deborah L., ed. 1990. *Theoretical Perspectives on Sexual Differences*. New Haven, Conn.: Yale University Press. {6.1.5}

Rietz, Thomas A. 1990. "Controlling Risk Preferences in Sealed Bid Auctions: Some Experimental Results." Northwestern University Working Paper. {4.2}

Roth, Alvin E. 1987a. "Laboratory Experimentation in Economics." In T. Bewley, ed., *Advances in Economic Theory, Fifth World Congress*. Cambridge: Cambridge University Press, pp. 269–99. {1.4}

1987b. "Bargaining Phenomena and Bargaining Theory." In A. E. Roth, ed. *Laboratory Experimentation in Economics: Six Points of View*, pp. 14–41. Cambridge: Cambridge University Press. {Appendix}

ed. 1987c. *Laboratory Experimentation in Economics: Six Points of View*. Cambridge: Cambridge University Press. {Appendix}

1988. "Laboratory Experimentation in Economics: A Methodological Overview." *Economic Journal* 98 (December): 974–1031. {4.8}

1990. "Lets Keep the Con out of Experimental Economics." University of Pittsburgh Working Paper. {6.2, 8.1}

1993. "Bargaining Experiments." In John Kagel and Alvin E. Roth, eds, *Handbook of Experimental Economics*. Princeton, N.J.: Princeton University Press. {4.8}

Roth, Alvin E., and Michael W. K. Malouf. 1979. "Game-Theoretic Models and the Role of Information in Bargaining." *Psychological Review* 86:6 (November): 574–94. {4.2, 9}

Roth, Alvin E., Vesna Prasnikar, Masahiro Okuno-Fujiwara, and Shmuel Zamir. 1991. "Bargaining and Market Behavior in Jerusalem, Ljubljana, Pittsburgh, and Tokyo: An Experimental Study." *American Economic Review* 81:5 (December): 1068–95. {4.8}

Samuelson, Paul A., and W. D. Nordhaus. 1985. *Principles of Economics.* 12th ed. {1.1}

Satterthwaite, Mark, and Steven Williams. 1993. "The Bayesian Theory of the *k*-Double Auction." In D. Friedman and J. Rust, eds., *The Double Auction Market: Institutions, Theories, and Evidence.* Santa Fe Institute Series in the Science of the Complexity, Proceedings. Vol. 15, Reading, Mass.: Addison-Wesley. {4.3}

Sauermann, Heinz, ed. 1967. *Contributions to Experimental Economics.* Vol. 1. Tübingen, Mohr Germany: J. C. B. (Paul Siebeck). {4.8, 9.4}

1970. *Contributions to Experimental Economics.* Vol. 2. Tübingen: Mohr.

1972. *Contributions to Experimental Economics.* Vol. 3. Tübingen: Mohr.

Sauermann, Heinz, and Reinhard Selten. 1960. "An Experiment in Oligopoly." In L. Bertalanffy and A. Rappoport, eds., *General Systems Yearbook of the Society for General Systems Research.* Vol. 5. Ann Arbor, Mich.: Society for General Systems Research. {9.4}

Savage, Leonard J. 1954. *The Foundations of Statistics,* New York: Wiley. {7.1, 9.2}

Schotter, Andrew, and Yale M. Braunstein. 1981. "Economic Search: An Experimental Study." *Economic Inquiry* 19:1 (January): 1–25.

Selten, Reinhard. 1967. "Invetitionsverhalten im Oligopolexperiment." Heinz Sauermann, ed., *Beitrage zur Experimentellen Wirtschaftsforschung.* Vol. 1. Tübingen, Germany: J. C. B. Mohr (Paul Siebeck), pp. 60–102. {9.4}

Siegel, Sidney. 1959. "Theoretical Models of Choice and Strategy Behavior: Stable State Behavior in the Two-Choice Uncertain Outcome Situation." *Psychometrika* 24: 303–16. {9.3}

Siegel, Sidney, and Lawrence E. Fouraker. 1960. *Bargaining and Group Decision Making–Experiments in Bilateral Monopoly.* New York: McGraw-Hill. {4.8, 9.3}

Siegel, Sidney, and D. L. Harnett. 1964. "Bargaining Behavior: A Comparison between Mature Industrial Personnel and College Students." *Operations Research* 12:334–43. {4.1.2}

Simon, Herbert A. 1955. "A Behavioral Model of Rational Choice." *Quarterly Journal of Economics* 69: 99–118. {9.2}

1956. "A Comparison of Game Theory and Learning Theory." *Psychometrica* 21 (September):267–72. {9.2}

Smith, Vernon L. 1962. "An Experimental Study of Competitive Market Behavior." *Journal of Political Economy* 70:2 (April): 111–37. {2.6, 7.1, 9.5}

1964. "Effect of Market Organization on Competitive Equilibrium." *Quarterly Journal of Economics* 78 (May): 181–201. {9.6}

1967. "Experimental Studies of Discrimination versus Competition in Sealed Bid Auction Markets." *Journal of Business* 40 (January): 56–84. {9.6}

1976. "Experimental Economics: Induced Value Theory." *American Economic Review* 66:2 (May): 274–9. {2, 2.2, 4.4.2, 9.7}

1982a. "Markets as Economizers of Information: Experimental Examination of the Hayek Hypothesis." *Economic Inquiry* 20:2 (April): 165–79. {2.6, 4.3}

1982b. "Microeconomic Systems as an Experimental Science." *American Economic Review* 72 (December): 923–55. {1.4, 2.2.4, 4.4.2, y 9.7}

1987. "Experimental Methods in Economics." In John Eatwell, Murray Milgate and

Peter Newman, eds., *The New Palgrave: A Dictionary of Economics*. Vol 2. New York NY: Stockton Press. {1.3, 8.4}

ed. 1990. *Experimental Economics*. Schools of Thought in Economics, Vol. 7. Aldershot, England: Edward Elgar; and Brookfield, V.: Gower Publishing. {Appendix}

1991. "Game Theory and Experimental Economics: Beginnings and Early Influences." Prepared for Conference on the History of Game Theory, Duke University, October 1990. {9.2}

Smith, Vernon L., Gerry L. Suchanek, and Arlington W. Williams. 1988. "Bubbles, Crashes, and Endogenous Expectations in Experimental Spot Asset Markets." *Econometrica* 55:6, 1119–52. {4.1.2, 8.3, 8.6}

Smith, Vernon L., and James M. Walker 1992. "Rewards, Experience and Decision Costs in First Price Auctions." *Economic Inquiry* (forthcoming). {2.3}

Strunk, William, and E. B. White. 1979. *The Elements of Style*. 3rd ed. New York NY: MacMillan. {8.3}

Sunder, Shyam. 1991. "An Introduction to Design, Planning and Conduct of Asset Market Experiments." Carnegie-Mellon University Working Paper. {Preface}

1992. "Market for Information: Experimental Evidence." *Econometrica* 60:3 (May): 667–95. {Appendix}

1993. "Experimental Asset Markets: A Survey." In John Kagel and Alvin E. Roth, eds., *Handbook of Experimental Economics*. Princeton, N.J.: Princeton University Press. {8.6}

Thrall, R. M., C. H. Coombs, and R. L. Davis, eds. 1954. *Decision Processes*. New York: John Wiley and Sons. {9.2}

Tietz, Reinhard, ed. 1982. *Aspiration Levels in Bargaining and Economic Decision Making*. Berlin: Springer-Verlag. {9.4}

1990. "On Bounded Rationality: Experimental Work and the University of Frankfurt/ Maine." *Journal of Institutional and Theoretical Economics* 146:4 (December). {9.4}

Torry, Saundra, and Mark Stencel. 1992. "Bush, Quayle Put Lawyers in Election-Year Docket." *Washington Post,* August 28, A, 16:1. {1.4}

Tufte, Edward. 1983. *The Visual Display of Quantitative Information*. Cheshire, Conn.: Graphics Press. {8.3}

1990. *Envisioning Information*. Cheshire, Conn.: Graphics Press. {8.3}

Van Harlow, W. 1988. "Economics Preferences and Risk Aversion: An Alternative Perspective." University of Arizona Working Paper. {4.2}

Van Huyck, John B., Raymond C. Battalio, and Richard O. Beil. 1990. "Tacit Coordination Games, Strategic Uncertainty, and Coordination Failure." *American Economic Review* 80:1 (March): 234–48. {9.9}

Van Huyck John B., Raymond C. Battalio, S. Mathur, A. Ortmann, and P. Van Huyck. 1992. "On the Origin of Convention: Some Evidence from Coordination Games." Texas A&M Working Paper, March. {9.9}

Vickrey, William. 1961. "Counterspeculation, Auctions, and Competitive Sealed Tenders." *Journal of Finance* 16 (March): 8–37. {7.5}

Von Neumann, John, and Oskar Morgenstern. 1944. *Theory of Games and Economic Behavior*. Princeton, N.J.: Princeton University Press. (Note: the second edition of 1947 is more readily available.) {9.2, 9.8}

Walker, James M., Vernon L. Smith, and James C. Cox. 1990. "Inducing Risk Neutral Preference: An Examination in a Controlled Market Environment." *Journal of Risk and Uncertainty* 3: 5–24. {4.2}

Wells, Don. 1991. "Laboratory Experiments for Undergraduate Instruction in Economics." *Journal of Economics Education* 22 (Summer): 293–300. {1.5}

Williams, Arlington W. 1980. "Computerized Double-Auction Markets: Some Initial Experimental Results." *Journal of Business* 53 (July): 235–58. {5.1, 8.6}

Williams, Arlington W., and James M. Walker. 1993. "Computerized Laboratory Exercises for Microeconomics Education: Three Applications Motivated by the Methodology of Experimental Economics." *Journal of Economics Education* (forthcoming). {1.4, 4.1.3, 5.3.4}

Williams, Fred. 1973. "Effect of Market Organization on Competitive Equilibrium: The Multiunit Case." *Review of Economic Studies* 40 (January): 97–113. {9.6}

Woodford, Michael. 1990. "Learning to Believe in Sunspots." *Econometrica* 58:2, 277–308. {5.5.3.2}

INDEX